If it's about the human condition and David ~~~~~~~~~~~~~~~~. This is what you'd expect from Powlison: good illustrations, great questions, unflinching diagnosis, and hope for redemption. I never thought of myself as an angry person . . . until I had a lot of kids. Now I know I need a book like this.

**Kevin DeYoung,** Senior pastor, University Reformed Church, East Lansing, Michigan; author of *The Biggest Story*

"*Good and Angry* by Powlison now takes its rightful place as my number one recommendation on anger—not to mention it now stands as the fullest and wisest Christian response to the sub-theme of self-hatred and self-anger I have ever read."

**Tony Reinke,** Desiring God.com; host of the *Ask Pastor John* podcast; author of *Newton on the Christian Life: To Live Is Christ*

"If there is any counselor on the planet who is qualified to come alongside you and point you to the truth about yourself and the Lord who loves you, it is David Powlison. For decades now he's been the primary voice of grace-saturated counsel and he speaks from a position of deep wisdom and careful exegesis. If you or someone you know has a problem with anger, this book is for you. In other words, everyone should buy it."

**Elyse Fitzpatrick,** Author of *Counsel from the Cross*

"Endorsing something that has occupied fifteen years of the 'salt n' light' life of Dr. David Powlison is a privilege. As an Anglican priest of an inner-city parish in Charleston, SC; having struggled with and viewed anger 'up-close-and-personal' in our community, the 'God tools' and experiences within the pages of *Good and Angry* are personally germane to me. And will enable me to teach others how to biblically 'reframe anger.'"

**Dallas H. Wilson, Jr.,** Vicar, St. John's Chapel, Charleston, South Carolina

"David Powlison does not treat anger as a disease to be cured or a vice to be crushed. After all, the Bible depicts both Jesus and his heavenly Father as sometimes angry. Expect no comforting nostrums from these pages. Here, instead, you will find biblically faithful probing and gospel hope that will make it possible to be *good* and angry."

**D. A. Carson,** Research Professor of New Testament, Trinity Evangelical School, Deerfield, IL; cofounder of The Gospel Coalition

"'This book is vintage Powlison—balanced, insightful, and richly nuanced. Powlison maps our anger (both good and bad) not on a sprinkling of Bible verses but on the gospel and the breadth and depth of biblical narrative. This is one of those books you not only read, but buy copies to pass to friends."

**Paul Miller,** Director of seeJesus, author of *A Loving Life*

"I've had righteous anger before, I think, but not very often. Most of my anger is more than a little bit unrighteous. In this wise and immensely practical book, David Powlison brings a lifetime of skill at understanding the human heart to help us deal with one of the world's biggest problems: anger, and everything that leads up to it."

**Philip Ryken,** President, Wheaton College

"It is a rare thing to find a fusion of biblically accurate and personally applicable insight in much that is written about anger. Dr. David Powlison is a stunning exception. He wields his written insight with all the wisdom and care with which a shepherd carries a staff to direct and defend the sheep dearly loved by the greatest Shepherd. His grasp of the Word of God and the heart of humanity is startlingly clear, compelling, convicting, and comforting."

**Joseph Vincent Novenson,** Senior Teaching Pastor, Lookout Mountain Presbyterian Church, Lookout Mountain, Tennessee

"*Good and Angry* is the best book I have reviewed related to the heart of anger. David Powlison gets the nuances of the heart, and his careful and thorough understanding of anger from a biblical perspective is a significant contribution to the biblical counseling movement. He shows us that with Christ as our example and the gospel as our guide we can forgive, be motivated to mercy, and even learn to love our enemies. I recommend this book to anyone who has ever been angry, loves someone who struggles with anger, and especially to those who don't think they have a problem with anger. I pray this book is as helpful to you as it has been to me."

**Garrett Higbee,** Executive Director, Biblical Soul Care Ministries

"David Powlison helps us to think clearly about our anger, no matter which form it tends to take. This book really is a one-size-fits-all, and the format is like interactive counseling. Whether or not you are already aware of your anger problem, you need this book. *Good and Angry* is an exceptional resource for everyone—from parents and teachers to pastors and missionaries."

**Gloria Furman,** Cross-cultural worker; author of *The Pastor's Wife* and *Missional Motherhood*

"The great thing about David Powlison's counseling and writing is that he is willing to get his hands dirty as he brings the gospel into the root problems of our lives. His discussions not only deal with the realities of our struggles but the realities of his own grappling for help—at a depth most of us are not capable or daring enough to consider. Yet, as troubling as are the problems he tackles, so refreshing and realistic are the gospel truths he unearths for us. He digs into his own heart to help us know how to bring gospel restoration to ours."

**Bryan Chapell,** Pastor of Grace Presbyterian Church, Peoria, Illinois

"This is the most complete, biblical, insightful, and practical book on anger that I have ever read. The concepts are clearly explained with plenty of illustrations from the biblical record as well as from our daily lives. It is obvious that the author is quite experienced in this field, knowing the personal and interpersonal conflicts that trigger the angry reactions in us. It is hard to think of a person that would not be helped by this book."

**Miguel Núñez,** Senior Pastor, International Baptist Church of Santo Domingo; President, Wisdom and Integrity Ministries

"*Good and Angry* masterfully captures the way every last one of us needs our anger redeemed and brims with practical wisdom to help that happen. This book moves far beyond anger management, consistently reorienting us to God's redemptive purposes for anger against real wrongs, while unveiling the lies that fuel destructive rage and cold-hearted grumbling. I have not read a more soul-searching and refreshing book in a long time."

    **J. Alasdair Groves**, Director of Counseling, CCEF New England

"*Good and Angry* takes a comprehensive look at good anger and destructive anger. I especially appreciate how David names the more covert forms of anger such as indifference, withdrawal, and contempt as being just as sinful and destructive as the more aggressive anger of rage and bullying. I will encourage my clients who are in destructive relationships to study this book to gain greater self-awareness of what's driving them when anger overwhelms them."

    **Leslie Vernick**, LCSW; relationship coach; speaker; author of *The Emotionally Destructive Marriage* and *The Emotionally Destructive Relationship*

"Far too often in Christian circles our approach to emotions tends toward simplistic and negative. 'Anger is bad. Stop it.' That's why I'm so grateful for David Powlison's robust, redemptive wisdom found in *Good and Angry*. David teaches us how Christ's gospel of grace emancipates our hearts so that even the messy emotion of anger can fruitfully and beautifully reflect the holy love of Christ."

    **Bob Kellemen**, Biblical Counseling Chair at Crossroads Bible College; author of *Gospel-Centered Counseling: How Christ Changes Lives*

"I struggle with sinful anger every day. This book is an excellent source of help in understanding my problem, discerning my motives, examining the lies I tend to believe, and diagnosing the deep roots of sin that compel me to explode in rage or retreat in cold, hateful disdain. In his chapter on anger toward God, Powlison invites us to a courageous honesty that puts us on the pathway to repentance, the sweet and rugged landscape of every believer's life."

    **Barb Duguid**, Author of *Extravagant Grace*

"David Powlison helps us to see that anger is not a problem to be solved but a natural human response to injustice, things we believe to be 'not right.' The problem we face is how to respond to what is 'not right' without sinning. Powlison helps us by encouraging us to admit our sinful anger problems, exposing the roots of sinful anger, and teaching us how to 'express the right kind of anger in the right way.' I needed this book! And if you're anything like me, you need it as well."

    **Juan R. Sanchez**, Senior Pastor, High Pointe Baptist Church, Austin, Texas

"Throughout the years, Powlison's works have been such helpful resources to turn to in pastoral ministry. *Good and Angry* proves to be no different as it provides keen insight into a very prevalent human emotion. From layperson to seasoned pastor, this book helps all those looking to investigate the root of anger. While doing so, Powlison artfully and tenderly brings his readers into the embrace of God's mercy."

**Stephen T. Um,** *Senior Minister of Citylife Presbyterian Church*, Boston, MA

"With characteristic humility and wisdom, David Powlison has produced a rich resource on understanding anger. He moves us beyond our reflex to repress and repent and shows us how our anger can increasingly reflect the loving purposes of God in Christ. The 'constructive displeasure of mercy' is a phrase that I will be meditating on for a long time."

**Winston Smith,** Faculty, Christian Counseling and Educational Foundation

"All of us struggle with the hot unpleasantness of emotions and desires on the spectrum of anger. This problem frustrates us, saddens us, and often enslaves us. We need a wise and gracious guide to point us to the mercy of God's Word. David Powlison is a man of peace and his words in this book breathe wisdom and point to Christ's own grace for change. Since anger is all of our problem, we all need this book."

**Heath Lambert,** Executive Director of the Association of Certified Biblical Counselors and Associate Pastor at First Baptist Church Jacksonville, FL

"David Powlison is never simplistic. This biblically rich, psychologically insightful analysis puts anger under the microscope and shows us just how complicated it can be. It also shows us how to relate anger to the really big themes of Scripture—grace, redemption, and the restoration of all things. Read this book and see why anger matters far more than you ever thought it did. Read this book and learn how to be both angry and good."

**Steve Midgley,** Executive Director, Biblical Counselling UK

"David Powlison's *Good and Angry* will serve as a seminal work in the arena of biblical care. Providing the reader with a sound conceptual understanding of anger while suggesting rich biblical insights for change, this book contains truths that equip the believer to more effectively address the struggle of anger in its varying forms. Powlison's style and wisdom are always profound and refreshing. This book is no exception."

**Jeremy Lelek,** President, Association of Biblical Counselors

"This is the opposite of a self-help book; it is a God-help book. Here we find readable, pithy, and searching reflections on what God says about anger—and its redemption by grace—in the Bible. Highlights include Powlison's treatment of the exemplary nature of God's anger, the multitudinous ways in which our anger falls short of God's, and the confusion of Christian defenses of anger against God. Again and again, this gentle sage of sanctification leads us back to the one who overcame our anger, and his, at the cross."

**Eric L. Johnson,** Lawrence and Charlotte Hoover Professor of Pastoral Care, The Southern Baptist Theological Seminary

# Good and Angry

Redeeming Anger, Irritation,
Complaining, and Bitterness

DAVID POWLISON

New
Growth
Press
www.newgrowthpress.com

New Growth Press, Greensboro, NC 27404

Cover Design: Faceout Books, faceoutstudio.com
Typesetting and eBook: Lisa Parnell, lparnell.com

ISBN 978-1-942572-97-8 (Print)
ISBN 978-1-942572-98-5 (eBook)

Library of Congress Cataloging-in-Publication Data
    Names: Powlison, David, 1949– author.
    Title: Good and angry : redeeming anger, irritation, complaining, and
        bitterness / David Powlison.
    Description: Greensboro, NC : New Growth Press, 2016.
    Identifiers: LCCN 2016012175 | ISBN 9781942572978 (print) |
        ISBN 9781942572985 (ebook)
    Subjects: LCSH: Anger—Religious aspects—Christianity.
    Classification: LCC BV4627.A5 P693 2016 | DDC 241/.3—dc23
    LC record available at https://lccn.loc.gov/2016012175

Printed in the United States of America

26 25 24 23 22 21 20 19        5 6 7 8 9

I dedicate this book to Mark and Karen Teears,
Barbara Juliani, and New Growth Press. Thank you.
Through your persistence, humility, and helpfulness,
we have been able to bring this book to publication.

*We have witnessed a miracle of grace that makes the angels rejoice!*

# Contents

# Acknowledgments

I am grateful that my faith was formed and is still being nurtured by men and women who understand that to live as a Christian is a synonym for living as an honest, wise, and humble human being. Every human capacity, every human activity, every sphere of human life is meant to be "very good"—as we once were by creation in God's image, as we never are because we have fallen hard, as reappears in the person of Jesus. Because he cares, his anger works as anger is meant to work, and his mercy speaks the final word in all who love him. Because he cares, he is remaking all things human—even this difficult, unruly, and destructive thing we call anger—so that we become like him.

# Introduction

We all have firsthand experience with anger gone wrong. We've dished it out. We've been on the receiving end. We've heard and seen others get angry at each other. At some point in each day you are probably affected by some form of anger gone bad—either your own or someone else's.

Often it's mild—frustrations, complaining, irritation. Often it's veiled—judgmental thoughts, passive aggressions. Often it's buried—hidden from conscious awareness, painted over with pleasantries, anesthetized by distractions, busyness, or mind-altering substances. All too often it's intense—bitterness, hostility, violence. It's no surprise that when the apostle Paul lists typical sins, half his list belongs to the anger family (Galatians 5:19–21).

And yet anger done right is a great good. It says, "That's wrong" and acts to protect the innocent and helpless. It says, "That's wrong" and energizes us to address real problems. God, who is good and does good, expresses good anger for a good cause. Jesus gets good and angry—in the service of mercy and peace. He is willing and able to forgive us for our anger gone bad. He is willing and able to teach us to do anger right.

But it is hard to sort out the good from the bad in anger, isn't it? And it's even harder to change when anger has gone bad. Why are problems that are so common so difficult to solve?

All of us are in this boat. It's hard to do anger right. Unless you have somehow numbed yourself to the human condition, every one of us struggles with anger. My chief goal in this book is to teach you *how* to more fruitfully and honestly deal with your anger. Your struggle with anger (and mine) will last a lifetime, but it can go somewhere good. We can learn to deal with anger differently.

This book is not about "solving" anger problems. That word *solve* suggests that we can arrive. Give us some answers, change some behaviors, and—just like that—no more problems. It suggests that bad anger is simply a bad habit. But anger is not a problem to solve. It's a human capacity—like sex, happiness, and sorrow. It is a complex human response to a complex world. And like all human capacities and responses, it sometimes works well, but too often goes bad. Anger creates problems. But having and expressing the right kind of anger in the right way is a good goal.

I can't promise you a technique, insight, or strategy that's fool-proof. (When it comes to anger, nothing is foolproof!) I won't offer you self-affirming truisms to reframe your self-talk so your moods even out. I am not going to give you deep-breathing and relaxation techniques to help you keep your cool. And I definitely won't encourage you to get in touch with the real you and tell the world how you really feel.

But I do promise you that there are ways to think through and work through your anger that are wise and true. There are ways of handling anger that produce *good*. There are ways to become more peaceful in many situations and more cleanly angry in the situations that call for it. There are even ways to fail well, so you learn how to find mercy and pick yourself up again after blowing it.

## What Do You Bring to the Table?

We are going to talk about hard topics. Will you join in? Will you think hard? Will you speak up honestly? Will you take constructive action? We're talking about anger, after all. It's the dark, turbulent emotion of destruction.

We'll examine incidents that leave a bitter taste, and whole lifetimes that go sour with accumulated bitterness. We'll look at volcanic wrath, but also the momentary irritations. I've often found that we learn the most from the little things, the everyday disappointment, frustration, disagreement, and complaint. What we learn transfers to the big things. It's like learning to walk before learning to walk a tightrope.

If you're willing to enter the conversation, this book will prove to be about *your* anger.

You picked up this book for a reason. In a constructive atmosphere, in the pursuit of true and living wisdom, why not tackle big things? We can talk straight and think carefully about things that really matter.

- Anger really matters.
- To mess up when it comes to anger is to mess up your life.
- To get anger straight is to get your life straight.

Think about reading this book as an honest conversation about something that really matters. We are sitting down together at the kitchen table for a long, slow heart-to-heart talk. A good conversation includes pauses to think, sometimes lengthy pauses. Sometimes you have to come back later and finish what you couldn't quite put into words.

This book is divided into four sections. The first section will help you ask questions and explore your particular experience of anger. The second section will answer the question what is anger? The third section will tackle how destructive anger is changed into something constructive. Then the final section will look at particular difficult cases.

## Three Suggestions

Let me suggest three things about how to read this book. Each is a different way to take your time as you read.

First, read *with a pen in hand*. Right from the start I'm going to ask you to stop and respond. I'll make statements. So take the time to write down what you think. Give an example. I'll ask you questions. Take time to ponder, explore, and reflect. Jot down your answers. Keep your pen at hand so that you can write down the gist of what you're thinking, what you wonder, and where you struggle. Get *your* real life into the mix. Of course, as the author I get first say on the printed page. But your details will make the story come to life. Each chapter ends with a section entitled "Making It Your Own" that gives you an opportunity to interact with and respond to what you've read.

Second, read with a yellow highlighter next to your pen. What strikes *you* as you read? Take the time to highlight one sentence on each page or in each section. At the end of each chapter go back and reread your highlights. Then pick the one sentence from the entire chapter that most strikes you, and consider the following questions:

- Why did you choose this?
- What does it mean to you?
- If you agree, how would your life change if this sentence became true of you?
- If you question or disagree, put it into words.

Using your pen and highlighter will help you to notice, stop, and consider so that you can respond.

Third, pay close attention whenever you find yourself thinking, *but what about . . . ?* The But-What-Abouts—BWAs—are *very* important. They are the places you collide with what I write. You sense that something you want to know hasn't been said yet. The key questions that *you* are asking come to the surface wherever you find yourself wondering *BWA* _____? Your questions bring into focus the perceptions and the life experiences that *you* must make sense of. This book is the product of hundreds of BWAs that I've asked about anger over many years.

The BWAs can create a problem. They get distracting if they talk too loud and too soon in the process. We stop listening. No conversation takes place. Don't let your BWAs hijack the process. Write them down and save them for later.

This book invites you to a slowly unfolding meal. If in the middle of appetizers, you suddenly cry out, "But what about the dinner rolls? What's for dessert? Who's doing the dishes?" then you never taste the hors d'oeuvres. An important question may pop into your mind as you read chapter 2, but it might not get answered until chapter 8. You may strongly disagree with something you read in chapter 5, for which you will find a satisfying explanation, or at least a plausible suggestion worth considering, in chapter 17.

The topic of anger bursts with big questions. At any moment we may only be snooping around one small answer, but it may build toward an answer to your big questions. So take note of your BWAs, and keep reading.

If you take this book to heart, you'll get anger right more often. Yes, you'll still fail. Perhaps you already know your typical pick of the poisons—whether your angers are mild, veiled, buried, or intense. Perhaps you've already learned wise things about how to deal constructively with failure. But wherever you find yourself in the process of facing and dealing with anger, God is merciful. He is not surprised by our blind spots. He is not surprised by our failures. God is merciful. He willingly meets us. He works patiently and persistently. He is merciful and will not give up on you. He will complete the good work that he begins.

As you read and ponder this book, I trust that you will grow in self-knowledge. I trust that you will grow more aware of your need for God's mercy, strength, and protection. You will grow in knowing your Father, your Savior, your life-giving Spirit. We have it from Jesus himself, sealed with his blood. Ask—he will give. Seek—you will find. Knock—he will open the door and welcome you in. There is no script, of course. I know that you will grow in ways impossible to predict. Sometimes you will be dismayed and discouraged at how hard the road seems.

If you lack wisdom, ask God. He does not reproach you for needing his help (James 1:5). Sometimes you will be delighted and encouraged at how directly and immediately the Lord helps you. And I know that in the end, you will be filled with joy. "I am sure of this, that he who began a good work in you will bring it to completion at the day of Jesus Christ" (Philippians 1:6).

》》》

## Making It Your Own

1. Were there any places in this introduction where you thought, *but what about . . . ?*

(I'll make the questions harder in the future!)

2. Go back through this introduction with your highlighter and single out the sentence that most caught your attention. Why did you choose this sentence?

# SECTION 1

# OUR EXPERIENCE

The next three chapters aim to give you a feel for the destructiveness of anger and for its constructive potential. They aim to help you think clearly about your own tendencies. Seeing yourself more clearly sets the stage. Then explanations and solutions that come later will *connect* to where you actually struggle.

# CHAPTER 1

# Angry People

Perhaps you can identify with George Banks in the movie *Father of the Bride*. George (played by Steve Martin) gets into a conversation with his daughter's fiancé. He describes her this way,

> Annie is a very passionate person and passionate people tend to overreact at times. Annie comes from a long line of major over-reactors. Me, I can definitely lose it. My mother, a nut. My grandfather, stories about him are legendary. The good news, however, is that this overreacting tends to get proportionately less by generation, so your kids could be normal.

Passionate people, major over-reactors, people who lose it. In the hands of Steve Martin such behavior is hilarious to watch, a bit maddening to live with, and touchingly human all the while.

But in real life, anger is the reaction that incinerates marriages and disintegrates families. It energizes gossip and guns down classmates. It divides churches, turns friendship into enmity, and erupts in road rage. It is the stuff of every form of grievance and bitterness. The fact that some of us overreact in less colorful ways does not mean that those who are quiet are not angry. Anger is also the basic DNA of complaining, brooding, irritability, and bickering. The "shoes" of problem anger are like a pair of open-heeled bathroom slippers. One size really does fit all. The crucial issues in anger touch every one of us.

This book is for all of us because we all experience anger. If you've always been strong-willed, argumentative, and volatile, you are in these pages. If a lifetime of disappointment and disillusionment has left you embittered, this is for you. And even if you're quieter, you're in this book too. In the way we do anger, some of us explode, some of us simmer, some of us seem dormant—but all of us experience anger. And if we don't, it's because we've anesthetized ourselves or detached.

For example, I was born easygoing. I can take no credit that my innate disposition is low-key. For many years I didn't think I had an anger problem. I found angry people puzzling and a bit intimidating. Why do they bother to get so bent out of shape over *that*? But either I've become a worse person as I've gotten older, or I've learned to know myself a bit better. Quiet brooding, defensive withdrawal, judgmental thoughts, low-grade irritability, a critical attitude, avoiding outright conflict, indifference to reparable wrongs—these are just my less dramatic brands of an anger problem. My personal tendency has never been to go on the offensive with frenzied hot war. I've specialized more in keeping a safe distance from conflicts—and, if necessary, engaging in a cold war.

*[margin note: I can certainly relate.]*

Why would I of all people write a book on anger? My interest in anger has grown as I have come to realize that I too (in my own quiet way) am part of the problem of anger, not simply an observer or victim of others' anger. At the same time, I'm trying to help other people, some of whom operate in the incendiary mode, some who are deeply embittered, and some who are rather like me. We all need help.

I've known lots of angry people. During my last year in college I worked as the Saturday night bouncer at the Club Casablanca. On numerous occasions I got up close and personal with extremely surly customers. One reeling drunk got so incensed when I escorted him out of the bar that he threatened to come back with a gun and kill me. I quit on the spot rather than waiting to find out if he meant it.

Working in psychiatric hospitals for four years provided a steady education in the out-workings of bitterness and hostility. Forty hours a week on locked wards is an education in the dark things in the human soul. A lot of anger comes out in a psychiatric ward. And it has many unhappy companions: confusion, heartache, deceit, self-pity, fear, and—saddest of all—false hopes, shattered hopes, and no hope. I became familiar with an abyss of miseries to which none of us is immune.

Yes, I've known lots of people—including the person I see in the mirror—for whom anger goes bad, rather than doing good. Now, after more than forty years of doing counseling ministry, I could assemble a Hall of Fame—a roster of bitterness, destructiveness, and sheer unhappiness—called "Angry People I Have Known." Let's look at several examples.

## Domestic Gunslingers

Anger is not just a strongly felt emotion that takes place inside us. It's interpersonal. It affects others. I once counseled a couple who had a gunfight in their suburban house. Willy was upstairs with the pistol, Brenda downstairs with the rifle. They'd had words— the usual, daily bickering. It had gotten more heated than usual. Finally, ugly words escalated into domestic World War III. A half-dozen rounds of live fire zinged up and down that stairway! Their marital dispute blasted bullet holes in the sheetrock, scared the daylights out of the neighbors, and brought police sirens wailing to their door. Talking with me was part of their court-mandated alternative to felony charges. For some reason I've never forgotten this story!

You've probably never been in a gunfight. I never have either. But one landmark in understanding my own anger came when all I did was move a magazine two inches.

It was about ten o'clock one evening. My wife Nan and I had just gotten our fussy two-year-old off to bed. Dinner dishes overflowed the sink. Toddler debris had turned the living room into a FEMA disaster site. A basket of clean laundry needed folding.

Oblivious to it all, I sprawled full length on the couch to read the latest issue of *National Geographic*. Nan walked in a few minutes later and said, "It sure would be nice to have some help cleaning up." I lowered the magazine two inches closer to my face and buried my nose in my reading.

I realized, *I'm angry*, though I hadn't said a word. But inside I was saying plenty: *It's been a long day. I need a break. If only she'd asked more nicely. I don't feel like doing it now. We could do it tomorrow. Go away and don't bother me. Why is this happening to me?* But amazingly, sanity also intruded: *You're angry. Love is patient, but you're being impatient right now. Love is kind. You're being unkind. Love gives. You're being selfish. Your withdrawal is a form of hate.* I was arrested by what is true, by words of God that he made personal. I came to my senses and got up.

A gunfight is one way to cut another person off and protect your turf. Burying your head two inches deeper in a magazine is another way. But that night I made peace with the God who is patient, kind, and giving. And I also made peace with Nan, asked her forgiveness for my selfishness, and we tackled the dishes together.

## The Volcano

Anger outbursts are not just isolated events. The underlying attitude can become a life-defining characteristic. Helen was in her sixties and so consumed with hatred that her hands and voice shook when she introduced herself. Her anger had destroyed her marriage, intimidated and alienated her children, cost her job after job, and driven away every person who ever tried to be her friend.

She spoke of grievances that went back decades. For example, years earlier she had run the audio ministry of a church. The minister would routinely preach for thirty-two to thirty-five minutes, rather than the twenty-eight minutes that allowed a sermon to fit neatly on a half-hour audiotape (yes, it was a long time ago!). Helen's bitterness and gossiping (she had scores of similar grievances against scores of similarly benighted persons) eventually split that church.

Helen's wrath on the day I met her was as fresh and fierce as if all offenses had occurred twenty seconds ago, not five, twenty-five, or fifty years in the past. Her rage seethed continually, barely controllable, on the edge of exploding. She was "Mount St. Helens" (her son's wry nickname for her, and the reason he kept both his distance and his sanity). Sadly, she took every bit of alienation that she caused, every negative consequence, every broken relationship, and converted it into one more good reason to be angry at all those terrible people that life had inflicted on her.

You're probably not as petty and destructive as Helen. She was ready to go off without any provocation. But she's just an extreme version of a common problem.

When a little thing pushes your buttons, it says something big about the buttons inside you. When I moved that magazine closer to my nose, it didn't take any forethought. I just did it. If a moment of sanity had not arrested me and gotten me up off the couch, then that small grievance—and 10,000 more sure to follow—could have worked inside me to destroy our marriage. Bad anger doesn't just go away. It festers over a lifetime. And good, constructive, problem-solving anger—like mercy—doesn't just happen. It must be cultivated over a lifetime.

## The Iceberg

Anger is the "hot" emotion by which we vent our displeasure. But some of the most ominous forms can be cold as ice. Jimmy was sixteen. He sat in the chair next to me, quite composed, bored in fact. His parents thought he ought to talk to someone, but he wasn't much interested in talking to me. Eventually we got past the monosyllabic, awkward silence phase. As Jimmy opened up a bit, he told story after story about how he'd been mistreated by his family, classmates, teachers, God, and the whole godforsaken universe. He gave a detailed recitation of all the injustice, unfairness, betrayal, disappointment, offense, and plain old stupidity committed against him. He had a rap sheet on the whole world.

Jimmy played his parts to perfection: crime victim and aggrieved plaintiff, prosecuting attorney and hanging judge, unanimous jury, outraged public, and ever-so-willing executioner. Most of his stories seemed plausible, but none of the offenses sounded particularly outrageous. They were the things that happen to everyone. Two things struck me about Jimmy.

First, he spoke in an unvarying monotone. His emotions were flatline. He sounded like he was reading from a telemarketing script. This dull litany of grievance was scarier than outright anger. At one point I asked him, "Are you angry?" (I was inviting him to say the obvious, let it come out of his own mouth. It might move our conversation in a good direction if we could establish that at least we had something worth talking about.) Jimmy seemed taken aback for a moment. Then he recovered his cool, and said matter of factly, "Nah, I don't get angry . . . . *I get even.*" His anger was chilly, not hot. It was more "premeditated, cold-blooded murder" than "crime of passion." He was not going to waste emotional energy on the vermin and trash that he had to deal with in life.

Second, Jimmy lived in a universe that featured *him.* Everything was all about one all-important, all-offended being. Every scene in his film, every page of his book, every news story in his daily paper circled around Jimmy—but he was never an agent or cause of anything. Every person, event, place, and object existed only to the degree that it affected his pleasure or displeasure. And because every other character in the story had dedicated his or her life to making Jimmy miserable, he felt entitled to this *modus operandi* of bland, cold vengeance.

The monotone and logical paranoia chilled me. Here was anger in the genocidal mode: efficient, decided, as matter-of-fact as taking out the garbage or exterminating bugs.

*Jimmy is a malignant narcissist*

You're probably not as cold and vengeful as Jimmy. I'm not either. But lowering the *National Geographic* two inches? That was a cold moment. Some form of hostility lurks in every relationship characterized by a cool or chill. All human reactions and emotions, however complex, play variations on themes of love and hate. Distance and indifference don't look like anger on the surface, but when you poke at it, the anger will come out.

## The Morass, the Misery . . . and the Possibility of Hope

Anger plays a significant role in a morass of interconnecting problems. And yet, in an almost inconceivable way, the right kind of anger can play a key role in solutions. Sorting all this out is the goal of this book. Let me tell a story.

One wintry afternoon many years ago, I was in the grocery store picking up a few items for dinner. A young mother came into the store at the same time. She was pushing her cart up the aisle ahead of me, with her four-year-old boy tagging along. It was hard to say how old she was. I'd guess twenty-five, but she could have been in her early thirties. Hard lines were already forming in her face. She had long, uncombed, blonde hair and was wearing an army jacket and worn-out sneakers. Her eyes had a slightly haunted look, not quite here, as if inwardly preoccupied with troubles from elsewhere, embittered, restless. It was the kind of face that troubles and concerns you.

Her little boy started to fuss as they worked their way down the snack aisle. He wanted a candy bar, and she wouldn't buy it for him. He whined, "But I want . . ."

She cut him off, "NO!"

He whined a little more.

She lit into him. "How many times do I have to tell you? NO. NO. NO. I don't want to hear it out of you. If you know what's good for you . . ." Her threat trailed off. She stopped her cart and looked away, out through the plate glass of the storefront. I had stopped too, concerned how this drama was going to play out.

The boy sulked a moment, and then complained some more, tugging at her jacket. "But I want candy."

She cursed him. "You're a [blankety-blank] pest, and I don't know why I bother to take you anywhere." She looked away, glanced back at him with hatred, looked far, far away at nothing in particular.

He whined again. "But I want candy."

She turned and slapped him across the face. He started to cry. She looked away, down past the candy and chips, over the checkout lines, out across the parking lot. I thought that perhaps she was trying to keep herself from screaming or from killing him.

She suddenly turned at him again, and bent halfway down. She was in his face, looming over him, her right index finger at a forty-five-degree angle three inches from his nose. "If you don't shut the hell up right now, I'm going to walk right out of this store, and I'm going to leave you here. Do you hear that? I don't want to hear you, and I don't want to see your face. If you say one more word, I swear to God I'm going to get in the car, and I'm never coming back, and I don't care if I never see you again." She turned and made as if to walk away. After a couple of brisk steps, she turned halfway back to grab his arm with a jerk and say, "Just shut the hell up."

She pushed her cart up the supermarket aisle. The boy followed along, muttering to himself, looking down at that rubberized steel wheel shuddering across the linoleum. He didn't seem afraid of being abandoned. He lagged a good step behind his mother, and a step to the side, dragging just enough to irritate her, but not quite enough to detonate her.

They were a couple of really angry people.

It made me angry.

I felt angry at the mom. She was abusing her son. It's plain wrong to do what she was doing. I felt angry at the boy. He was tormenting his mom. It's plain wrong to do that. I felt angry at whatever background evils made this woman's life such a dark, hellish nightmare. All the things that are so wrong: boyfriends who don't care, parents who messed up their own lives too, drug dealers, poverty. And I felt angry at the choices she made in response to her difficult life.

The anger I felt seemed clean and constructive compared to the irritations I more often feel. I didn't hate that mother and child. I cared, however powerless I was to intervene. I was angry—I hated what they were doing—in such a way that I wanted to help. I wished I could protect them, give them mercy, and help them change. It was one of those too-rare moments when anger seemed motivated by love, not self-interest. But the good intention went nowhere that day. I couldn't think of how to make a connection.

Thirty-five years later, this book is part of that incident going somewhere. That incident is one of the BWAs that made me want to reckon more thoughtfully and constructively with anger.

These three angers in the supermarket aren't like anything in a self-help book. Half those books teach techniques for maintaining a degree of detachment so you can keep your cool amid the irritants of life. The other half urges you to stand up for yourself, to own your anger in order to feel empowered. Both kinds of advice sound plausible, sort of, sometimes, when the problem you're dealing with is a minor irritant, or if the things you're angry about can actually be fixed.

Sure, if you take a deep breath and visualize the beach when you're stuck in traffic, the world seems like a nicer place. Sure, when you verbalize your expectations in a non-demanding way, it's more likely people will give you what you want. Sure, acknowledge what you're feeling.

But this scene in the supermarket is not about irritants or about managing reality to get more of what you want and to feel better. It's about evils. It's about things that are wrong and destructive. They need to be made right. What it takes to make it right is not obvious, but the right kind of anger is part of the solution. Platitudes, affirming self-talk, mindfulness, self-assertion, or medication can never do what actually needs doing. None of these angers is explained or resolved by the self-help industry. But they are what life is about.

Think with me about what we witness in this story. I'll make some assumptions, but I think they're plausible.

First, the boy's anger was the kind we're most familiar with: "I want my way. When I don't get it, I make a stink. I feel sorry for myself. It's so unfair if I don't get what I want when I want it. I'll manipulate you to get my way, and bully if necessary. I'll punish anyone who crosses my will." This sort of anger springs up when you want something and don't get it. Anger whines and sulks. Anger persists. Anger makes a scene. Anger is savvy and strategic.

We're all familiar with the boy's kind of anger: been there, done a bit of that, and at the time felt justified. An identifiable desire gets frustrated, and anger powers up from within to attack whatever impedes your will. It's a way to get your way, or to punish those who cross you, or to register your complaint. That little boy had a very grown-up problem. For one thing, he could never love his mom as long as he was using her. For another, he was becoming like her.

The mom's anger was like in kind, but not so simple. Her anger includes, but isn't limited to, "I want my kid to be quiet and not embarrass me. He's bugging me so I'm angry." Her anger had ripened through the years into a more complex evil. It has more history tangled into it. It incorporates more strands of current events. It wraps the despair of a bleak future into its aggression. It came as a torrent of mixed feelings, blind motives, and bad experiences. It was raw hostility, and it was also despair, fear, habit, regret, hurt, disappointment, consequences of past bad choices, lack of good role models, accumulated provocations, tight finances, mutually destructive relationships, lies believed, lousy life options, accumulated resentments, futile goals, and perhaps a hangover.

Her anger is half-right—many of the things that happened to her are wrong. And her anger has gone all wrong. It is one distillation of life "having no hope and without God in the world," as Ephesians 2:12 puts it. Her anger at her son was cosmic in scope and scale:

*[handwritten margin note: The history of personal anger]*

"Right now this kid represents *all* the bad choices I ever made and *all* the bad things I ever suffered and *all* the life I'm never going to have. It's not just that he wants a candy bar . . . . It's that he exists, that I exist. I'm angry at everything." Many desires, many falsehoods, and many fears drive her complicated self-destruction. She can never deal constructively with her kid being a brat when she half-resents his very existence and has no hope for her own.

Most of us have known at least a taste of the mother's darker and more intricate passion. Often anger brings far more than current events onto the table. Often anger obeys more than one desire.

Perhaps you lived a period of your life in the waste of wraths and sorrows. Perhaps you're there now. No one wants life to be hellish. Maybe you hate yourself for being hateful. But you don't see any way out. You don't know where to begin. How do you untangle your own angry reactions?

Most readers have probably never gotten that far lost, but perhaps you've experienced pain from someone else's morass of anger exploding onto you. This mother and son were attacking and wounding each other in the aisle—you can feel what it is like to be treated that way. Rage brings misery to those on the receiving end. It is difficult to negotiate your way through life when you live in the shadow of the volcano. How can you go forward constructively rather than retaliating, cowering, or bolting?

Perhaps you are trying to help someone else who lives in the morass. If you've reached out to troubled people, you've often run up against such hopelessness. Many unhappy strugglers don't know where to begin and see no way out. A person like the mother in the grocery store often justifies and defends the very things that are destroying her. How can you help such tangled people? It's hard for a would-be helper to know where to begin and to see any way forward. A real understanding of anger and a true solution to anger problems must go as deep as these problems.

And it must go deeper. The story is also about the impulse toward a qualitatively different kind of anger—something good. I'm not so familiar with the kind of anger that I felt in the supermarket that day. It seemed right. I ought to feel that way more often. It was inextricably mingled with love. It was a kind of anger that cared. It intended to do something constructive, however small, amid the firestorm of evils. I hated what both the mom and the boy did to each other. But it was a loving hate. It seemed just: "That's wrong and unfair, and it should stop." It seemed merciful: "If only we could bind up what is so broken." It animated some sort of redemptive impulse: "How can what is now so wrong be made right again?"

All this is the deeper and wider problem of anger that I want us to grapple with together in this book.

## People Like You and Me

Anger stands out when it wears its colorful and dramatic costumes: violent, relentlessly embittered, ice-cold, or flailing in misery and confusion. But the difference in the angers described above and the anger that you or I experience is a difference of a degree, not of kind. We're all more alike than different. So I can get irritated when someone is guilty of disturbing the peace of my personal comfort and convenience. I can get irritated at incompetent customer service reps. I can get irritated when someone doesn't take the time to understand me accurately, caricatures what I believe and do, and disses me on the basis of what they've imagined.

You know some things about me and about people I've known. And I also know some things about you, even if we've never met.

First, you get angry too. Of course you are not exactly like Helen or me or other members of our rogues' gallery. Then again, the differences are probably matters of degree. You can probably identify with these people, even if your way of doing life operates in a different key or tempo or volume.

Second, I know that your anger is sometimes justified. Someone else did something truly wrong. We live in a world that contains significant provocations. There are evils worth getting upset about.

Maybe there have been times you handled the provocation rightly too. Just anger is supposed to motivate fair-minded, constructive, and energetic problem-solving. Have you ever had a taste of doing it right? Anger is meant to be laced with mercy and loving intent. Does that ring any bells? Have you ever experienced someone else—a parent, coach, coworker, teacher, pastor, spouse, friend—who got mad in a way that actually brought good? It sometimes happens.

Third, I know that many times your anger is not justified, or it gets blown out of proportion. You were irritable. You got into nitpicking or feeling sorry for yourself. Perhaps you take things personally that aren't about you. (Have you ever complained about the weather or cursed in a traffic jam?) Perhaps you misinterpret or exaggerate what someone else says or does. It can be hard to see and admit because we seem so plausible to ourselves. But I bet this is so. You were ruled by your agenda, your expectations, your convenience, your pleasure, and your fears. You couldn't see it at the time, but when somebody or something got in your way, you lost it.

Fourth, I know that there have been other times when it was right for you to be bothered about what happened, but your anger still got out of line. What you thought, what you said, and what you did was hostile, even mean-spirited. You got stuck in being judgmental. In a nutshell, you returned evil for evil, as if two wrongs could make it right. You became essentially destructive, not basically constructive. Your anger created more wreckage, more hurt, and more alienation, rather than positive solutions.

Fifth, I know that whether you were right or wrong to get upset, there have been times when anger at what happened hung around a lot longer than it should. You became bitter at a betrayal and couldn't let it go. You brooded, replaying video clips in your mind. You rehearsed. How wrong she was! How many reasons I have to be upset at him!

Sixth, if you've piled up some mileage on life's odometer, I know that your anger probably has accumulated some complexities. Anger isn't necessarily a cause-and-effect reaction to one particular event.

Often there's a cumulative effect to life's disappointments and frustrations. Take a daily dose of Sartre's "hell is other people!"[1] Mix in the reality that "hell is myself," and life simply grinds you down, burns you up, and wears you out. Disillusioned people may not fuel the hot fires of anger outburst. Why bother to get uselessly upset? They may not point to any one specific grievance that makes them bitter. But cynicism is a close kin to anger gone bad.

Seventh, I know something about you that we've barely mentioned but will discuss at some length in later chapters. There are times when you, like me, have the opposite problem. You really ought to get upset, but you don't. Something truly wrong is happening—not necessarily to you—and you don't care enough to care. You aren't wired to pay attention and react. You ignore or shrug off things that are wrong and ought to be tackled. Maybe you don't even notice. Maybe you even endorse and perpetrate the wrong.

In an odd way, absence of appropriate outrage is also an anger problem. It's not a problem anyone ever seeks help for. But we ought to. When the impulse to anger is rekeyed into something good and constructive, it includes the ability to be rightly aroused against true evils.

Finally, we know one more thing about each other. Every one of us has a hard time changing. It's hard to think straight about anger. It grabs you and it's got you. The ancient Romans had a saying, *Ira furor brevis est*, "Anger is a brief madness." Anger makes us crazy, blind, confused, and confusing. The beams of sanity are rare. Have you ever noticed and marveled later at your irrationality? *What came over me? How could I have thought that, said that, done that?* Sometimes the insanity is not so brief. It settles in and stays a while. Sometimes the habit runs on for a lifetime—a hamster wheel you don't ever get off.

How can you figure out what's wrong and needs fixing? How do you know what you should have done instead, and what you should do now? How do you separate the destructive parts of anger from the constructive parts? How can you learn to get upset about the right things *and* to express your concern in the right way? Where can you find help that really helps?

We need help. We need forgiveness. We need both vision and strength to change. We need a Savior—on scene, active, committed, practical, personal—to get mixed up with our troubles.

Anger? We're in this one together. And so is Jesus.

» » »

## Making It Your Own

1. This chapter has been packed full. Go back through and pull out your yellow-highlighted sentence. What about that sentence strikes you?

2. Of all the forms of anger portrayed, select two or three that are most characteristic of your life. Give a concrete illustration.

3. Have you ever had a taste of anger going right? Describe specifically what was happening. What did you feel, think, and do? What was the outcome? Have you ever witnessed someone else doing anger in a way that was truly constructive?

4. An ancient, wise, prayer makes this request of God: "Let the design of your great love shine on the waste of our wraths and sorrows, and give peace."

Wherever anger misfires, we have two needs. We need God to intervene in love, and we need to do something.

So ask God to help you. He willingly meets us in our need: *Lord, let the purposes of your compassion and mercy shine into the waste of my wraths and sorrows, and give me peace.*

And commit to work. You are already making time to read. Continue to put in the thought and effort to pursue greater wisdom.

CHAPTER 2

# Do *You* Have a Serious Problem
# with Anger?

Yes.

»»»

*If you'd ask me that question a week ago, I'd have said No. But now.......*

## Making It Your Own

1. How do you respond to this chapter? Go back and reread it a couple of times. (Don't you love short chapters?!) Think hard about what it says.

2. How do you react to the statement "*You* have a serious problem with anger"?

3. Turn this sentence over in your mind: "I do have a serious problem with anger." What comes to mind? Do you agree or disagree? Are you not quite sure? How is that statement true? Partly true? Partly false? Do you think it's not true at all? Collect your thoughts into words and specific examples.

Here is the sweet paradox in how God works. He blesses those who admit that they need help: The poor in spirit are blessed (Matthew 5:3). Sanity has a deep awareness, *I need help. I can't do life right on my own. Someone outside me must intervene.* The sanity of honest humility finds mercy, life, peace, and strength. By contrast, saying we don't need help keeps us stuck on that hamster wheel of making excuses and blaming others. The end result isn't life and peace; it's self-righteousness, self-justification, alienation, and bitterness.

CHAPTER 3

# How Does That Shoe Fit?

I can confidently write that *you* have a serious problem with anger because *I* do, because *we all* do. How do you react to that truth? This chapter will look at six common reactions to the hard statement that we all have an anger problem.

Each reaction expresses something of what makes anger so confusing. Each reaction contains a strand of truth—sometimes more, sometimes less—that makes it plausible. But the good gets easily tangled up with misperceptions and distortions, with blind spots and half-truths. Rarely, and wonderfully, anger arises as a simple and constructive good (more about that later). Far more often, anger acts in purely destructive malice, doing no good to anyone. Perhaps most often, anger is a crazy quilt of good and bad, of good-going-bad, of bad wishing it were better. In real life, anger most often comes mixed up. That mix-up makes it hard to define exactly what the problem is.

Perhaps one of these six reactions describes you?

## 1. Yes, I know I've got an anger problem. I feel guilty and discouraged.

Some people agree right away. "The shoe fits. I've got a temper. I hold on to bitterness and can't let things go. I react and say things that I later regret. Sometimes I feel regret even while the words are coming out of my mouth. But I can't seem to stop once I get going. Even when I'm not mad, I tend to be a pessimist, and always manage to see the dark side of whatever's going on. I complain and feel sorry for myself. I know I need help. I wish I could just snap out of it and get rid of my angry, negative reactions once and for all. That's why I picked up this book."

Is this you? You know that your anger goes bad. You wish you could quit losing it (temper) or holding onto it (bitterness) or grousing about it (complaining). You wish you could break the cycle of failure and regret. You see the damage your negativism causes in relationships. You freely admit, "I've got an anger problem," but you're stuck. You don't change. You feel discouraged, a bit hopeless, perhaps even cynical.

*Strand of truth?* Those of us who know we are temperamental—and feel guilty and discouraged—rightly know that irritability, hostile outbursts, bitterness, and complaining are wrong.

*Blind spot?* You can get mixed up about the goal of change. For example, the opposite of tantrums and bitterness is not a placid temperament and unflappable demeanor. And you can misunderstand the process of changing. For example, there is no technique or strategy to actually resolve what is going wrong. We need a different kind of help, a different helper, a different depth of self-understanding, and a different timetable for the process. And so your good intentions misfire because it's hard to see the way forward.

## 2. Maybe, but I know other people who have a lot bigger problem than I do.

Some people hedge a bit. You're willing to admit that the shoe fits, sort of, sometimes, maybe, *but* . . . "Yeah, I know I get a bit upset sometimes and get out of line. But I know some people with *serious* anger problems—and I'm not anything like them. I've got this friend who loses it when someone cuts him off in traffic. He throws a fit, yelling, making hand gestures, driving like a maniac. *He's* definitely got a problem with anger. And my uncle breaks things when he gets ticked off. He once destroyed his TV set with a lamp after the quarterback threw a fourth quarter interception that cost the game. Yeah, I know, I might get a bit irritated on occasion, but I usually control it and get over it pretty quickly."

Some of us aren't that bad, in comparison to others. Is this you? You're probably right. Compared to the outright barbarians and criminals, you're downright civilized—or at least semi-civilized—or at least, well, at least not as bad as you could be. You're not quite sure if the shoe fits. Maybe it sort of fits, but other people need a lot more help than you do.

*Strand of truth?* Those who feel relatively good in comparison with others know that some behaviors are worse than others. Mild irritation is not the same thing as reckless endangerment, destruction of property, or battering a spouse or a child.

*Blind spot?* They don't look deeply enough into their own motives. Is your seemingly smaller problem still a serious problem worth tackling? When does being comparatively not-so-bad drift into being self-righteous?

## 3. No, I don't have a problem. I've got good reasons to be angry and bitter.

Some people acknowledge they're angry, but they make a plausible case—in their own minds, an airtight case—that they've got reasons. "I know I've got anger issues, but look at what people did to me. It makes me so mad when my spouse or boss acts like a jerk. Anyone would get angry. And what can you expect when my parents were such lousy role models. Mom was verbally abusive to all us kids. And they were both so unfair: they'd let my younger brother get away with murder, but then they'd get on my case as though everything that happened was my fault. Of course I'm bitter. Plus, I've come from a long line of people who don't hold back their emotions. We don't really mean anything by it. It's just my personality."

Do you explain your anger by the list of grievances and reasons why, by the "buts" and "becauses"? If other people would only change, if things had only been different, if you weren't what nature and nurture made you to be, then you wouldn't have a problem.

*Strand of truth?* Those with justifiable reasons know that others do us wrong—sometimes grievous wrong. They know that anger usually arises in response to provocation. And temperament and cultural background do influence how we experience and express anger.

*Blind spot?* They act as if two wrongs (or twenty) make a right. They don't reckon with how plausible a blame-shifting stance seems, even while we are deceiving ourselves about ourselves. Could you be partly right and quite wrong at the same time? It happens all the time to all of us, which is why wise self-understanding does not reduce to a pat answer and an easy solution.

## 4. Well, I might get angry sometimes, but I'm not really an angry person.

Some people take this a step further and deny that they personally have a problem. "I'm not *really* an angry person. Deep down I'm basically a nice person. I get along great with the guys at work. But my wife is such a pain! When she goes on and on, you'd have to be a saint not to react. I lose it sometimes and get a bit out of control, but it's only when she provokes me. Left to myself, I'm easygoing."

Anger seems to invade from the outside, commandeering a well-meaning innocent party who's not really angry. Is this you? Your anger feels like an alien intruder, like a terrorist who temporarily seizes the controls of your airplane and crashes you into a building. It's not really you. The fault lies with the wife (or husband), that clueless teen (or parent), the impossible boss (or employee, or co-worker), that irritating pastor (or church member). You don't really have a problem; it's all *their* fault. The serious problem you see is that all those offenders keep doing the things that make you so mad.

*Strand of truth?* Those to whom anger seems like an invader from outside know that we react differently to different people, that others do wrong, and that our actions and reactions can contradict our conscious intentions.

*Blind spot?* They don't see themselves in the mirror in order to take responsibility for themselves. Are you really such a "nice guy" or "sweet lady"? Is your anger only an anomaly and alien intruder, the fault of others?

## 5. No way! I've found that anger is the empowering solution to personal problems and social injustice.

Then there are people who see anger not as a problem but as the solution. "I used to just go along with the status quo, but then I had an epiphany. I saw how often I was playing the victim role, how I'd believed the lies that people were telling me. I was passive, a doormat. Getting in touch with my anger has energized me and given me new identity and purpose. I no longer put up with being manipulated. I've learned to stand up for myself, for my opinions, for what I think is right, for what I want."

Is this you? Anger feels so right, so liberating. It empowers you to act for what you see as a good cause. And maybe you're right. You organize a chapter of Mothers Against Drunk Driving. You fight for racial and economic justice. You work to liberate women from sexism. You seek to stamp out child abuse. "We," the righteous, take a stand against "them," the perpetrators of evils.

How can something that feels so good be bad? Maybe you're partly right—but maybe you're partly wrong too. Have you ever noticed how dangerous it is to be right (or to think you're right)? How easily being right can ratchet up into self-righteousness, judgmentalism, self-pity, or entitlement? How easily the timid become the prickly? The aggrieved become aggressors?

*Strand of truth?* Those for whom anger is the empowering solution to injustice know that anger can be justified and can motivate constructive action. In fact, anger ought to energize action in order to right wrongs.

*Blind spot?* They don't see how easily the oppressed turn into aggressors, how subtly self-righteousness blinds us, how smoothly anger at real wrongs goes really wrong. Are you right about what's wrong, but wrong in your way of being right?

**6. Huh? I hardly ever get angry. Life's usually been pretty good, and I try to keep the problems in perspective.**

*[handwritten: This is me.]*

Some people are a bit mystified by the thought that they have an anger problem. "I'm basically a peaceful, easygoing person. Live and let live. I don't make huge demands or place unreasonable expectations on people. Nothing much tends to upset me. When something bad happens, I tend to put it in perspective: 'That's life. It doesn't matter that much. Not worth getting upset about.' I get along with most people. I try to think the best of others, do what's constructive, and look on the bright side. I'm basically an optimist. The cup is usually at least half full, and I look for the silver lining. I've gotten much more than I deserve, and achieved much more than I ever thought I would. There's no real reason to get upset. I've never ranted and raved or held a grudge for long."

If you don't care, you won't get angry. Is this you? Perhaps you were born with a sunny disposition, an easy-to-please temperament. You just can't identify. Or you've mellowed over the years and learned to be more philosophical about life. Or you've learned to detach, get a grip, and calm down. Perhaps do yoga. Take a deep breath. Or have a drink or take a drug that takes the edge off. Or maybe life's circumstances have been relatively kind to you. No real reason to get upset. In any case, the assertion that you might have a problem with anger—let alone a serious problem—doesn't seem to fit.

Maybe you're right. You aren't an over-reactor. But could it be that different shoes fit? Are you an under-reactor or nonreactor? Are

*[handwritten: Yes!]*

you too laid-back and indifferent? Do you keep your cool even when you *should* get concerned—and even a little hot and bothered? Do you put layers of insulation between yourself and the broken things in life?

*Strand of truth?* Those who see anger as other people's immaturity know that reckless desires and misplaced expectations provoke much ugly and pointless anger. There are many times we really have no reason to get angry.

*Blind spot?* Overly calm sorts usually have a hard time seeing that human beings ought to care enough to get angry sometimes. They keep their distance from life's troubles in order to keep life peaceful. And they may not see the subtler forms of anger that still inhabit them, like a virus incubating in some remote corner of the body. Or is it an indifference that makes me detached from what I ought to connect to?

These are six common responses. Do any of them capture your tendencies? But before we leave this section, it's worth adding one more important variable.

## When Anger Is Coming Toward You

Perhaps your relationship to anger takes yet a different shape. You face a serious anger problem—someone else's anger they aim toward you. If that is you, then you have a lot of company. The most immediate anger problem for many people is not what they do, but what someone else does to them.

They might say, "I have to walk on eggshells. I never know when the volcano will erupt. He (or she) is so volatile, so intimidating, so controlling. It's scary, unfair, and oppressive. I feel beaten down, and if I'm not careful, I get beaten up. Yes, I do get angry in response. But my fear and hurt seem more front and center than my anger. I wouldn't ever dare express anger, or even the mildest disagreement. Sometimes I don't even know what I want anymore. Shall we have pizza or Chinese for dinner tonight? I don't dare even think about what my preference might be, let alone say something. I just defer. I don't know what to do. I feel paralyzed, powerless, and overwhelmed by living in this atmosphere of hostility. Sometimes I even think it's all my fault, which is the very thing he accuses me of. If only I were different, then he wouldn't get so vile and violent. But in my saner moments, I realize that I am manipulated by his anger, and there's no excuse for how he treats me."

Is this you? Does violent anger come *at* you much more than it comes *from* you? Those for whom anger is an assault by others know how hurtful and intimidating it is to be treated angrily. Aggressors and abusers use anger as a power play, a way of manipulating, a reckless way of "winning." Their temper is cruel, threatening, overwhelming.

Right now, your biggest anger problem may not be your own anger. Getting immediate help to keep you and others safe is your first priority, and then you need long-term help to understand your fear, shame, and sense of powerlessness in the face of someone else's aggression. Please find a trusted counselor, pastor, or friend to talk with. Don't hesitate to call the authorities if you feel threatened (or those around you are threatened).

But I also hope that you continue to read this book. It might help you to grow in wisdom. Your own anger at the injustice you are experiencing can also become redemptive in the sure hands of your Redeemer.

>> >> >>

## Making It Your Own

1. Do any of these (or several of these) typical reactions describe your approach when things go wrong? Or are you a mix of two or three patterns? (Human beings never fall into neat categories.) Or is your biggest problem someone else's anger coming toward you?

2. Can you put the specifics of your experience with anger into words?

3. Your details will be different from mine. Yet, in different ways, every one of these reactions embodies a bit of what I mean by "a serious problem." Each reaction seems initially plausible. Certainly from the inside, we usually experience our own anger as a sense of *justified* outrage. But each reaction gets dislocated, out of whack, misshapen, misdirected—as is often apparent to those who know us, watch us, and experience us in action. Anger is most often a jumble. One of the goals of this book is to begin to sort it out with you.

At this point, let me simply ask, again, how does the shoe fit you? You may not agree that you have a *serious* problem with anger, but I hope you'll agree that you have some problem. We all do. Acknowledging your need for help and change is the first step in finding help to change. Which reaction most accurately describes your response to the sentence "You have a serious problem with anger"?

4. What is your yellow highlighter thought from this chapter? What did it say to you?

5. Are any But-What-Abouts rattling around inside you?

6. Francis of Assisi's prayer is perhaps the most well-known prayer outside of the Lord's Prayer. He longs for a better way to respond to the troubles, aggravations, and evils that we face. Notice what he asks.

> Lord, make me **an instrument of your peace.**
> Where there is hatred, **let me sow love;**
> Where there is injury, **pardon;**
> Where there is doubt, **faith;**
> Where there is despair, **hope;**
> Where there is darkness, **light;**
> Where there is sadness, **joy.**
> O Divine Master, grant that I may not so much seek
>     to be consoled
>     as to console;

To be understood as **to understand**;
To be loved as **to love**.
For it is **in giving** that we receive.
It is **in pardoning** that we are pardoned.
It is **in dying** that we are born to eternal life.

Notice each of the bold words. Each one is the opposite of unruly, confused, reactive anger.

Again, ask for help: Make me _____ . Grant me _____ .

# SECTION 2

# WHAT IS ANGER?

The next six chapters are the "engine room" of this book. What is anger? How does it work? What factors come into play? Why do we get angry? What goes into turning anger into a force for good? Anger is often confusing—"a brief madness"—or sadly, not so brief, but still confusing!

As our understanding grows, we become increasingly oriented. You know where you are. You can figure out where you need to be heading. The proposed solutions and strategies will be far richer and far more honest than strategies for anger management.

CHAPTER 4

# "I'm Against That"

What is anger?

That simple question quickly becomes complex. As we saw in the previous chapter, the anger we experience usually appears mixed up. In the most typical case, you see something wrong or bad happening. When a supposed friend betrays you, that's wrong, not right. When construction shuts down the highway and you miss an important appointment, that's bad, not good. You get angry when you experience what happened as a moral offense or an unpleasant frustration. So far, so good. In theory, your anger could be clean and constructive. Yet most often, our anger comes out grubby and destructive in complaining, throwing tantrums, displaying coldness, trying to get "even," and feeling self-pity. These are typical ways all of us return "evil for evil"—a natural response, for sure, but one that God identifies as the exact wrong response (Romans 12:17–21).

The question is also complex because each of us brings a certain set of associations with us into each angry moment. Particular memories, good and bad experiences, people who've hurt us or influenced us, the turmoil of emotions—these create a context that may be far more persuasive than any textbook definition of anger. Your instinctive, personalized definition may or may not be helpful in getting to the bottom of all that anger is.

Consider this analogy. Say the word *father*, and one woman thinks of a man who is gentle, strong, generous, protective, and reliable. She feels trust and pleasure at the thought. Another woman thinks of a man who was all those things, but he died last year. Her trust and pleasure are infused with grief. A third woman thinks of a man who is still a vicious drunk, betrayer, abuser, and hypocrite. She feels immediate fear, pain, and anger. A fourth woman thinks of a similarly harmful man . . . who died twenty years ago. Dark feelings are still present, but muted and colored with a sense of regret, of emptiness, even of thankfulness that her life was not destroyed.

The same word yields a completely different starting point for the train of thoughts and feelings. If you are trying to understand what a father is or should be, it's important to get your starting point out on the table. Only then can you start to think more widely and deeply.

It's no different with anger. What image or experience comes to mind when you hear the words "He's angry," or "She's angry," or "I'm angry"? What do you picture taking place? Do you think of a hostile exchange between two people? A particular person's facial expression, hostile words, and violence? An overwhelming burning inside? The way that you react fearfully to an angry person? An angry crowd of protesters? What is *your* association?

Here are six common wavelengths within the spectrum of bad anger. Perhaps one of these is what first captures your attention.

- *Irritability* is anger on a hair trigger. Do you live or work alongside someone who is easily set off? Are you cranky, grouchy, and testy? (The English language contains such wonderful words for this!)
- *Arguing* is the disagreeable "he said, she said" of interpersonal friction. Anger is the emotion that inhabits interpersonal conflict, and it takes two for a fight. Is quarreling your first association?
- *Bitterness* expresses how anger can last a long, long time. People recycle old hurts and nurse grievances and grudges. They never get over it.

- *Violence* expresses·the sheer destructiveness of angry behavior. Anger attacks, hurts, destroys, and even kills, finding pleasure in inflicting pain.
- *Passive anger* hides behind surface appearances and even beneath conscious awareness. As long as it remains undetectable by the person who is angry, it cannot be addressed. But it is not without its side effects—depression, lethargy, and pessimism can all stem from a passive anger toward others.
- *Self-righteous anger* enjoys the empowering sense of grievance, of getting in touch with honest emotion and expressing it freely. It feels good to let it out, and it often gets results.

Each of these six problems matters hugely. Anger flares too quickly, alienates too many relationships, burns too long, causes too much pain, hides too well, and feels too good.

But these various anger *problems* aren't the whole story. What connects them? Do they have anything in common? They can't be the essence of anger. These are some distorted versions, misdirected expressions of something deeper. They pervert something intrinsic to human nature that can be remade right.

We must bring the deeper definition to light. Only then can we cultivate a new association to anger operating as it should. *Good and angry* is the polar opposite of all forms of bad and angry, and it acts constructively in the presence of wrong. Then we can also add that other problem we've mentioned before: *absent anger* that fails to get aroused when real wrongs are occurring because it's easier to remain indifferent and detached.

The problems that arise are not the essential DNA of anger. They are the mutations and corruptions. It is important that we get the DNA straight. Then we can make sense of the mutant forms of anger that make up 99 percent of the anger that is expressed in interpersonal experience.

So what *is* anger? What common thread runs through every form of anger, whether good or bad?

At its core anger is very simple. It expresses "I'm against that." It is an active stance you take to oppose something that you assess as both important and wrong. You notice something, size it up, and say, "*That matters . . . and it's not right.*" You encounter something in your world that crosses the line. Anger expresses the energy of your reaction to something you find offensive and wish to eliminate.

The DNA is *not* a heightened pitch of emotion. It's *not* the surge of adrenaline. It's *not* any particular way of expressing anger. It's *not* which events or people happen to tick you off. It's *not* whether you get into arguments. The underlying essence is the negative evaluation: *active displeasure toward something that's important enough to care about.*

Human beings come wired with the capacity to react with displeasure toward real wrongs and to act forcefully to make wrongs right. In other words, we are moral beings. We are made in the image of God. So we are wired to operate in anger's logic: That matters, and it's wrong. It displeases me, and I am against it. I should change it, remove it, destroy it. The core is that something important is not the way it's meant to be, and we are moved to take action.

Anger is about displeasure. When you are pleased about something, it's impossible to feel angry. You approve, so no offense is taken. Or if something doesn't much matter or you don't even notice it, again no anger, no offense taken. But in each variant of anger, we assess something that happens. We care, and we take the stance of critic, judge, activist, enemy, and plaintiff: I disapprove. That's wrong. I feel offended. I want either to make it right or get rid of it.

This evaluative core *underlies* our more narrow associations to anger. Every incident has three things in common.

1. I identify some *perceived wrong.*
2. I take a *stance of disapproval* and feel displeasure.
3. In some way I'm *moved to action*—to say or do something about it. (At minimum, there's an implication of potential action.)

All of our more specific associations, what each of us calls to mind as "anger," are variations on this theme.

If this is the DNA, then anger is "judgmental" by nature. Everything else is variable. Getting the common denominator straight lets you flex with all the variables. It helps you cut to the core for proposing solutions.

Consider the wide range of possible *emotions*. On one end of the spectrum are angers that express a mere flash of irritation or mild complaint. At the other end, anger can be keyed to a ranting rage or an all-consuming quest for revenge. But whether the tremor is mild or fierce on the emotional Richter scale, the common denominator operates inside. The degree to which something matters to you, the degree to which it cuts you to the quick, will intensify or diminish your emotional fire. But momentary complaint, vocal argument, brooding resentment, and murderous frenzy all share the same anger DNA.

Similarly, the *actions* can vary greatly. Depending on the particulars, a person might actually commit murder in the first degree— or in the third degree, a crime of passion. In other cases, you might file a lawsuit, start a protest movement, or go to the defense of a victim. You can *always* get in an argument. Or you could try escape—move to a tropical island, avoid that person, pretend it doesn't bother you, or drink a few beers. Or you might do nothing. Your actual response might be fair or unfair, merciful or merciless, constructive or destructive. But the common thread within every action is the same: "That's wrong." What you do or don't do about it is variable.

The *objects* that trigger displeasure also vary widely, though the common core—"I'm against that!"—operates in every case. We can take a stand against just about anything. You can get mad at people, at animals, at ideas, at the weather, at machines, at God. We can oppose what is evil and be angry at things that truly abuse and misuse people. But we can also get angry at the smallest thing that happens to go against what we want. We can be angry with people who have done genuine harm to us, and we can also be angry with people we ought to love.

The *duration* of your reaction can vary. Your negativism might be a passing fancy, a frustration in traffic that you've forgotten in three seconds. Or anger can define the moral cause and settle into the hostility that will dominate and define the rest of your life. Whether short or long, it's still fire, registering "I'm displeased."

## Value Judgments

All this is to say that anger always makes a value judgment. Anger is always a moral matter. It has rightly been called "the moral emotion" because it makes a statement about what matters. Human beings make moral judgments, therefore human beings do anger. Period. Like God, you come wired to size things up, to feel displeasure at wrong, and to act in order to do something about it.

Would you want to live in a world with no value judgments? Not on your life. When the standard of judgment is accurate and the way of reacting is constructive—then clear-minded, hearty disapproval is one of the best things going. If you were indifferent or approving toward child abusers, terrorists, or cheats, you'd be morally defective. Moral sanity must disapprove of wrong, and that disapproval is the essence of anger.

Every time you get angry, you make your values and point of view explicit. But anger isn't the only reaction that proclaims what you value. In fact, every time you open your mouth (or don't open your mouth) you are broadcasting your values to others. This is what is meant, for example, when Jesus said that "every careless word" will be evaluated and that the mouth speaks from what fills the heart (Matthew 12:36; Luke 6:45). Every word you say—including small talk—tells something important about you. What you choose to talk about (or never think of saying) broadcasts what matters to you. Your emotional reactions and your choices always proclaim your values. Stir in a bit of emotion—because you care, because something that matters is going wrong—and you can get the reaction we call anger. Every time you get angry (or don't get angry) you broadcast what matters to you.

Throughout this book I use the flexible word *anger*. It naturally will focus on the negative value judgments we make. But always in the background I'll work within this broader description of our evaluative capacity as human beings. We evaluate everything—ourselves, others, weather, animals, ideas, dinner, God, prices, current events, you name it. Thumbs up or thumbs down. You can't escape working the way a human being works. Anger simply expresses with particular force and emotion our negative evaluations. Where does the emotional charge come from? The more something matters, the more you care, the more important it is—the more you value something—the more force you'll pour into your displeasure.

What is anger? It's the way we react when something we think important is not the way it's supposed to be. Consider several examples from the Bible that illustrate how anger is aroused, and how the emotions move us to action. In particular, notice what both bad anger and good anger have in common. And pull out your pen as you think through what is happening in each story.

1. The king Ahasuerus wants to show off his trophy wife:

> When the heart of the king was merry with wine, he commanded [his servants] to bring Queen Vashti before the king with her royal crown, in order to show the peoples and the princes her beauty, for she was lovely to look at. But Queen Vashti refused to come at the king's command delivered by the eunuchs. **At this the king became enraged, and his anger burned within him.** . . . [He called his advisors together, and they said], "Let a royal order go out from him [the king], and let it be written among the laws of the Persians and the Medes so that it may not be repealed, that Vashti is never again to come before King Ahasuerus. And let the king give her royal position to another who is better than she." (Esther 1:10–12, 19)

What does the king perceive as wrong? *Queen's disobedience*
How does he feel? *Betrayed*
What does he do? *Shuns her*

2. A young man sees the self-righteousness of Job and the accusatory attitudes of his three friends.

> **Then Elihu . . . burned with anger. He burned with anger** at Job because he justified himself rather than God. **He burned with anger** also at Job's three friends because they had found no answer, although they had declared Job to be in the wrong . . . I also will declare my opinion, for I am full of words. (Job 32:2–3, 17–18)

What does Elihu perceive as wrong? *Job was not owning it.*
*Friends were really condemning*
How does he feel? *Angry*
What does he do? *Verbal eruption*

3. A king sees another man's success and the way others praise him.

> And the women sang to one another as they celebrated,
>     "Saul has struck down his thousands,
>     and David his ten thousands."
> **And Saul was very angry, and this saying displeased him.** He said, "They have ascribed to David ten thousands, and to me they have ascribed thousands, and what more can he have but the kingdom?" And Saul eyed David from that day on. (1 Samuel 18:7–9)

What does Saul perceive as wrong? *David's popularity is a slight towards him*
How does he feel? *angry*
What does he do? *Became distrustful of David*

4. Shortly after being rescued out of slavery the Israelites throw a party to celebrate a bull calf they had cast from molten gold. Moses was delayed on Mount Sinai, and so the people said to Aaron,

"Make us gods who shall go before us. As for this Moses, the man who brought us up out of the land of Egypt, we do not know what has become of him." So Aaron . . . received the gold and made a golden calf. And they said, "These are your gods, O Israel, who brought you up out of the land of Egypt!" When Aaron saw this, he built an altar before it. And Aaron made proclamation and said, "Tomorrow shall be a feast to the LORD." And they rose up early the next day and offered burnt offerings and brought peace offerings. And the people sat down to eat and drink and rose up to play.

And the LORD said to Moses, "Go down, for your people, whom you brought up out of the land of Egypt, have corrupted themselves. They have turned aside quickly out of the way that I commanded them. They have made for themselves a golden calf and have worshiped it and sacrificed to it and said, 'These are your gods, O Israel, who brought you up out of the land of Egypt!'" And the LORD said to Moses, "I have seen this people, and behold, it is a stiff-necked people. Now therefore let me alone, that **my wrath may burn hot against them and I may consume them,** in order that I may make a great nation of you." (Exodus 32:1–10)

What does the LORD perceive as wrong? *in Fidelity*
How does he feel? *Angry / wrath*
What does he propose to do? *consume them and start over*

5. In a synagogue encounter, both Jesus and his enemies feel intense displeasure toward each other.

[Jesus] entered the synagogue, and a man was there with a withered hand. And they watched Jesus, to see whether he would heal him on the Sabbath, so that they might accuse him. And he said to the man with the withered hand, "Come here." And he said to them, "Is it lawful on the Sabbath to do good or to do harm, to save life or to kill?" But they were silent. And **he looked around at them with anger, grieved at their hardness** of heart, and said to the man, "Stretch out your hand." He stretched it out, and his hand was restored. The Pharisees **went out and immediately held counsel** with the Herodians **against him, how to destroy him.** (Mark 3:1–6)

What does the Jesus perceive as wrong? *violated a rule*
How does he feel? *agrieved @ their narrow murderess*
What does he do? *Heals*
What do the Pharisees perceive as wrong? *Jesus out of bounds and unrepentet*
What is their preset attitude? *Black/white*
What do they do?
*Seek to destroy him*

In the next chapter we will look at all that comes into play when a person gets angry. We will build toward explaining why anger seems essentially destructive in some of these cases, while in other cases it seems essentially constructive. The motives at work are the deciding factor.

» » »

## Making It Your Own

1. What is your key highlighted sentence from this chapter? Why did you select that?

2. This is a crucial chapter. We're starting to move from description to explanation. What do you make of the main point: anger is an assessment you make and a stance you take—"That matters . . . and it's wrong"?

3. Where did you find yourself asking, "But what about . . . ?" How would you answer your own question, even tentatively? How do you think that I might answer your BWA?

# CHAPTER 5

# *All* of You Does Anger

When something crosses the line and you get angry, how much of "you" is involved?

All of you. Anger is something *you* do.

Seems obvious. Why is this so important? It's important both because it's true and because it hardly ever gets said.

Usually angry people and those who give them advice focus on only one part of what is going on in anger. And, curiously, the part they focus on is not *you*. Anger becomes something that is happening to you or in you. *You* deal with "it," or harness "it," or liberate "it," or manage "it," or rid yourself of "it." But you are not intrinsically responsible for "it." "It" is going on inside you, but you aren't doing it.

One key to getting anger straight is to understand that when you are angry, *you* are doing something. Anger is not an "it." Anger is not just one part of you. Anger does not "happen" to you. You do anger.

Anger is a single complex system. It's something *you* do with all your heart, soul, mind, and body. You size something up in a flash, "I don't like that!" As your adrenaline surges, your body wakes up, heats up, tightens up. You feel intense emotions, which emote into your tone of voice, decibel level, body language, and facial expression. You think quickly, rehearsing what happened, imagining scenarios, evaluating, planning, and choosing. You go into action, choosing what to do and say (or not do and not say). Your desires and expectations are active. You want fairness, or to be proved right, or to be treated lovingly, or to get to your appointment on time, or to protect someone, or to get your way.

Is one part of your anger reaction primary and everything else merely a by-product? No. Your anger operates as a whole system of interlocking components. That unified complexity doesn't reduce to either adrenaline or emotion or thoughts or actions or motives. In anger everything works together.

If you don't understand that anger is something that *you* do—every part of you working in concert—you'll head in the wrong direction. Let me illustrate with a series of snapshots and examples. When *you* get angry, *all* of you gets involved. We will look at your agitated body, your heated emotions, your judgmental thoughts, your aggressive actions, and your godlike motives.

## Your Body Operates in the Agitated Mode

Anger involves physiology and anatomy. It has a marked bodily component, especially obvious in the more dramatic forms of anger. A general nervous tension pervades your body. Your adrenaline surges. The muscles in your face and chest—maybe your fists too!—clench. Your stomach churns. The sympathetic nervous system fires up. You actually feel hot, as blood rushes to your muscles preparing you for action. Your face gets red. Your eyes glitter—you've heard of a person having "fire in his eyes"! Your brow and mouth tighten into a disapproving scowl and frown. You're in a state of high alert with alarm bells clanging. The limbic system of your brain lights up the MRI scan with anger's distinctive neuro-electrical pattern.

Modern neuroscience has revealed more of the inside details, but this physical agitation is common-sense observation. It's fascinating how the very words for anger play off these visible, palpable effects in your body. For example, our English word *ang-er* comes from a word that captures the distress of a person who feels contorted with

intense pain and trouble: *ang-uish* and *ang-st*. You feel all twisted
up inside when you are mad; you are literally "bent out of shape."
Others can see it too; can sense it by reading your body language.
Anger is a tension state, not a calm state. In fact, our word *rage*
comes from the same root as *rabies* and *rabid*—a violent, raving fit!
A "mad dog" goes "mad" in both senses—both aggressive and out
of its mind.

A little lower on the Richter scale of emotion, the face of an
angry person looks as if something left a bad taste in his mouth, like
the sour taste of stomach acid. The French word for anger is *colére*,
from the facial grimace identical to when the bitter taste of bile or
gall is in your mouth (*choler* in Latin). Those digestive secretions
themselves have a long history as synonyms for anger. A person with
a choleric disposition is always in a bilious mood and easily galled
by what happens!

People have long been struck at how we breathe with loud, irregular snorts when we're ticked off, our nostrils flaring. One Hebrew
word for anger is the word for nostrils! Another Hebrew word expresses a different bodily experience: burning. Blood floods your
capillaries, heats your skin, and flushes your face. You literally "see
red" and "get hot under the collar." That blood flow also produces
swelling in your face, popping veins in your neck, and bulging eyes.
That hot swelling gives the Greek language its two words for what
they saw in an enraged person: "steaming (or smoking) hot" and
"swollen."

So it is no accident that many of our vivid expressions for anger
play off the physiological effects. When you get "steamed up" you
"breathe fire." A "hot-blooded" person does a "slow burn" and then
"erupts" in a "volcanic" outburst. Anger is unmistakably physiological. Your blood gets flowing. Hormones, blood flow, tense muscles,
grimaces, and a neuro-electrical firestorm register anger. But dramatic as this is, there's more to it.

The *whole* person does anger. The body no more explains the
core reality of anger than the physics of a flat-screen TV explains the

movie that's being televised. Electrons underlie everything on TV, but who would dare blame (or credit) the electrons for bringing us reality TV, infomercials, and the Golf Channel? Your body operates in the agitated mode, but what else kicks in at the same time?

## Your Emotions Operate in the Hot Displeasure Mode

Anger is a *feeling* of distress, trouble, and hatred. When someone says, "I'm angry," we usually think first of an emotion of intense displeasure. Your emotional equilibrium is upset, not calm or happy. When you don't like what's going on, anger adds the emotional charge that says, "I *really* don't like that!"

For example, I don't happen to like the taste and texture of lima beans. I'll eat them if they're served, but offered the choice, I'll always pass. I don't get worked up to any pitch of antipathy against the lowly lima bean. The threat of "lima beans for dinner!" became one of the standing jokes in our family. It's a healthy food after all, and my wife loves lima beans. Stranded on a desert island, even I would give thanks for them every day (while keenly anticipating the day of dietary deliverance).

But I *really* don't like it if someone lies to me, manipulates me, or cheats me. The "really" sets mere dislike on fire with emotion. Nobody likes betrayal, whether you're stranded on a desert island or comfortably settled at home. It's not merely a matter of taste and preference. It's a matter of active evil. Evil hurts, and anger kicks into gear.

Anger is a passion. As we just saw, when you *feel* angry your body gets fired up. But you aren't only sensing what your body is doing, as if emotions reduce to physiology. No actual human being would say, "When you mocked me, my body started to react with those physiological processes that people term the emotion of anger, but we both know that it's just my body reacting." No way. You are reacting, with feeling. "When you mock me, *I* get disturbed." Anger is a high energy state for both body and soul.

Intensity levels vary tremendously, of course. The emotional Richter scale can range from a shrug of mild irritation to a holocaust of blind rage. Or, as we saw with sixteen-year-old Jimmy and the Pharisees in the synagogue, sometimes anger comes across as flat, chilling, and calculated, not agitated, heated, and impulsive. But poke around, and you'll always get down to fire.

We've noted how your body gets agitated and your emotions feel hot displeasure. But there's more. Your physiology and your emotions connect to thoughts. You don't only feel angry; you think angry.

## Your Mind Operates in the Judicial Mode

Anger actively involves your *thought life*. Any dullness of mind instantly departs. You think vividly and quickly. When you're mad, an intense mental conversation takes place inside. You watch the video replay in the inner theater of your graphic imagination. Anger involves pointed, articulate attitudes and judgments that express the criteria by which you evaluate something as acceptable or unacceptable. You run what happened through the analytic grid of those criteria. All your reasoning powers come to bear (however unreasonable at the moment). You remember. You imagine. You weigh what happened. You run scenarios of what you should do. You form words. You weigh your possible reactions. You plan. Whether or not you are doing anything outwardly, when angry you furiously think, and what you think makes a judgment. *You idiot! That's not fair. I can't believe she did that to me.*

Your internal video camera not only replays clips from what happened, but you also script and rehearse imaginary scenarios: violent retribution or a conversation in which you give the perfect unanswerable comeback that leaves the other speechless or groveling in guilt. Words and actions get thought, planned, and practiced, whether or not you ever say or do what you're thinking inside your head.

In fact, a microcosm of the criminal justice system plays out in the courtroom of your mind. You play all the prosecuting roles simultaneously! You are the innocent victim and offended plaintiff. You are the zealous investigator, the sheriff serving summons to the offender, the D.A. pressing home irrefutable charges. You provide eyewitness testimony to the crimes, and you are the stern judge ready to mete out just punishment. You are the unanimous jury disposing of every thin alibi and extenuating circumstance, finding the accused "guilty as charged." You are the jailer of convicted felons, and the hangman ready to administer capital punishment to evildoers.

But there's usually something else distinctive about this courtroom. The trial is rigged. It's a kangaroo court and the verdict is predetermined. The punishment is vigilante justice. With rare exceptions, in this private courtroom of the mind the accused is allowed no defense attorney, no character witnesses, no due process, no extenuating circumstances, no evidence to the contrary, no second chances, no plea of innocence, no possibility that the accuser got it wrong, no possibility of mercy for the guilty!

The judicial mental attitude is written deeply into the nature of anger. One goal of this book is that you will think more carefully about *how* you think when angry, so that your inner courtroom will grow more just. Anger is the attitude of judgment, legal condemnation, and moral displeasure. But judgment can show good judgment—and even mercy.

Your thoughts operate in the judicial mode. But this is not a detached courtroom simply rendering pronouncements. It's a battlefield on which enemies will be smitten.

## Your Actions Operate in the Military Mode

Anger doesn't only operate in your body, feelings, and mind. It breaks out into *behavior*. And that behavior—whether words or deeds—is about conflict and combat. Anger goes into action as a military operation. It's about winning or losing, identifying enemies and allies, attacking and defending. Anger is fight-or-flight arousal in the body, the attack-and-defend emotion, the administration of battlefield justice. We don't ever say of someone "He got fighting sad or fighting glad." But we do say with good reason, "He got fighting mad."

Anger is a way of declaring war against a world that seems to have gone wrong. It's a way to engage, to take a stab at fixing things (though it often makes things worse). It gets rid of problems by using force (though it often backfires). If you reduce your anger to physiology, or emotion, or thought patterns, you'll lose sight of how anger significantly engages the real world in which you live. Anger—whether warped or wholesome—is an action-response to a troubling life context. You do and say things in order to change things. You "attack the problem."

Like the bigger wars, our private wars are an action adventure. They include sneak attacks, *blitzkrieg*, and strategic retreat; intelligence operations and propaganda campaigns; artillery bombardments and hand-to-hand combat; hot war and cold war; sniper fire and major offensives; giving no quarter and temporary truce. There are a thousand angry behaviors between gunfire and silent withdrawal.

Anger does things. It appears in accusatory words, sarcasm, threats, and curses. It adopts that tone of voice. Gestures and body language speak loudly: hitting the dashboard, giving a disgusted sigh, walking out of the room, raising the decibel level, rolling the eyes, scowling. You do anger with all that you are, and you do it as an inter-*action*.

Often anger is chiefly described as a personal problem or a psychological reaction. But it's important to stress that anger has an *object*, a target. It's a military engagement, not just an internal emotion. And anger is usually an interpersonal event. Of course people can become angry at nonhuman things too. Complaints about food and the weather seem endemic to human nature. People get mad at their animals, cars, TV sets, and sometimes take it out on mere objects or dependent animals. But usually "going to war" takes place against human enemies.

So problem anger isn't just a "personal" problem or an "emotional" problem. It busts out into interpersonal conflict. Anger is a central feature wherever conflict occurs: marriages, families, churches, workplaces, neighborhoods, and nations. People use anger to get what they want and to defeat other people. While the courtroom convenes in your mind, the battlefield unfolds before your eyes. Anger is a weapon to coerce, intimidate, and manipulate others—and it is a shield to defend yourself. Perhaps in your family, workplace, or church there are people who "walk on eggshells" or "duck into a foxhole" in relation to one explosive member.

To understand anger, we must look beyond ourselves to see how we engage the real world. But we also must look deeply inside ourselves. Anger happens for reasons that arise from who we are and what we want.

## Your Motives Operate in the Godlike Mode

Anger occurs not only in your body, emotions, thoughts, and actions. It comes from your deepest motives. Underlying *desires and beliefs* are at work—always. Motives run far deeper than our conscious thoughts. We often feel, think, act, and react without being aware of our motives. But they are the organizing center of who you are, and what you live for. The smallest incident of irritation or the merest lingering bitterness reveals vast truths about you—if you're willing to look.

To tease out the motives underlying anger, ask "What are my expectations?" That simple question helps you stop and think. And the answer often comes in layers, not all at once. Self-knowledge is both a simple gift and a hard-won achievement. You might be aware of your expectations at one level, but gradually come to understand more profound levels. It's hard to see our motives. It's even harder to see them for what they are. Part of the problem comes because anger feels so "righteous"—and bad anger is so self-righteous. "I'm so *right*, because you are so *wrong*." That same passionate desire to think well of ourselves, to assert and defend ourselves continually, gets in the way of seeing and facing our motives.

But taking an honest look will bring light to the reasons for your anger. Here are some questions that will help you uncover expectations and motives that underlie your anger:

- When you get upset, what do you *want*? What does that desire mean to you? Why does that thing matter so much to you?
- When you fire into anger, what do you *believe* about the significance of what just happened to you?
- What are you afraid of? (Fear is desire turned backwards: "I *don't want* that to happen.") What dire thing do you believe might happen?
- What *intentions* guided you during that interaction? What are you after? When you become bitter and can't shake it, what do you hope for and wish? What are you living for—right now, not in theory?

These questions dig deeply into the springs of anger. They reveal your heart—what you crave, what you trust, what you hate, what you love. When anger goes astray, it says something about how we are going astray inside, about who is the center of the universe. When anger runs amok into temper, grousing, or bitterness, you don't just need a technique to calm yourself down. You don't just need your circumstances to change. You don't just need other people to change. Your core motives must change. The god you worship (my will be done, my kingdom come . . . or else) must be overthrown.

And overthrowing a false god takes something much deeper than simply learning conflict-resolution skills, valuable as those are. It calls for more than altering how you talk to yourself, though that also will change. It takes more than finding some technique, recreation, or medication that works to calm you down. Sure, take a deep breath or count to ten. But motives are the goals around which you organize your life.

Motives are your core values and commitments, what you base your identity on. They shape and energize your emotions, thoughts, and actions. They determine how you treat people. They determine how you react to pain, loss, or threat (the provocations to anger). They determine how and why you get angry—and whether your anger is radiantly healthy or somehow diseased.

Trisha and Ryan give us an example. They are dating and they often argue when they cross wires about plans for the evening. It just happened again. Ryan showed up late for a dinner date, and they started to bicker. A video of the argument captures the time, the place, who said what when, their supposed plans, and what extenuating circumstances played in whose favor. It also captures the pouts, the shocked expressions, the frowns, the eyes rolling, the edge in the voice, the rising (or lowering) decibel level that registers hostility. As the argument escalates, the words turn from current events into personal accusation and damnation. On Trisha's side, "You always do this. You're impossible. You're so selfish and inattentive. You never listen."

And, like any war, offense encounters defense. Once Ryan heard her opening salvo, he rebuts: "I don't *always* do this. Just this morning I suggested the sushi bar, but when you mentioned Italian I said that sounded great. I'm here now. What's the big deal? So I'm ten minutes late." And then (partly because he is actually closer to twenty minutes late) he launches a counteroffensive, "You never cut me any slack. You're so judgmental and controlling."

So far, so bad. It's a typical dating couple argument. Now scratch for motives. What do these two aggrieved people *really* want? Is the argument only about the difference between 7:00 and 7:18? Is it only about whether or not his reasons for not getting in touch are valid? Is it only about whether either one of them is listening? Is it only about body language, hot feelings, hard thinking, and then the insulting and defensive words they are saying to each other? Even if we add the element of history ("always" and "never" refer back to something specific), we still haven't gotten to the root of it. Underneath, you find motives. You find other stories that were not mentioned out loud.

People rarely share these things when under attack and attacking back. The combatants are often not even aware of their motives. The noise of hostility and hurt drown out conscious awareness.

On Trisha's side: *I want you to love me. If you cared for me, you'd be on time, or let me know, or at least say you're sorry. Instead, you're obsessed with proving you're right and I'm wrong. Your lateness and defensiveness mean you don't love me, and you don't care about how I feel.*

On Ryan's side: *Your anger means you don't love me. I want you to treat me with common courtesy. I fear your rage. If you respected me, you'd care to find out what really happened, and what I was thinking, and that I was thinking about you and felt bad that I was late. You'd believe me, and not just get angry because you feel put out. You couldn't care less about me as a person.*

We can understand, and perhaps sympathize, with both parties when we hear what they want. It sounds so plausible. Our motives are a curious thing. On the one hand, they are fine china, delicate and vulnerable. Anger makes you feel strong (or at least you can pose as strong, covering over the vulnerabilities). But admitting the motives in a lovers' quarrel exposes you as weak. This couple could talk about their motives in a way that expressed simple hurt or perplexity, not vast hostility, grievance, and disdain. Such a conversation might even help them understand each other better and learn how to love in more thoughtful ways.

So why does it go so bad? Why can't they talk over the miscommunication and disappointment in a constructive way? Why don't they communicate their desires and hurt without adding large doses of hostility and self-righteousness? Why don't they work toward mutual understanding and a better life together?

Motives are not only the fine china of plausible desires and honest hurt. They are also the steel and high explosives of all-consuming self-will. When anger goes bad, it's because motives operate in the godlike mode. "I want my way. I demand that you love me on my terms. I will prove that I am right at all costs. Proving that you are inexcusably and outrageously wrong is one way to prove that I'm right, and that I'm a victim of your ridiculous iniquity. I want to be in control. You should obey me, listen to me, attend to my every want. How dare you cross my almighty will?"

How might we describe this basic *modus operandi* that happens on the inside of bad anger? It's rather like the MS-DOS operating system hidden beneath a Microsoft Windows interface. The surface of any argument is like the documents, folders, icons, and windows. But far underneath is the code that makes it all go. Let's look at that code from three complementary angles.

**First, Trisha and Ryan are each saying, "I WANT MY WAY."** Anger goes bad because of a demand. A simple desire (and the simple pain that comes when we do not get what we want) becomes magnified into something I *must have*. The wrong in my desires is often not what I want, but that I want it *too much*. My desires become my *needs*. I must be loved. I demand your respect. I need you to treat me the way I want. I command that you cut me slack. I insist that you be understanding. I demand that you be affectionate. "What I want is right; therefore I am right to be angry at you." Even if what you want is a good thing (e.g., your boyfriend to come on time and to have the thoughtfulness to phone if he's delayed), you want it so much that it devours you. Simple desires mutate into demands that must be met *or else*!

**Second, Trisha and Ryan are each saying, "I'M AN AGGRIEVED VICTIM."** In my anger, I put you on trial for crimes against humanity and punish you as a criminal. I'm the victim of your felonies (real or imagined). Victimhood becomes my identity. It mutates and grows all-consuming. Self-pity and self-righteousness are strong narcotics. It feels so good to feel so bad because it proves you are so bad and I am so good.

**Third, Trisha and Ryan are each saying, "I AM GOD."** There's something high and mighty about anger, when distilled to its basic elements. Anger goes wrong when you get godlike. Your desires become divine law. Poke your way into every example of bad anger, and you'll find god-playing. Whether I'm really ticked off, just a little irritated, or deeply embittered, it's all about almighty me. Anger is demanding and entitled: This is what I want. My will be done. It's superior: The world and all that is in it are subject to me. All persons, objects, and events are subject to my opinion and evaluation. It's accusatory: You have violated my will, and you deserve punishment.

When anger goes right, there's always something higher, some higher purpose or person who puts a cap on anger, who sets a limit on bitterness, who gives reasons not to whine and complain. The most high God, his higher law, his loving mercies, and his higher purposes transform anger. Something miraculous happens when I no longer say, "My kingdom come, my will be done on earth." My motives no longer operate in the God-usurping mode. The mercy that humbles us begins to master us, and my universe returns to reality.

It's only then that we shed the arrogance, self-interest, jealousy, and hostility that Ahasuerus, Saul, and the Pharisees expressed in stories we read at the end of the last chapter. It's only then that Trisha and Ryan became sane, humbled by mercies they need, grateful for mercies God gives. The quality of our anger decisively changes for good. This doesn't mean you never get upset. You read good examples in the anger of Elihu, the LORD God, and Jesus. The essential inner logic of anger changes.

What made the difference? In each case, larger purposes controlled. Elihu was justly angered when he witnessed the clash between Job's self-righteousness and his friends' accusatory counsel. He leaped to God's defense. But though Elihu couldn't say it as well as God would, his words introduced the pointed love of God's anger as he challenged both Job and the three friends. The end result? Mercy and humility triumphed over fruitless wrangling and mutual accusation.

Similarly, the LORD God was justly angered by his people's idolatrous carousing. What resulted? God's justified anger prompted Moses's faith as a Christ-figure to his people, alternately interceding for mercy and expressing God's just anger. The end result? In the scene that followed we hear a revelation of the core DNA of the entire Bible. In Take Two on Mount Sinai, we witness the double-stranded helix of God's spectacular goodness toward straying people.

> "The LORD, the LORD, a God merciful and gracious, slow to anger, and abounding in steadfast love and faithfulness, keeping steadfast love for thousands, forgiving iniquity and transgression and sin, but who will by no means clear the guilty." (Exodus 34:6–7)

God is good—justly angered at all who turn against him and others. God is good—incalculably merciful toward all who acknowledge their need.

In the same way, Jesus was justly angered by the stony-heartedness of men who hated him and were indifferent to the sufferings of others. But what such men meant for evil, God worked for our incalculable good. Jesus healed a disabled man on a Sabbath and for such "wrongdoing" faced death at the hands of murderous men. The end result? He himself bore the sins of stony-hearted men and women. The core DNA of the entire Bible took on flesh, the Son of Man, walking among us and then dying for us. He lives now, forgives us still, and renews us into the image of his just anger and his abounding mercy.

When God's larger purposes are in control, the poisonous evil of anger is neutralized. Anger becomes a servant of goodness. The anger becomes just, and the purposes become merciful to all who will turn and trust and become conformed to his image. He changes our motives.

In a later chapter, we will explore our motives more deeply. We will weigh them for what they are, both the good and the bad. And, most importantly, we will look at how the grace of Christ enters in to forgive and then sets to work altering our motives. At this point simply take to heart some basics. Motives operate below the body's agitation, the emotional firestorm, the mental courtroom, and the military action. It is possible (and hugely illuminating) to describe the motives that operate below the he said/she said of any argument. We can name them for what they are. In other words, we can know ourselves in ways that our culture's current theories on anger never notice.

» » »

## Making It Your Own

1. What is the key sentence for you in this chapter?

2. What are the implications? Why is this important to *you*? What difference would it make if this became a controlling perspective from the bottom of your heart?

3. Any BWAs?

CHAPTER 6

# Nature, Nurture . . . and Human Nature

We have seen that anger is a moral response saying "That's wrong and it matters." We have seen that you *do* anger—all of you, body and soul—and you do it for personal reasons. But how does it arise, and what factors shape the particular forms it takes?

In this chapter we're going to stand back and admire a feisty little girl. We'll witness God's common grace in action. We'll think about the original equipment with which human nature comes wired. And then we'll look at the way we each pick up patterns and develop habits. This chapter aims to give perspective before we dive into the deep waters of radical thinking about our goals.

## Anger Is Natural

I don't remember much from fourth grade. But I do remember Leanne. She was a fiery little girl. She could be imperious and opinionated, giving teachers fits and wearing out her best friends. When something or someone crossed her will, you knew about it: the toss of her head, the fire in her eye, the quick comeback, the heels dug in for a fight to the finish with no quarter asked and no quarter given.

But Leanne could also be a heroine. One day on the playground after lunch I was a bystander to her moral outrage.

Mark was another classmate, a small fourth-grader. He was an awkward, shy kid, who was often teased. This afternoon he was being picked on by three, big, fifth-grade boys. The bullies had trapped him in a ring and were shoving him around. When he started to whimper, they began to mock him in singsong, "Marky is a baby, cry little baby. Marky is a baby, cry little baby."

Suddenly Leanne ran up to them. She was smaller even than Mark. But she broke right into the ring, stood up to the bullies, and started berating them. "You stop that. It's wrong. You're just being mean. You should be ashamed. Look how big you are. Look how little Mark is. Look how many of you there are, and only one Mark. Go pick on somebody your own size. You should tell him you're sorry for what you did." She made quite a scene. She was mad. It was the perfect combination of courage, love, and outrage.

The rest of us kids started to gather around, instead of hanging back in apprehension. The bullies stopped. They glanced sidewise at the gathering crowd, and looked down at the ground. Then they edged away, scuffing the dirt with their feet, and shrugging. Leanne had won the day. Mark had been rescued from their torment.

Nobody told Leanne to have a keen sense of justice. I bet she hardly thought about what she did. She simply saw an unfair, mean thing going on—and her anger carried her into action. It was an act of temper—spontaneous, loving, and good!—on behalf of someone who was being harmed. It came naturally.

Leanne, like you and me, like all humankind, is wired to discriminate between kind and cruel, fair and unfair, and right and wrong. Something about "cruel, unfair, and wrong" bothered her. Unless you have numbed yourself to meanness, or hardened yourself by becoming mean (and both of those things often happen as a life unfolds), then you too will get upset at what seems wrong and unfair. It's something in the way *human* nature comes wired. Leanne instinctively *knew*—without lengthy reflection or careful analysis—that what those boys were doing was an evil to be opposed.

Anger is the fighting emotion. Anger is the justice emotion. Anger is the deliver-the-oppressed-from-evil emotion. It stems from love for the needy. All of us come wired with a sense of justice. We can override it or pervert it. We can direct it to wholly selfish purposes. So a bully's sense of justice might only kick in when *he's* being mistreated—or when *he's* being fairly called to account. Have you noticed how huffy and outraged some people get when they are caught doing something wrong?

Your sense of justice can be bent in many directions, for good or ill, but you cannot erase it. It's part of the original equipment in human nature. What's the term for this? "The image of God" is the shorthand way of describing the way we were all meant to be. You identify something wrong and harmful. It matters. You are created to get upset about it. You speak and act forcefully to address the problem. When human beings work this way, it's beautiful. It's constructive. Our anger is natural. It is a capacity given by creation in the image of the God who is just.

In the Garden of Eden there was already evil to be angry at. As image bearers, loyal to God, Adam and Eve should have gotten angry at the Liar and Murderer. They should have picked up sticks and stones and killed the serpent who lied by suggesting to them that God was the liar. So the first act of anger would have been in Genesis 3, instead of Genesis 4 (when Cain murdered Abel).

If only Adam and Eve had been angry at the right time and in the right way. If only you and I got angry at the right time and in the right way. But, sadly, anger is "natural" in a second way. Creational good is entangled with and distorted by fallenness and innate evil that has become "second nature." *Eye opening.*

Have you ever been around children who were whining? Whining is the fingernails on the blackboard of human relationships. Or have you ever seen a child throw a full-volume tantrum? Or have you ever listened to children as they are manipulating their parents? "But I *want to* watch TV." "But I *don't want to* eat my dinner." "You *never* let me do what I want." Where on earth did they learn such behavior?

They didn't learn it. Yes, skill in the habits of whining, temper, and manipulation can be learned (more on that later in this chapter). A newborn is utterly dependent and comes wired to need and trust parents who nourish and protect. A parent is God's *in loco parentis*, a powerful and loving god in the infant's small universe. And then a transition happens as the child's willfulness emerges. A new god comes forth: "I am god, not you."

When Jesus said, from within, out of the heart of man, come evil thoughts, coveting, wickedness, deceit, envy, slander, pride, and foolishness, he did not exclude children.[1] That litany of human sinfulness uses the grown-up words for what children do, no less than adults. We come hardwired for sinful anger.

So to be human means you come created with a capacity for just anger. And to be human means you come fallen, with a bent toward bad anger. The potential is hardwired into us in two different ways. Good and evil cohabitate. We aren't talking physiology, but in human nature, the givens of our moral makeup. We are a living contradiction. Something about anger is very good, and something is very bad. We are attuned to know the difference between fair and unfair, love and hate. But we are also out-of-tune so anger gets petty, self-serving, and vicious. This fact doesn't need to be proved. The contradiction in our nature is obvious. It operates in my life and in yours too.

A lot of what makes anger so hard to sort out is our difficulty in figuring out and accounting for these two sides of human nature. You and I are paradoxical. No one can understand a person who isn't willing to hold two opposites together. You can't understand yourself without holding the creation and fall together.

Optimists see all the evidence for the image of God and creational good when they talk about anger. "Human nature is basically good. Open your eyes. Look at the noble actions, the courage, and the self-sacrifice for others. Consider the creativity and the

generosity of which people are capable. The causes of bad all lie outside of you, those forces of nature or nurture that negatively impact
upon you. You have every right to your anger because other people
do you wrong. The problems in life, the distorted forms of anger,
can be fixed through science, medicine, social reform, education, en-
lightenment, and good intentions." Optimists think they see clearly,
but they only half-see.

Pessimists are more cynical and see all the evidence for the fall
when they talk about anger. "Human nature is basically self-serving, destructive, and duplicitous, so what else can you expect? Open
your eyes. Look at all the bullies, liars, and manipulators. People
are selfish and think they're better than they are. Real life is a jungle
of competing self-interest and spin-doctoring. Since you are part of
people, don't kid yourself. You do whatever is required to get by in
personal relations, the workplace, or politics." Cynics think they see
clearly, but they too only half-see.

They're both half right and all wrong. When you wake up and
look reality in the eye, you can't remain either a tender-hearted
optimist or a tough-minded pessimist. Thoughtful wisdom says,
"So much good and so much bad, all at the same time, in every
heart. The bad so often perverts the good in hostility and bitterness. Thankfully, the good often subverts the bad in acts of kindness
and in the hard work of peace making. None of us are as bad as we
could be (though some people come close). None of us are as good
as we should be (and the more you know yourself, the more you see
how you fall short). Each of us is a microcosm: a perpetual skirmish
in the Great War between good and evil." Anger comes naturally
to you and me. Both the good and the bad are part of the package
called a person.

So angry people come with a package of both good and bad.
Your anger is both brilliant and appalling. The shifting line between
good and evil plays out when it comes to your anger, like everywhere else. Your anger is Godlike to the degree you treasure justice
and fairness and are alert to betrayal and falsehood. Your anger is

devil-like to the degree you play god and are petty, merciless, whiny, argumentative, willful, and unfair.

## Anger Is Learned

Our capacity for anger is a given of human nature, but at the same time, our patterns of anger are also learned through human nurture. You learn exactly how to be angry in two different ways. You pick it up from others, and you develop your own style through long practice.

First, anger is taught and modeled to us. We learn many things from other people about how and when to be angry, for good and ill. We learn what to get upset about (and what to ignore). We learn how to show our displeasure (and how to mask it).

Let me give a simple example. I live in Philadelphia where, on occasion, we get a heavy snowfall. Is a snowstorm something to enjoy or something to get angry about? Is a snowstorm a beautiful sight with a built-in opportunity to meet neighbors, exercise by clearing the walkway, and have fun sledding and cross-country skiing? Or is it a frustration, with the inconvenience of shoveling and the financial hit of customers staying home? Either attitude rubs off on the people around. Unlike experiencing betrayal or being given a surprise gift, a snowstorm doesn't come with a cue card telling you whether to "get mad" or "get glad." Your response to snow is often shaped by how the people around you react.

What habits, styles, and tendencies to bad anger did you acquire from others? Some children never thought of letting fly an angry curse—they had never even heard the bad words. They surprise themselves when a graphic obscenity slips out a week after first riding on the school bus. Parental shock perhaps quickly nips habit formation. But later, when those kids grow up and live in a college dorm, start their first job, or join the military, maybe the four-letter words creep in as all-purpose modifiers: "Pass the %$#@! butter" wasn't necessarily learned at home, but it was learned.

Other children were raised to curse. A father who routinely damns the weather, yells in traffic, and demeans his wife is training his children to do likewise. Angry and hostile curses become routine ways to respond to the mildest frustration. Or consider a mother who pretends she's never angry, but then withdraws with tight-lipped disapproval and often blames and criticizes others. She is training her children to do the same. Our parents, our peers, and the media give us models for how one ought to handle the minor frustrations of daily life. Emotions are highly catching.

A wise proverb says, "Do not make friends with a hot-tempered person, do not associate with one easily angered, or you may learn their ways and get yourself ensnared" (Proverbs 22:24–25 NIV). Do you have bad anger habits that are affected by friends, family, or co-workers? We learn many things by example. The capacity for anger is a given of human nature, but the form anger takes is greatly influenced by human nurture.

Constructive anger is also learned from role models. It would be an exaggeration to say the habit of patience and constructive anger are *easily* acquired from others! Somehow germs seem more catching than good health, and a bad attitude travels faster than a good attitude. But it can happen. Did you ever know a parent or close friend, a teacher or coach, who was patient and generous with others, not easily set off? Did he or she save their anger for when there was a wrong that really mattered? Was anger expressed cleanly and constructively, as part of love for others that tackled wrongs? You may well have picked up a good thing or two. Another wise proverb puts it this way, "He who walks with the wise grows wise" (Proverbs 13:20, author translation). There's nothing like a good role model to give you a vision for how it's possible to do life well.

Many of the details of your style of anger may be influenced by parents, peers, or ethnic group. Cultural differences in expressing emotions can be marked. Norwegian anger and Italian anger often differ drastically in modes of expression. The habits of the former should not form our image of ideal self-control. The habits of the latter should not form our image of ideal emotional expressiveness. You're hardwired for anger, but the exact form anger takes often is nurtured.

We are all learners, sponges absorbing the values, assumptions, attitudes, and expectations that surround us. The modern words for this process are enculturation and socialization. The old-fashioned way to say the same thing is to note how we are all being "discipled" into the image of the significant people from whom we take our cues. Sometimes what we learn is conscious; most of the time it is simply the air we breathe.

Anger is learned in a second way. We practice. It can become "second nature," a habitual way of responding. "Practice makes perfect" in anger as with many other things. Perhaps every time you think about your tight finances, you get uptight. The day you pay bills, you're testy. Every time, twice a month on the Saturday after payday, your family learns to avoid you because you bark and holler. Or perhaps you get in the same argument over and over and over again. You could almost mail in the tape and spare yourself the trouble.

A few weeks ago my wife and I were driving on an unfamiliar road, trying to find an unfamiliar destination. I slowed down and was a little tentative about which driveway to turn into. (I swear that I had *not* been indulging in my love of slow driving before that. I'd been moving along at a normal speed, and I'd given the truck driver behind me no previous reason to be irritated!) But as I slowed and wavered, that driver leaned hard on his horn. Then as we started to turn left, he accelerated up next to us on the shoulder, and leaned out his window, face contorted with rage. He let fly a blast of obscenities. Employing a vivid mix of anatomical, excretory, sexual, and hellfire vocabulary, he concisely summed up my character, intelligence, mother, and right to be driving on that particular road, making his life miserable. I marvel that he could pack so much content into such a brief moment. The verbal tirade was accompanied by creative use of finger gestures. Then he gunned the accelerator and shot off down the road. I think it's fair to assume that I was not the first slow driver to receive the full treatment at his hands. I had run up against a well-practiced habit.

Patterns of anger—both bad and good—become characteristic. Some people always hit the roof and then get over it. Others go into their shell. Some go on the rampage for days, muttering, gossiping, rehearsing, or exaggerating. Other people raise their voices. Some get quiet, fearful, and discouraged. Others pretend nothing happened. Some don't recognize that they're bothered and can't acknowledge anger even to themselves. Others take it out on an innocent party, or with a hard workout. Some people give plenty of signals that they are angry. Others make guerrilla strikes out of nowhere. Some use anger to intimidate and control people. Others use anger to sulk and avoid people.

And, wonderfully, some people express anger in ways that tackle problems to solve them. Blessed are the peacemakers. To respond constructively to trouble is a fine art, gained through long practice. We develop a "lifestyle," a characteristic manner of doing life.

These last few chapters have sought to orient our thinking to basic truths about anger. I have wanted to give you a richer repertoire of terms and ideas with which to think about anger. But they've also been fightin' chapters in a sense. For me to say that *you* do anger as a moral response by a morally responsible human being is the simple truth, and essential for true self-knowledge and for becoming rightly oriented in this complex world. But it is a tough sell when so many other voices tell you to look in other directions for the essential factor. The things you say to yourself in your head? How your family raised you? How the evolutionary history of the human race shaped your genetics? The devil taking up residence and taking over?

In order to hear a simple truth clearly and walk out the implications, we've had to clear out a lot of underbrush. Anger arises in your body, but your body is not the crucial issue. Anger is learned from people around you, but their model is not the crucial issue. Anger is affected by the things you tell yourself, but your thoughts are not the crucial issue. Anger gets pent up, but releasing energies is not the crucial issue. Anger is devilishly hostile, but exorcising dark powers is not the crucial issue.

The crucial issue is *you*. And you are the complex human being we've been looking at for the last few chapters.

» » »

## Making It Your Own

1. Key sentence and why?

2. BWAs?

3. What do you make of the idea that a *paradox* operates within your experience of anger?

4. Where have you seen the good side of indignation arising from the sense of justice and compassion for the victimized? Have you ever thought of this as part of the practical meaning of the phrase "image of God"?

5. Where have you seen the evil side of petty hostilities arising from the perversion of our sense of right and wrong? Have you ever thought of this as part of the practical meaning of the phrase "fall into sin"?

6. Do you have a tendency to be more of an optimist (focusing on what's good) or more of a pessimist (focusing on what's bad)?

## CHAPTER 7

# The Constructive Displeasure of Mercy, Part I: Patience and Forgiveness

Now we turn the corner from understanding the problem to addressing it. So these next few chapters are the heart of this book.

We have looked closely at anger's essential DNA: displeasure at wrong. And we have traced in some detail the ways that our displeasure itself goes wrong. But along the way, we have caught glimpses of how anger might be redeemed. How does anger actually become constructive? How can displeasure at wrong become an expression of faith in God, and then an expression of love for people? The concern I felt for that troubled mother and son in the supermarket intimated that anger might be transformed into something loving. Leanne's bold defense of her helpless classmate demonstrated that anger in action can accomplish something truly good.

It is possible to say "That's wrong!" and yet express our displeasure in ways that prove truly constructive. Actually loving. Even beautiful. Jesus saw wrong, called it wrong, and called out wrongdoers. Here is how he describes his purpose:

> God did not send his Son into the world to condemn the world, but in order that the world might be saved through him. (John 3:17)

We justly deserve anger and condemnation. But mercy's purposes control how God expresses his displeasure. This chapter is about good anger.

Let's give this good anger a name: *the constructive displeasure of mercy.*

Think about that description: constructive . . . displeasure . . . of mercy. Each of those three words matters. Good anger operates as one aspect of *mercy.* It brings good into bad situations. It stands up for the helpless and victimized. It calls out wrongdoers, but holds out promises of forgiveness, inviting wrongdoers to new life.

Your anger and mine can be remade into God's image. Of course, when we react to one bad with another kind of bad, we always compound problems. The typical bad angers are all versions of returning evil for evil. But, where intelligent mercy flows, then mercy's displeasure brings a powerful good. Strong mercy is the DNA of the entire Bible. Clear-minded mercy is the DNA of redemption. Jesus gathers up our angers, not to neuter our sensitivity to evil, but to redeem how we respond.

By definition, mercy is a response to feeling *displeasure.* When someone is going wrong, when someone is suffering wrong, when things are going wrong, both pleasure and indifference are wrong. Goodness, if only we did not suffer and did not sin! We would have no need to receive God's mercies—his paradoxical, lovely expressions of his displeasure with how things are. If this world did not throb with sufferings and sins, we ourselves would not need to learn how to also feel mercy's energetic displeasure with the status quo. Strong, clear-minded mercy is the way we are meant to transmute feeling disturbed, uncomfortable, and bothered by what is.

And by definition, mercy is consistently *constructive.* Mercy intervenes to address and solve whatever problem is in view. Jesus embodies this constructive displeasure of mercy. It is a rich, complex way of responding to life.

- Faced with the death of Lazarus and with the sisters' grief, Jesus is successively angered, distressed, grief-stricken, and indignant at death, loss, and suffering (John 11:33, 35, 38). In mercy, he raises Lazarus to life.

- Jesus meets a man with a withered hand in the synagogue at Capernaum. He is resolved to heal the man. But Pharisees are also present, and out to get Jesus. In mercy to the man, he looks at the Pharisees with anger, grieved at their hardness of heart (Mark 3:1–5). Then he heals the man.

- When Jesus calls Matthew to follow him, he is calling a bad man. He eats with Matthew and a crowd of other bad people. Pharisees raise questions. Why would Jesus eat with tax collectors and sinners? He responds that doctors work with sick people, not healthy people. I am calling sinners, not those who think they are good enough and better than other people (Matthew 9:9–13). In mercy, Jesus does life-giving good for sinners. He willingly dies for weak, ungodly, sinful enemies of God (Romans 5:6–10).

Mercy. Because Jesus hates suffering and loves sufferers, sufferers find help and joy. Mercy. Because Jesus hates sin and loves sinners, sinners find forgiveness and joy.

This response to something that is wrong in our world is complex. It involves a constructive mix of justified anger combined with mercy and active efforts to make true peace where there is trouble. *The constructive displeasure of mercy* traverses exactly the same ground as simple anger. But it's on a different spectrum altogether. It does not act like the typical hostilities. Like simple anger, it says, "That matters. It's wrong and offensive. I want to do something about it." But unlike just getting mad, it says, "That's wrong—and I will be constructively merciful in pursuing whatever is just, whatever makes things right, whatever does good."

Mercy is an entirely different way of reacting to offenses, to things we think are wrong. Think about this: mercy is not a non-reactive indifference—because it *cares*. And it's the furthest thing from approval—because what's happening is *wrong*. Mercy includes a component of forceful anger, but anger's typical hostility, vindictiveness, and destructiveness does not dominate.

True mercy proceeds hand in hand with true justice. It brings mercy to victims by bringing justice. While working hand in hand with justice, it offers mercy to violators. Mercy contains a combination of attitudes and actions that proceed in a constructive, instead of destructive, way. Mercy, including its component of constructive anger, is an amazing act of love. It's how we love in the face of something wrong. I can know something is utterly wrong, yet I can act constructively.

Let me give an example. We've all known people who bristle at the slightest hint of criticism. But have you ever seen someone respond *well* to unfair criticism? I'll never forget watching a public speaker respond when he was sharply attacked by someone in the audience during the Q&A session after his talk. The critic erupted with hostility and made an outrageous caricature of what the speaker had just communicated. She accused the speaker of arrogance, ignorance, and incompetence (because she disagreed with one particular implication of his politics). Her behavior was completely out of line. Even if there were legitimate grounds to disagree (I didn't completely agree with the speaker either), her way of disagreeing was outrageous.

But that speaker did something amazing, something I've always remembered. He did not take the tirade personally, get defensive, or counterattack. Instead his response was clarifying. He acknowledged valid concerns in what she'd said—good points hidden within the hostile accusations we'd all just heard. In fact, he argued her case better than she did, noting its strong points! He was personally conciliatory: "Let's talk more later. Come seek me out after the meeting breaks up." He didn't back down, but he did not get his back up. He defended what he'd said, but not defensively. Instead, he handled a volatile situation constructively.

The verbal attack had prompted an awkward moment for the whole group of some 300 people. People were squirming during her rant. But our speaker deflected some of the awkwardness with a bit of gently self-deprecating humor. In response to one of her barbs—"What gives *you* the right to stand up there and pontificate?"—he answered, "Well, our hosts *did* invite me to speak, and I *do* hope they'll pay me, even though they now know what I think." That bit of gentle humor took the attention off of the critic, who by now looked like she felt embarrassed that she'd made such a scene. As far as I could tell, the speaker was at zero on the personal anger scale, and marvelous on the constructive response scale.

That public speaker gives us some hints about this curiously merciful way to stand against someone. He didn't react in the ways that come so easily to us all. He didn't bristle or retaliate. At the same time, I'm sure he did not approve of her venomous attack on him. He certainly wasn't feeling pleasure!

It was a tense moment. He disagreed with her accusations and with the way she accused him. It was a very unpleasant public scene. He was not indifferent to being publicly caricatured and maligned. He didn't shrug it off. But he demonstrated the constructive displeasure of mercy. His response was full of vitality, purpose, alertness, and emotional energy, just like anger. But his displeasure did something wonderfully constructive.

The speaker was demonstrating constructive displeasure. The way he responded to the attack looked and sounded like mercy. This good version of anger takes careful thought to understand. It turns the world upside-down. It changes you into an agent of good, engaging a world of bad. You can really only learn it from Jesus Christ. It's the quality of true mercy that he shows you and me. He's willing to spend your life teaching you. It is a most beautiful, non-intuitive wisdom.

Would you like to grow in expressing the constructive displeasure of mercy? I know I would. At home, at work, at church—I would like to respond to wrongs with constructive mercy instead of making a bigger mess. And the good news is that we can all grow in these things. To grow in mercy is a long, slow process, but it starts with understanding what we are aiming for.

## Four Key Aspects to the Constructive Displeasure of Mercy

There are four key aspects to the constructive displeasure of mercy. Each of these four, like anger, implies active disapproval of what's happening. But unlike the vast bulk of anger, each breathes helpfulness in how it goes about addressing what it sees as wrong. These four characteristics are:

1. Patience
2. Forgiveness
3. Charity
4. Constructive conflict

We often lack a rich sense of exactly what such varied aspects of mercy actually do and mean. We can understand displeasure, indifference, and pleasure. But though constructive displeasure is the key to becoming both sane and humane, we lack a category for it.

Patience, forgiveness, charity, and constructive conflict sound "religious," and for good reason. The actions and attitudes that express constructive displeasure of mercy are *exactly* how the Bible portrays the man Jesus in action. And Jesus is the incarnation of God-in-action who intervenes in what goes wrong. The God who reveals himself in Scripture is not a theological abstraction. He is an active, morally discerning person. He sees, evaluates, speaks, and takes action. These four actions within the constructive displeasure of his mercy describe the crucial way—the stunning way—that he acts.

They also describe how a wise person acts. They describe someone who is becoming like Jesus. Because of the sort of world we live in and the sort of people we are, these four activities describe beautiful necessities. You can't live without them. They describe love and goodness—the opposites of hate and evil.

These words describe rare qualities. They are difficult to do—actually impossible, without the help of God himself. They don't come naturally to anyone, religious or irreligious. But, you can't "do" anger right without the constructive displeasure of mercy. It rolls up its sleeves. It tackles the toughest problems you will ever face in life and in yourself. It redeems anger.

We must grasp the workings of merciful displeasure in order to think rightly about anger. How does the in-working of such mercies into your experience *change* the way you feel displeasure? How does their outworking in how you live change the way you face life's provocations, disappointments, frustrations, and betrayals? Patience, forgiveness, charity, and constructive conflict put a qualitatively different spin on troubles and problems. All four necessarily go together. If any one of them goes missing, you've lost something crucial. This chapter will discuss in greater detail the first two—patience and forgiveness. The next chapter will take a close look at charity and constructive conflict.

As we look closely at these four aspects of the constructive displeasure of mercy, we will notice that they express the most powerful interpersonal dynamic imaginable. It is Christ himself, the Word becoming flesh and dwelling among us, full of grace and truth. It is the engine of peacemaking. It is the triumph of love over hate, indifference, and living for personal pleasure.

### Patience: In It for the Long Haul

*Patience* is a curious response to something that is wrong. Why is it curious? Because when you are truly patient, you agree with the moral evaluation that anger makes: "That's wrong. What you're doing does not please me. It offends me. It hurts people." True patience is not about passivity, indifference, or tolerance of evils. You do not just put up with bad things. It's not an easygoing tolerance and neutrality. It does not accept anything and affirm everything. Patience hates what's happening. Then it rolls up its sleeves to redress what is wrong.

Patience sees wrong, but it is "slow to anger." This is a prime characteristic of the Lord God. He is gracious, compassionate, and slow to anger (Exodus 34:6). It is the first characteristic of love. "Love is patient" (1 Corinthians 13:4). God is love, and God is slow to anger. He intends to make us like himself. To be slow to anger means you are willing to work with wrong over time. "The Lord is not slow about his promise as some count slowness, but is patient" (2 Peter 3:9). God chooses to work over a scale of moments, days, years, decades, centuries, millennia. And he will accomplish what he has set out to do.

Patience is an intelligent, feeling act. When you are patient, you often see the wrong more clearly. You feel its knife edge more keenly. You actually notice more and deeper wrongs than when you react resentfully. Our resentments are often petty. But patience takes personally wrongs that don't necessarily slap our own private agendas in the face. It notices others' sufferings. And it doesn't take so personally the wrongs that do slap us in the face.

Patience hurts. It's hard to learn. You struggle within yourself so that you don't react immediately in the wrong way. You bear with difficult people and events, not out of indifference, resignation, or cowardice. You hang in there because you are driven by a different purpose. You are willing to work slowly to solve things. Patience is not passivity. It is how to be purposeful and constructive in the face of great difficulties. You are even willing to live constructively for a long time within seemingly insoluble evils. By definition, patience means that what's wrong doesn't change right away.

It's so easy to get ticked off, fed up, I've-had-it-and-I'm-out-of-here. But have you ever known anyone who did not do that? I have a friend named Enrique who has learned to love his wife even though she makes it very hard to love her. Cheryl Ann is a difficult person. Her intense self-absorption, hyperactive imagination, and suspicious temperament make for highly combustible emotions! Unpredictably, she will erupt with accusations against Enrique that have no basis in reality. Then, turning on a dime, she'll be filled with remorse, self-loathing, and fears. Spinning again, she'll turn giddy with high hopes and wild desires that promise trouble-free heaven on earth—only to come crashing back into difficult reality. Our culture labels such people. It throws up its hands, saying, "She's impossible!" But over many years Enrique has learned to love her.

How? Christ is patiently shaping his life to a different purpose. His reactions were not always loving. Retaliatory anger, escape into fantasy, discouragement, and self-protection came naturally. But haltingly, amid ups and downs, he is living his life in order to learn how to love her, even when, and especially when, it is difficult. He confronted his own lack of love, rather than blaming Cheryl Ann for his failures. Like all of us, Enrique instinctively lives on either pleasure or indifference or displeasure spectrum. But Jesus has been purposefully patient with him, showing him the constructive displeasure of a powerful mercy.

A tender hymn captures the dynamic.

My song is love unknown, my Savior's love to me,
Love to the loveless shown that they might lovely be.
O who am I that for my sake
My Lord should take frail flesh and die?[1]

And Enrique has responded—love to the loveless shown that they might lovely be. He has learned—he is still learning—to approach Cheryl Ann's shortcomings with purposeful patience. It is lovely to know such a man.

One near-synonym of patience is forbearance. To forbear means to hang in there with people or events that remain wrong and hurtful. This is more than brute endurance. It does not mean that you just keep on keeping on, merely gritting your teeth. Forbearance is committed to changing the world—and willing to hang in there for as long as it takes—not simply to endure the world. The willingness to work over the long haul is the first piece of the constructive displeasure of mercy.

### Forgiveness: The Willingness to Not Get Even

*Forgiveness* is a second mercy, another curious and complex response to true wrong. Forgiveness also looks wrong in the eye. By definition, it names wrong for what it is and feels the sting. Then it consciously acts "unfairly" in return. Anger is all about fairness (however accurate or distorted our perceptions of fairness might be). But forgiveness is *mercifully unfair.* You choose not to give back what only seems fair, just, equitable, or reasonable.

If I throw a china teacup onto a slate floor, I deserve its shattering. If I betray your trust, I deserve your wrath. But if that teacup bounces and remains whole, I receive a most astonishing and undeserved gift. And if you forgive me, you do me an undeserved kindness. Forgiveness does not ignore what's wrong. It does not excuse what's wrong. It does not pretend that the person didn't really mean it. Instead, recognizing that a debt is owed, it forgives the debt.

What is the dynamic? Pay close attention to how Psalm 103:8–13 unfolds. It begins by remembering how God described himself to Moses when they met on Mount Sinai:

> The LORD is merciful and gracious,
> slow to anger ["patient"] and abounding in steadfast love. (v. 8)

These words express the genetic code of the Bible. This DNA comes in the flesh in Jesus Christ. This is who he is and what he is like. It is what it is like when Enrique or you or I live out the image of God. A different life purpose makes all the difference. May it be said of you and of me, "He is merciful. She is gracious. He is patient. She abounds in steadfast love." Your anger experience changes as you are refashioned in this image.

He will not always chide,
nor will he keep his anger forever. (v. 9)

God's anger is always justified and just. But he does not give his anger the final word. Just displeasure serves within the larger constructive purposes of mercy. This means that God is *spectacularly unfair* to us:

He does not deal with us according to our sins,
nor repay us according to our iniquities. (v. 10)

*Forgiveness* means you don't get what you deserve. Think about that. Because God is "unfair," we have hope. Instead of fairness, you get someone who is deadly serious about wrong but acts on your behalf in ways that are inconceivably unfair.

For as high as the heavens are above the earth,
so great is his steadfast love toward those who fear him. (v. 11)

To fear God is to wake up to who he is, to know my dependency on him, to realize that his opinion of me is the opinion that matters, to feel my vulnerability before him. He is good and I am not. But his steadfast love has found expression in this constructive displeasure of mercy.

Think for a moment about the night sky. How high is the visible universe above where you and I are sitting right now? One night while walking around our neighborhood, I spotted my favorite dark sky object, the faint blur of light that we call the Andromeda Galaxy. At the speed of light it takes 200,000 years to flash from one side of that tiny disc to the other. This light takes two and a half million blazing fast years to reach our eyes. God's steadfast love is that high.

As far as the east is from the west,
so far does he remove our transgressions from us. (v. 12)

His forgiveness is that wide—from one end of the universe to the other.

> As a father shows compassion to his children,
> so the LORD shows compassion to those who fear him. (v. 13)

His compassion is that tender, that tangible, that considerate of our needs and our limitations.

To know such a Savior is to be in awe of him and to love him. By receiving forgiveness in our need, we become able and willing to give forgiveness to others. Being released from the guilt of real moral wrong, we become able to release others. Is it easy? No. One and done? Rarely. Entirely possible? Yes. Christ shows love to the loveless that they might lovely be.

God's mercies in Jesus Christ are like taking in the sun full strength. Our love for others is at best a flickering three-watt nightlight. But light is light. And in a dark house, in a relationship torn by conflict, that three-watt night-light makes a huge difference.

Real forgiveness does not fall for a cheap substitute. Let's revisit Trisha and Ryan. Once again they are in the middle of a conflict. It's a lot like their last fight over dinner plans (and our conflicts do tend to be about the same issues, don't they?). This time Ryan forgets that they had made plans to visit Trisha's family this weekend. He double books himself, goes to the beach with his buddies, forgets his cell phone charger, and is once again unreachable. When he finally connects with Trisha the next day, she is mad. His string of lame excuses reveals that he doesn't treat what happened seriously and is mainly concerned with being defensive.

Trisha reams him out, recounting his present and past faults in videographic detail. She charges him with a variety of malicious motives. This latest crime against humanity is only one of a string of perpetual iniquities. Global accusation is a typical pattern in angry people: "You *always* _____ . You *never* _____ ."

Ryan gets increasingly hostile, and entrenches in a defensive position. Trisha calls in the heavy artillery. She vents expletives, calls Ryan names, and pronounces curses (more typical anger strategies). She trumpets her own righteousness (again, typical): "*I* would never do that. When *I* promise to do something for you, *I* do it. *I* make an effort with your family." Then she stomps out, leaving Ryan to squirm in his guilt and silent wrath. Both of them kill off any present-tense relationship.

Later, however, Trisha feels bad for getting so riled up. She goes back to Ryan and says, "I'm sorry for what I said. I didn't mean it. I was overtired and upset."

"That's OK," he answers. They kiss and make up.

End of incident? No. That's not forgiveness, either sought or given. Nothing has been confessed. Nothing has been forgiven. She *did* mean what she said (though now she regrets it and wants to make up). And it's *not* OK (though now he also wants to let it go and patch things up). They are both making excuses. They have not created any true, substantial peace. Their making up is only a truce, a temporary cessation of hostilities that might break out again at any moment.

True forgiveness (both sought and given) looks wrong in the eye. It makes no excuses. But it does not hold the offense against you. It lets you go (when it could hang on). It covers over (when it could hold it over you). True forgiveness looks more like this:

> Trisha: "What I said was wrong. I am so sorry for my hurtful words. I exaggerated in order to hurt you. I acted like I'm never wrong. Please forgive me."

> Ryan: "I forgive you. Thank you. And I was wrong first. Please forgive me for not following through on what I said I'd do. I'm sorry for hurting you by thinking first of myself and what I wanted to do and then making it worse with my excuses."

> Trisha: "I do forgive you. Thanks."

They kiss, because they've made up. They've been honest. They've dealt with what really happened. They have made actual peace where there was actual war.

What if the other person does not ask forgiveness or even admit any wrong? The Bible addresses this in a deft way. Forgiveness comes in two forms. First, and foundationally, you forgive another person before God, whether or not that person admits or even recognizes any wrong. This is *attitudinal forgiveness*. Listen to how Jesus speaks of this vertical-dimension forgiving of another person:

> "Whenever you stand praying, if you have anything against anyone, forgive, so that your Father also who is in heaven may forgive you your trespasses." (Mark 11:25)

> "Pray then like this: 'Our Father in heaven, hallowed be your name. Your kingdom come, your will be done, on earth as it is in heaven. Give us this day our daily bread, and forgive us our debts, as we also have forgiven our debtors. And lead us not into temptation, but deliver us from evil.' For if you forgive others their trespasses, your heavenly Father will also forgive you, but if you do not forgive others their trespasses, neither will your Father forgive your trespasses." (Matthew 6:9–15)

In both cases, you are talking with God, not the person who wronged you. That person is not part of this conversation. You stand alone before God your Father dealing with your own attitudes. In the Mark 11 passage, Jesus says to deal with *whatever* you have against anyone else. He doesn't even tell you to try to sort out what really happened, and whether it was a real wrong or only a subjective feeling of offense. Conflicts can be impenetrably complex. Did you actually do something against me? Or did I misunderstand what you were doing? Or was I just being hypersensitive? Often it's hard to know what really happened because so much was happening in both parties. Trying to figure out the definitive explanation leads to more disagreement and outrage. Instead, Jesus simply says that if you have anything against anyone, forgive.

In the Matthew 6 passage, Jesus emphasizes dealing with real wrongs: "our debtors" are people who owe us. The mercy of God, our Father in heaven, (remember Psalm 103's fatherly compassion) is front and center in helping us. This vertical aspect of forgiveness deals with our attitudes. Its purpose is to change *you*, not to deal with the other person. It prepares you, so you will go to the other person already willing to be merciful. You are no longer holding the grudge, building up bitterness, on the defensive, on the offensive.

The second aspect of forgiveness is *transacted forgiveness*. Again, listen to how Jesus describes it: If your brother sins, bring it up with him directly, and if he repents, forgive him, and if he sins against you seven times in the day, and turns to you seven times, saying, "I repent," you must forgive him (Luke 17:3–4, author's paraphrase).

> "If your brother sins against you, go and tell him his fault, be-tween you and him alone. If he listens to you, you have gained your brother. . . ." Then Peter came up and said to him, "Lord, how often will my brother sin against me, and I forgive him? As many as seven times?" Jesus said to him, "I do not say to you seven times, but seventy-seven times." (Matthew 18:15, 21–22)

Notice that here Jesus envisions a conversation with the other person. You bring it up constructively; the other person asks to be forgiven. The interpersonal interaction is able to be both candid and full of mercy (a rare combination!) because the attitudinal forgive-ness has already happened. It is also worth noticing that in both cases, Jesus chooses to portray the other person as a repeat offender! He or she keeps doing it, even after admitting it's wrong. That's realism. That's why we need patience. That's why we are continu-ally driven back to our Father to seek forgiveness ourselves and to again work out the attitudinal forgiveness. Then we can again move toward the other person to seek transacted forgiveness.

This combination of attitudinal and transacted forgiveness helps make sense of many common and extremely tangled situations. I'll mention three. First, what if the other person won't hear you out? He or she gets defensive and self-righteous, counterattacking when you were seeking to be constructive. Again, we are driven back to our Father to forgive attitudinally. This vertical dimension of forgiveness must always happen, and it keeps your attitude in check. The horizontal dimension is a more uncertain and hazardous road, a goal to pursue, not a certainty. It takes two to reconcile, just like it takes two to make a war. But one can forgive, even when the other is still at war. It is called loving your enemy.

Second, what if the person who hurt you is off the scene—perhaps dead, perhaps long vanished out of your life, perhaps too hostile or even dangerous to approach? The attitudinal forgiveness means you can always deal with the things that poison your own heart. Transacted forgiveness and actual reconciliation are desirable fruits, but not always attainable. But, by God's mercy, we can always establish our hearts in mercy. We are not left in limbo when there is no possibility of a reconciling interaction.

Third, seeing that our forgiveness of others has two interconnected parts helps us navigate the opposite messages that one often hears in Christian circles. Some in the church teach, "If you forgive from the heart, then you don't need to go to the person." Others teach, "Unless the other person asks for forgiveness, you don't need to forgive." Each focuses on a half truth—and draws a false conclusion. When you put together both halves of what Jesus did and taught on forgiveness, you get a coherent truth.

So if you forgive from the heart, then you become able to go constructively to the other person when it is called for. Not to go would be not to love. But, if the other person will not ask for forgiveness or if it would not be wise to approach the other person, then transacted forgiveness and reconciliation can't take place. But you are reconciled with God and able to forgive. Not to forgive would be to harbor bitterness.

Forgiveness is a conscious choice formed through knowing God's mercy to you. It clearly recognizes that what happened was wrong. It makes no excuses for what happened. And *then* it lets it go.

Patience and forgiveness are the first two key aspects of the constructive displeasure of mercy for a reason. As we respond with patience and forgiveness to wrongs we have experienced, we have gone a long way toward redeeming anger. But there is more—we also need to respond to true wrongs with charity and constructive conflict. To have a complete picture of what it means to become good and angry we will take a close look in the next chapter at how kindness and constructive conflict can actually go hand in hand.

## Making It Your Own

1. Can you identify one example from your life of seeing the constructive displeasure of mercy on display?

2. Why do you think patience is the first characteristic of love that Paul mentions in 1 Corinthians 13?

3. Where, today, do you need to grow in patience?

4. How do you respond to the thought that forgiveness is "mercifully unfair"? How might you apply that to your life?

5. Does understanding the difference between attitudinal forgiveness and transactional forgiveness change how you think about forgiveness? Why or why not?

CHAPTER 8

# The Constructive Displeasure of Mercy, Part 2: Charity and Constructive Conflict

Our discussion of the constructive displeasure of mercy would not be complete without adding two more key aspects: charity and constructive conflict. Charity moves toward the person who has done wrong with undeserved kindness. But there is also a place for entering into constructive conflict when wrongs have been done. Mercy doesn't stand idly by while others go in the wrong direction or when someone—oneself or another—is being mistreated. Mercy wades into difficult situations and is willing to get involved. It's willing to raise difficult issues, apply justice (when needed), and persevere to see good come out of evil. Constructive conflict continues the work that patience, forgiveness, and charity have begun. Let's start by considering charity.

## Key Aspects to the Constructive Displeasure of Mercy

### Charity

Anger alone, whether rightly or wrongly energized, operates out of a strictly punitive sense of fairness and justice. But charity looks at what happened and says, "That's wrong," and then it does the

undeserved generous act of kindness. This calls for the most difficult self-confrontation of all: "Love your enemies." Really? That's
hard to do. Impossible, actually. It's an unnatural act. How can I see
wrong and be wronged and yet do right?

> But if God is actually merciful to you and me, his enemies . . .
> And if Jesus Christ lived this out consistently in how he loved
>     us . . .
> And if this is the very image of God that he intends to form in
>     us . . .
> And if the Holy Spirit is for real and will actually work with
>     you and me to bring forth this fruit . . .

Then it stands to reason that the Lord means it when he says, "Love
your enemies" and "Be imitators of God, as beloved children; and
walk in love, just as Christ also loved you" (Luke 6:27 and Ephesians
5:1–2 NASB).

It is easy to glaze over when you hear, "Love your enemies, do
good to those who hate you." It is easy to write off Jesus, as if he
must not really mean it, as if in saying this he is being a rather gen-
tle-souled, naïve idealist. Does Jesus's call imply that he hopes that
people can "Just be nicer to each other"? Is Jesus unaware that this
sounds like, "Let people walk all over you"? Nothing of the sort.
The love and goodness he is talking about has more grit than sweet-
ness, more hard-as-nails realism than niceness. You can't separate
what he did for us—blood, and sweat, and tears—from what he
calls us to do. He means what he says.

> If you only love people who love you, what does that prove?
> Even sinful people love those who love them. If you do good
> only to people who do good to you, what does that prove? Even
> sinners do the same with each other. (Luke 6:31–33, author
> paraphrase)

To do good to someone who does wrong, who has hurt you or
others—this is a marvel. It's so much easier to give back in kind.

Charity does what the recipient doesn't deserve. Someone deserves payback because they did you or others wrong. But you do charity.

The piece of folk wisdom that says, "Love the sinner, but hate the sin," is one attempt to capture the constructive displeasure of mercy. In fact, you can fiercely disagree with a person and actively dislike what he or she is doing—all the stuff of anger—and yet you can still do genuine kindness. Anger grips tightly a wrong, points it out, prosecutes it, punishes it. Mercy acts generously toward a wrongdoer, rather than claiming your pound of flesh. Anger thinks this way: "I've been wronged, so I will deal out fair and just punishment to the malefactor." But generosity, like patience and forgiveness is "unfair." You treat with purposeful kindness someone who treated you or others badly.

What does this look like? Let me give you several snapshots that give us a feel for how a charitable person approaches life. Unsurprisingly, Jesus tells us that God is the first person we should watch.

> "You have heard that it was said, 'You shall love your neighbor and hate your enemy.' But I say to you, Love your enemies and pray for those who persecute you, so that you may be sons of your Father who is in heaven." (Matthew 5:43–44)

That word on the street is Philosophy of Life 101 for most people. You scratch my back, I'll scratch yours. You do me wrong; I hold a grudge or get even. That's the easy way—and it's the recipe for disaster, estrangement, and war. Jesus turns the tables. Our Father doesn't operate by that philosophy. He brings up his children in a way that's hard, but good. It's the path to reconciliation and peace. He wants us to understand love in reality, not theory, so he gives us three pictures.

> First, notice the weather. "Our Father . . . makes his sun rise on the evil and on the good, and sends rain on the just and on the unjust" (Matthew 5:45). We need sun and rain in order to

have food, and God doesn't discriminate in doing basic good. Can you do that too?

Second, notice how even bad people treat their friends right. "If you love those who love you, what reward do you have? Do not even the tax collectors do the same?"(Matthew 5:46). Can you take it a step up from bad people?

Third, notice how all people everywhere recognize a special bond between family members. "If you greet only your brothers, what more are you doing than others? Do not even the Gentiles do the same?"(Matthew 5:47). Can you take it a step up from the us-them loyalty that comes naturally to everyone?

If you are a child of our Father, then "You therefore must be perfect, as your heavenly Father is perfect" (Matthew 5:48). Charity toward people who displease you is the "perfect" response—it's the way things ought to be. And it's not just niceness. It's not just the right thing to do. It has a bigger goal.

Our second example takes us toward that goal. In Romans 12 Paul gives detailed instructions about how to think and what to do, and why to think and do those things. He unpacks what it means for us to live "by the mercies of God" that come to us in the many gifts of Jesus Christ and the Holy Spirit. We pick up his discussion in 12:17–21.

Retaliatory anger comes easy. It takes hard thought—forethought, planning, prayer—to lean against what comes naturally. "Repay no one evil for evil, but give thought to do what is honorable in the sight of all" (v. 17). People know the difference. We have radar for when someone adopts an attitude, or has that tone of voice, or mocks us, or avoids us. And we have radar for when someone treats us right. But for us to do right takes work.

Remember, you never know how things will turn out, but you are fully responsible for what you are bringing to the table.

"If possible, so far as it depends on you, live peaceably with all" (v. 18). Those words set a challenging goal and embed that goal with the realism that we can't control how life plays out.

God gives powerful reasons for becoming peaceable rather than vengeful—a curious and unexpected combination of reasons. "Beloved, never avenge yourselves, but leave it to the wrath of God, for it is written, 'Vengeance is mine, I will repay, says the Lord'" (v. 19). First, trust that when the Lord calls you his "Beloved," he means it. If he loves you, then all is well. Second, trust that his just anger will destroy all evil and will right all wrongs when the time is right. If he is powerful and just, then all will turn out. Third, beware, because if you return evil for evil, you yourself are an evildoer. If you play for the wrong team, you play God, which means playing with explosives.

A specific kind of action is called for. Love for someone who wrongs you does not mean working up feelings of affection, attraction, and attachment. It means a policy of doing tangible good. "To the contrary, 'if your enemy is hungry, feed him; if he is thirsty, give him something to drink; for by so doing you will heap burning coals on his head'" (v. 20). Charity is a powerful weapon—of good.

All these thoughts, actions, and reasons are going somewhere. "Do not be overcome by evil, but overcome evil with good" (v. 21). God himself is about the business of good destroying evil. You have the privilege of playing a small part in The Great War.

The constructive displeasure of mercy calls for a kind of charity that shines very brightly in very dark places. It is our privilege. Mercies needed and received lead to having mercies to give away.

For our final illustration, consider an example from American history. The genius of Abraham Lincoln's leadership lay in the profoundly practical way he loved his enemies. Doris Kearns Goodwin's *Team of Rivals* probes this character quality. Lincoln's cabinet members were political rivals who often worked against him. But he was spectacularly and consistently fair, generous, and forgiving. He did not slam his political enemies. He looked hard for reasons to pardon Union soldiers charged with desertion or dereliction of duty. He sought merciful release for Confederate soldiers taken prisoner. He sought to provide honorable citizenship to former slaves and to create honorable ways for former rebels to be welcomed back into the Union.

One of the most striking examples of Lincoln's large-heartedness occurred when he decided to appoint Salmon Chase as Chief Justice of the Supreme Court. Chase was extremely competent, but was feverishly ambitious to be president himself. While serving as Treasury Secretary, he had both overtly opposed and covertly sought to undermine Lincoln. When people reminded Lincoln of what Chase had done against him, Lincoln responded, "Now, I know meaner things about Chase than any of those men can tell me, but we have stood together in the time of trial, and I should despise myself if I allowed personal differences to affect my judgment of his fitness for the office." Lincoln's personal secretary later commented, "Probably no other man than Lincoln would have had, in this age of the world, the degree of magnanimity to thus forgive and exalt a rival who had so deeply and so unjustifiably intrigued against him."[1]

True charity is *magnanimous*. We don't use that word much anymore, but it is worth reviving. It means being large-hearted. Refusing to be petty and sectarian. Willing to forgive. Pursuing a consistent policy of generosity and kindness in dealing with fellow human beings. Lincoln was magnanimous—and gives clues to someone even better at it. We know the LORD, who is all that and more: gracious, compassionate, slow to anger, steadfast, faithful and forgiving iniquity, transgression, and sin.

Yet Lincoln was not soft. He exercised decisive authority. He pursued a cause, prosecuted a war, and was willing to fight to the finish. And the LORD is not soft either. He deals straight with people, seeking to win them to mercy, willing to lose them to their own hard-heartedness, and mercifully protecting his people from their hostility. That leads us to the fourth lovely quality that characterizes the constructive displeasure of mercy.

### Constructive Conflict

Patience makes you hang in there through the process. Forgiveness makes you let go of getting even or of holding on to bitterness. Charity makes you generous to those who do not deserve generosity. But these three mercies don't make you "nice." They make you the right kind of tough, able to do the fourth mercy as needed: *constructive conflict.*

The displeasure of mercy enters forcefully into conflict in order to redeem. There is no one-word summary for this most rare form of goodness. Forthright problem-solving goes about seeking to right what is wrong. Constructive anger steps into wrongs with conviction and force. It tackles evils head-on. It means a willingness to start a necessary conflict in order to solve a real problem. It means a willingness to go through the messy process of engaging in constructive conflict. It means a willingness to pursue necessary justice—giving mercy and protection to victims; in effect, protecting evildoers from their own power to do wrong and holding out God's mercies to those willing to reckon with what they have done. You raise the problem that wrong creates. Do that in the right kind of way, and you create the right kind of trouble.

Mercy is not a free pass. It is an invitation to turn and repent. It is not inconsistent with facing consequences. Innumerable felons have experienced the combination of paying for their crimes and being forgiven by the blood of the Lamb, coming to life-changing faith while in prison. The repentant thief crucified next to Jesus entered into eternal life in the hours before he died, and then entered the paradise of God's presence.

God consistently reveals who he is in the inconceivably wonderful dance of mercy and justice. Perhaps the most vivid expression of the moral richness of his mercies appears when he showed himself to

Moses on Mount Sinai. He approaches us with mercy upon mercy, inviting our faith.

> "I will make all my goodness pass before you and will proclaim before you my name 'The LORD.' And I will be gracious to whom I will be gracious, and will show mercy on whom I will show mercy. . . . The LORD, the LORD, a God merciful and gracious, slow to anger, and abounding in steadfast love and faithfulness, keeping steadfast love for thousands, forgiving iniquity and transgression and sin. . . ." (Exodus 33:19; 34:6–7)

People who go wrong are invited into his life-giving goodness. But he is not indifferent to unacknowledged and unrepentant wrong. So the sentence continues:

> . . . but who will by no means clear the guilty.

This can perplex us. Is God patient, or is he impatient? Does God forgive, or is he unforgiving? Does he show love, or does he not show love? He shows the constructive displeasure of mercy . . . and that creates a conflict with our sins. His mercy is not niceness. His mercy is not blanket acceptance of any and all. Mercy to us costs him—the blood of the Lamb. And mercy comes to us at the cost of our sins and pride. His kindness is an open invitation to turn to him in repentance and faith, to come to him in our need for mercies freely offered, and our trust in mercies freely given. But a hard, impenitent heart rejects the offer, goes its own way, and will experience the fair consequences.

To what extent does our mercy mirror this? What we do is infinitely smaller in scale, but like in kind. Earlier in this chapter, in discussing forgiveness, I used the metaphor of the night-light. God's mercies are the blazing sun; ours is a flickering three-watt night-light. But light is light. So we orient ourselves to the realities of God's nature. There is a carefully defined place for candor, conflict, and consequences—for a just indignation in the service of mercy.

The technical term for all this is *redemption*. Jesus was a redemptive troublemaker. Truth is always a troublemaker. It shakes up the wrong in what is happening. To actually *make* peace, where open wrong, hostility, and destruction now operate, is the hardest and best work in the world. It involves saying true words that some people might not like to hear: "That's wrong. Let's solve it." It involves confronting evils, rescuing victims, calling wrongdoers to accountability: "You can't treat people that way." It involves anger on behalf of victims and to the face of victimizers. But such merciful anger always maintains its sense of proportion, its perspective, and its constructive purpose.

The process of problem-solving, of peacemaking—of making right what is wrong—is often long and hard. It takes honesty. It's almost always complicated and uncomfortable. You'll need patience yet again. You'll need to forgive again. You'll need more charity. You'll need to check your attitudes, words, and actions. You'll need the Holy Spirit to mediate the mercy and strength of Christ in order for you to do it in some semblance of the right way. You will often need forgiveness yourself as you stumble in your peacemaking. When you fail to be merciful as your Father in heaven has been merciful to you in Christ, you will have to call out for mercy from above. And yet you'll continue to pursue the constructive conflict with darkness because that is the way redemption is accomplished.

Think with me about two wildly different ways of expressing displeasure with what is happening. Here are two lists of energetic ways of speaking up to wrong:

| List 1 | List 2 |
| --- | --- |
| rebuke | attack |
| reprove | criticize |
| admonish | accuse |
| exhort | moralize |

| confront | condemn |
| judge fairly | be judgmental |
| warn | threaten |
| talk directly | talk aggressively |
| righteous indignation | self-righteous hostility |

Do these lists sound rather similar? How are they alike? How are they different?

In fact, they are as different as heaven and hell. List 1 gives voice to goodness and love when we are concerned to address and redress a real problem. List 2 gives voice to evil and hate in the act of condemning. But, unfortunately for the clarity of our mind and emotions, both lists tend to call up the same connotations. When people say they "rebuke," they most often attack. When they "confront," they most often condemn. When they "judge," they are most often judgmental. Both lists sound aggressive, as if both lists express different ways of "getting it off my chest" and "letting you have it."

It's true that both lists have something wrong in view. And both lists can express the emotion of anger. In other words, they are both on the spectrum of displeasure toward whatever is going on. But the motivation, the intentions, and the way of coming across are opposite. When List 1 is done right, you act in the image of Jesus. You work to redeem. When you do List 2, you act out in the image of Satan. You murder verbally.

List 2 words are innately destructive. These are ways to attack people, not problems. They "take out the speck in your brother's eye" by swinging a 2 x 4 at his face. They are harmful, not helpful, in addressing problems. These are hostile, unkind acts. When you are judgmental, you will find that other people, without fail, react to you with fight, fright, or flight. The war continues.

List 1 words intend to capture something utterly constructive and life-giving. These are ways of expressing firm, candid love.

Indignation, for example, is a just and energetic response to some-thing mean, evil, unjust, plain wrong. For you to do the difficult kinds of wisdom expressed on List 1, you must care enough to tackle a real problem directly. You must aim with all your heart for a con-structive solution. If you are lovingly direct, you will find that other people sometimes (and amazingly) respond extremely well. (Not al-ways; there are no guarantees in interpersonal relationships.) You are an agent of peacemaking in a world at war.

I have tried to describe this most rare and wonderful form of anger. But you've got to see it to believe it. As you start to do it, even haltingly, you will become convinced that this is the way of life and love in a world of wrongs. A story is the best way to begin to catch a vision, so listen in.

## The Constructive Displeasure of Mercy in Action

Winston Churchill's memoirs of World War II contain a fascinat-ing portrayal of how the constructive displeasure of mercy operates, culminating in his willingness to get angry and engage in construc-tive conflict. As prime minister of Britain, Churchill had to work closely with the USSR's Josef Stalin in alliance against Adolf Hitler. He found Stalin to be "surly, snarling, grasping, ungrateful, suspi-cious, bullying, accusatory, and manipulative." During the years from 1939 to 1941, Stalin had shown himself "utterly indifferent to our fate." He not only joined Hitler in plundering Eastern Europe, but he generously supplied the Nazis with oil, iron, tin, and grain to assist in their war effort against Britain. But in 1941 Hitler betrayed him and invaded Russia, leading to the largest, bloodiest battles in the history of the human race.[2]

So Stalin and Churchill became odd allies. Britain immediately and consistently poured massive relief aid and war materials into Russia. But Stalin's response was demanding and suspicious, rarely grateful, never trusting. He frequently blamed Britain for Russia's troubles. In responding to Stalin, Churchill was unfailingly patient, forgiving, and generous—as a matter of policy, not pleasure! He repeatedly displayed those first three attributes of mercy's constructive displeasure. He kept in view the larger purpose of their alliance. Churchill consistently bore with the unpleasantness of his ally rather than taking offense and cutting him off.

But such love is not sentimental or nice. It is not blind to real wrongs. On one occasion the Soviet ambassador met with Churchill in London.

> The Ambassador emphasized the extreme gravity of the crisis on the Russian front in poignant terms which commanded my sympathy. But when presently I sensed an underlying air of menace in his appeal, I was angered. I said to the Ambassador, "Remember that only four months ago we in this Island did not know whether you were not coming in against us on the German side. Whatever happens, and whatever you do, you of all people have no right to make reproaches to us."[3]

Notice the bluntly appropriate, "I was angered." Notice that he minced no words in confronting the problem.

Churchill's expression of just anger did not rupture or even threaten his relationship with the Soviets. Britain continued to work patiently and generously with the Soviets, as a matter of policy. Stalin's menace and manipulation threatened the relationship. Churchill's constructive anger worked to strengthen the relationship. He voiced sharp displeasure *because* he valued the alliance, and *in order to* build a better working partnership, with the *purpose* of destroying the Nazis. It did not contradict his consistently constructive attitude—it was part of it. He called wrong "wrong," with some force and fire. Constructive ends mastered and directed his anger at wrong. And it is not surprising that constructive ends were achieved. The ambassador changed his tone, as did Stalin himself in a similar incident a year later.[4]

Churchill stood up to a bully without becoming one, and Stalin respected that. Constructive conflict is part of the redemption of a bad situation. It is the only merciful alternative to giving up in exhaustion, disgust, or fear. It's the truly merciful alternative to papering problems over with mere politeness. It's not out to destroy (like raw anger); it's out to make something good out of something bad.

So even anger can express the true kindness that comes through patience, forgiveness, and generosity. You care enough to care about solving something wrong. It's what good parents and teachers keep doing with troubled and troublesome kids. It's what good employers, pastors, counselors, social workers, spouses, and friends keep doing.

I've been privileged to know many unsung heroes through many years of counseling and teaching. I know a mother and father whose teenager is throwing his life into the vortex of drug abuse, promiscuity, rage, deceit, and self-destruction. That child's life is going seriously wrong. He tries to bully his parents and manipulate them. Most parents in this situation are mastered by their rage, fear, despair, confusion, and self-righteousness. Out-of-control kids often provoke out-of-control parents, and *vice versa*. But these two parents have been fundamentally mastered by God and his sort of mercy. Neither of them is a perfect person. But they fight against their tendencies and temptations to raw anger, anxiety, discouragement, confusion, or self-righteousness. They admit their faults, even while grieving over and addressing their child's self-destructive ways. They don't always know what to do. But on the overall balance sheet, they simultaneously exhibit patience, forgiveness, charity, and the firm clarity of appropriate consequences as they seek to bring constructive truth into a very difficult situation.

I've known wives and husbands who have redemptively confronted spouses who were deceitful, domineering, hostile, or immoral. I've known friends who redemptively took on a longtime friend who was acting destructively. All these people could have given fair and just reasons for giving in to disgust and wrath, seemingly good reasons for giving up. But all these people showed the constructive displeasure of mercy. They treated the wrongdoer unfairly, like the vast and generous unfairness of the God who had loved them, who "does not treat us as our sins deserve" (Psalm 103:10 NIV). I count it one of the joys of my life to witness such love in action.

The constructive displeasure of mercy is about real life, not some spiritual sphere of life. It's about both public and private actions, not just some self-improvement project to solve a few personal problems. In the best sense of the word, it's a matter of "policy"—a committed stance and course of action. It is God's "policy" toward us. Our Father loves his beloved children who were formerly his enemies. He intends that it becomes our policy toward all others.

## Conclusion: Reverse Gear, Neutral, Forward . . . and Vertical?

Indifference and delight are the obvious opposites to the displeasure of most anger. Our usual responses are either "I don't like that," "I don't care," or "I like that." These three easy responses come naturally. We might liken this to a car with reverse, neutral, and forward gears. But we have been considering a whole new spectrum of responses—the wild, complex music of merciful displeasure.

The hardest, best response is this odd fourth gear—"I don't like that; I care; and I will act in constructive love." Maybe we should call this gear "vertical"! To shift into vertical reaches higher and cuts deeper. It's a whole different way of reversing the tide of something wrong. It woos us and challenges us . . . to grow up. It has the ring of what a human being is meant to be.

Why does this description of mercy seem so intuitively right? Even if you rarely (or never!) act this way, even if most humans only choose from three gears, this vertical gear makes profound good sense. Why does it inspire something in us to know that our capacity for anger at wrong might take the form of such mercies? It is because we are wired to understand the image of God as something even deeper than the sense of justice. Justice and mercy meet. The constructive force of love harnesses the destructive force of displeasure, and puts displeasure to work as a form of love. It's almost too good to be true—but it makes perfect sense.

These last two chapters have drawn a portrait. It's not a "religious" portrait. It's a portrait of the truly human. You haven't been reading about some plaster saint or haloed icon, serene above the fray and fret of human troubles. This isn't someone who wears weird clothes and talks funny.

This fourth gear is exactly how the Bible portrays Jesus in action. With a world of wrongs in his face, he's patient. He forgives, at great personal cost. He goes about the business of practical generosity, touching the exact points of human need. And he pointedly confronts people: "Who are you living for? How are you living? Who do you say that I am?" Then in mercy he bears the very anger that our bad answers deserve.

Matthew, Mark, Luke, and John never portray Jesus as some static ideal of remote, humanoid perfection. He is not a calm, cool, and collected Hindu guru or cognitive therapist offering to help you become more serene. The Jesus on their pages takes on people— people like you and me, people who refuse to shift into that fourth vertical gear—with his own constructive displeasure of mercy. He said, Come and "learn from me" (Matthew 11:29) because the thing he was best at is the thing we find hardest to do.

It is grasped only by revelation, and then received as a gift. The *constructive displeasure of mercy* means the redemption of the world. It is the glory of God and the love of God. It is God reforming you into his image.

》》》

## Making It Your Own

1. Let me ask you a "But What About _____ ?"
Are you interested in adding a vertical gear to your natural forward, neutral, and reverse gears to the ways in which you approach your world? Why or Why not?

Jesus is deeply interested in helping you learn the constructive displeasure of mercy.

It is the meaning of wisdom.

It is the meaning of love.

It is the meaning of the image of Jesus.

It is the meaning of being "holy unto God."

It is the meaning of being human.

2. What might be different about your everyday, natural responses to a situation where something that matters is wrong? Make a list.

3. Think about the last time you got angry. What would it have looked, sounded, and felt like for you to add that vertical gear of the constructive displeasure of mercy to your response?

4. The chapter ended on a high note. You might want to put the book down for a bit and let what you've just read sink in.

## CHAPTER 9

# Good and Angry?

Let's take the next step. Let's dig into the good reasons to become good and angry. Where can we find an excellent example? Winston Churchill gave us a glimpse, but on the larger scale Churchill's ego made him far from a role model for all godly attributes! Abraham Lincoln also gave us a glimpse, but his uncertain appreciation for Jesus Christ makes his example less than complete as well. Where can we find someone who is completely honest about anger, and that anger operates as a good? Let's start in an unusual place—but one that makes perfect sense when you think about it.

## The "Wrath of God"

All through the Bible we witness the nasty effects of grumbling, hostility, and conflict. But alongside and intersecting that sinful anger, the Bible captures an entirely different picture of anger in action. No other biography or autobiography gives so much detail about how good and justified anger works. It's candid. But it is admirable and appropriate, not embarrassing or overblown. Jesus said, in his matter-of-fact way, "There is only one who is good"—the God portrayed in the Hebrew Bible. Every other character in Scripture has feet of clay. Moses lost his temper. David was coldly vindictive to a man who did him no wrong. Jesus's disciples argued with each other about who was the greatest.

The only one who is good also happens to be the best-known *angry* person in all history and literature! No other person in history has ever allowed his or her anger to be so carefully detailed and held up for public inspection. No book ever written tells so much about one person's anger—and portrays it as essentially and coherently good. Never capricious. Never irritable. Never selfish. The Hebrew Bible and the New Testament that consistently builds upon it offer an extended, coherent case study. Among other things, it's a case study in the inner workings and the outworking of healthy anger.

Put aside whatever you *think* the "wrath of God" is all about. Come look at how it's actually described. Climb inside it. I think you'll find it very surprising. We've all had the experience of our stereotypes being turned upside-down by firsthand experience. I think you'll find it very illuminating, perhaps wondrous, sometimes disturbing, always challenging—but in a way that makes great good sense.

Whatever you currently think about God, come and take a close look at the most famous angry person in history. You will discover that there is no one whose anger is so like your own and yet so refreshingly different. Remember that we were made in his image, with the *potential* for holy indignation at evil. And however twisted and upside-down our anger has become, the Lord lovingly intends to remake us into that very image. The remaking is actually far richer and more complex than the original making.

Our re-creation is not simply as a pristine potential. What emerges—slowly and imperfectly—is seasoned and deepened by life experience. We learn the image of Christ out of the wreckage of our firsthand participation in evil. We grow in his image as our salvation in Christ gradually unfolds, as he gradually works out what he has begun. We learn in the midst of a continual baptism by fire—being called to live out that image in a world of wrongs, as Christ himself did.

I'm persuaded that we can learn a great deal about ourselves and others by slowing down and taking an actual look at this thing termed the "wrath of God." It's the clearest example I know of how to get *good* and angry—and be patient, merciful, and generous at the same time. You will have to discard prejudices and preconceptions. Many people, whether religious or irreligious, envision the God of the Bible as ill-tempered, exacting, and capricious—rather like us at our worst. Particularly in his Old Testament incarnation, he's supposedly a looming storm cloud of petty, harsh, vengeful wrath.

But I'm not sure what "Scripture" such folk have been reading. The god they describe sounds uncannily like *us* when anger goes sour: demanding, arbitrary, irritable, and judgmental. It sounds nothing like the person actually portrayed in the Bible.

Jesus is portrayed as the explicit image of the God of the Old Testament. He is the "I AM" come in the flesh—generous mercies and just angers perfectly joined. He is the most admired person in human history, for good reason. Jesus gets just as angry as the God whose character he expresses. And Jesus is the archetype of courageous, self-giving, tender love. When you consider how God describes himself in relationship to anger, you will see why Jesus's approach to anger is so much different than what comes naturally to us.

## God Is Slow to Anger and Quick to Show Mercy

Consider this example first. "The LORD is gracious and merciful, *slow to anger* and abounding in steadfast love. The LORD is good to all, and his mercy is over all that he has made" (Psalm 145:8–9, author emphasis). Notice, in particular, the description "slow to anger." It doesn't mean he's so easygoing or indifferent that he never gets upset. That same psalm says "all the wicked he will destroy" (v. 20).

But God's anger follows a certain pattern. It is embedded in tangible goodness and mercy. It arises slowly, and when it arises it is actually an aspect of his moral goodness. He attacks *only* what is truly evil. He does great good to all (Matthew 5:45). And only after the insult of endless ingratitude and life-defining rebellion does he cut off evil. The Greek word for *patience* literally says that God is "long-tempered." It's just the opposite of someone with a short fuse. God is patient in that he continues to actively treat people well, even when they are offensive and ungrateful. God does get angry, but it's the opposite of spiteful and irascible.

Consider that one of the prophets actually got mad at God because God was too patient for his taste and preferences. Jonah said, "I *knew* it! I ran away from you because I know you are so slow to anger. If I warned the Ninevites to straighten up, I *knew* you'd let them off the hook. I want you to destroy my enemies—not show compassion" (Jonah 4:1–3, author paraphrase).

God responded by dealing gently (and pointedly) with Jonah's anger, in one of the most comic scenes of the entire Bible. He lets Jonah gets mad about a shade bush that wilts, then says, "You care when a plant dies, because it inconveniences you. Shouldn't I care if people die?" (Jonah 4:10–11, author paraphrase). God gets angry— at Jonah, at Nineveh. But God is *slow* to anger and *quick* to show mercy.

Jesus makes the same point in the New Testament, putting a further twist to it: "Love your enemies . . . and you will be sons of the Most High; for He Himself is kind to ungrateful and evil men. Be merciful, just as your Father is merciful" (Luke 6:35–36 NASB). To become slow to anger is to become like God. It is a quality that frequently describes God and frequently describes what we are meant to be.

### God's Anger Is Fair-Minded

We've seen how anger intrinsically makes a moral statement. It is about right and wrong. It is about fairness. God *is* slow to anger, patient, and generous. But he also gets angry—*really angry*. At the same time, he is always fair. He is fiercely fair-minded.

In reference to God, *wrath* and *fury* don't describe a mere irritable mood or a momentary tantrum. They express God's whole-hearted decision to destroy things he finds utterly despicable. There's no contradiction at all between slowness to anger and fierce indignation. In fact, it's because God loves so intensely that he must get angry. "That matters . . . and it's wrong!" Without such anger, so-called love would be a bland, detached tolerance. If he's going to get up close and deal personally in a world that has a lot of wrong in it, then he must get angry. God is angry at those who victimize and oppress others. He defends the victim. He must stand up for the weak and powerless. He considers wrongs done and takes them in hand (Psalm 10:14). His anger rights wrongs and overturns injustices.

It's the same in both the Old and the New Testaments. Jesus ("gentle Jesus meek and mild"?) blazes with anger both before and after he tells us to be as loving and tender as God is with the people who make us mad! He says, "Woe to you, woe to you, woe to you. If you condemn others, God will condemn you. If you don't listen to what I'm saying, you will be destroyed!" (Luke 6:24–26, 37, 49, author paraphrase).

There are passages in the Bible where heat blisters the page. But it's never irascible. Churches that talk about God's wrath usually portray it only as threatening. Churches that criticize those churches don't offer a corrective view of wrath, but simply eliminate God's anger as unfitting. But rarely are the beauty, internal logic, and necessity of God's wrath communicated.

Here's one particularly sizzling example: "The anger of the LORD burned against that land, to bring upon it every curse which is written in this book; and the LORD uprooted them from their land in anger and in fury and in great wrath, and cast them into another land" (Deuteronomy 29:27–28 NASB). Moses uses up just about all the synonyms, doesn't he? What can we learn by studying such concentrated outrage?

Don't let any preconceptions you have about "the wrath of God" keep you from stopping to examine the inner logic of how God's anger works. His anger always arises for a good reason. It's never a fit or spasm or bad hair day. It's never brooding hostility just waiting to explode on some innocent, well-meaning bystander who happened to get caught in the cross fire. The causes are clearly identified and they make perfect sense when you stop, listen, and think about it.

In the passage just mentioned, astute observers are witnessing the impact of God's anger at work. It's as if they are walking through the rubble of a Nazi munitions factory in June 1945. The Allies bombed this building for some good reason. The people ask the logical question, "*Why* did the LORD do this to them? *Why* this great outburst of anger?" (Deuteronomy 29:24, author paraphrase). They didn't deny God's evident anger. But they were curious about the reasons.

The answer came simple and clear: "These people betrayed me. I loved them, but they proved to be traitors" (vv. 25–26, author paraphrase). That makes sense. It's not irritation or nit-picking to be upset at *treason*. People who have every reason to be loyal, thankful friends instead betray him. And their betrayal of God led them to betray others. God haters become people haters who abused and destroyed others.

This instinctively makes sense to each of us. As you grasp it, "the wrath of God" seems not only logical, but right. You'll become clearer in thinking about your own anger too. If he's good, how could God *not* get angry at things that are plain wrong? Consider the following examples of things that elicit righteous anger, in order to get a feeling for the inner logic of God's anger. It will help you understand your own anger at its best. It will shed more light on where your anger goes bad. It will point in the direction of remaking your experience and expression of anger for the good.

- Betrayal and treason
- Lies, gross misrepresentation of another, character defamation
- Hypocrisy
- Laziness, workaholism, or a harsh taskmaster
- Stubbornness, rebellion, and back talk
- Murder and physical abuse

- Sexual betrayal or abuse
- Cheating and stealing
- Slander and gossip
- Entitlement and greed

Even people who claim that there are no moral absolutes tend to get distressed by such evils.

Now take another look at that list. Have you ever seen a list like that before? If they sound vaguely familiar, it's because they precisely mirror the Ten Commandments God gave us in the Bible.

1. You shall have no other gods except the true God—don't betray him.
2. Don't worship lies and self-serving fictions. No idolatrous substitutes for the real thing.
3. You shall not take the LORD's name in vain, mouthing God-talk while living a life of pretense and contradiction. (That's actually the core meaning of this commandment; profanity and cursing are secondary meanings.)
4. Your life needs a rhythm of hard work and true rest to evidence trust in God as your provider and to bring joy to the weary.
5. Honor your father and mother, rather than rebelling against them.
6. Don't murder or do any other harm to another or express unjust and damning anger.
7. No immorality of any sort. Your sexual ethic should protect others rather than use them.
8. Don't steal in any way, shape, or form.
9. Don't lie or speak evil of others, bearing false witness.
10. Don't organize your life around "I want, I want, I want."

These things that arouse anger in anyone with a conscience are simply the familiar Ten Commandments, paraphrased a bit, and adapted to our everyday experiences. When your anger is justly aroused, it operates along the lines of the Ten Commandments. Like God, you are displeased at betrayals of love. Selfishness, backstabbing, hypocrisy—all those things that anger you anger God as well. More to the point, the *reason* these things anger you is because they anger God. He describes us as "made in his image." We are hardwired morally to know that some things are plain wrong and need to be dealt with.

You actually work the way that God says you work. You have the capacity for just outrage because he does. Notice, God's anger is not unpredictable and mean-spirited. Far from being a contradiction to love, God's anger comes from love. It's the product of love betrayed (when he's the one being done dirty) and of compassion for the victims of injustice (when others are the ones being hurt).

Not only did God publish this list in the Ten Commandments and not only do violations of these things occasion your actual real-life anger, but, it's no accident that these things also form the explicit or implicit basis of our laws protecting persons, property, and reputation. Theft, murder, defamation of character, reckless endangerment, pedophilia, terrorism, treason, and the like not only call forth personal anger, they call for criminal proceedings.

This points us to something else very important to understand about God's anger, something that also illuminates your own anger. To betray God and to do what harms other people is to break God's commandments. Perhaps you are familiar with what Jesus called the two greatest commandments, on which everything else hinges (Luke 10:27):

- You shall *love* the Lord your God with all your heart, soul, strength, and mind.
- You shall *love* your neighbor as yourself.

Why does God say this? "Because I have loved you, you are made to love me. Because I have made you in my image, you are made to love other people. If you don't love me or others, you betray a relationship."

What is the technical word that describes wronging God and others by being unloving? *Sin.* The word means something that wrongs a relationship. It's different from *mistake* or *error* or *failing.* It describes a relational betrayal, not just a personal failing. Sin means to wrong God by betraying love for him. Sin means to wrong other people by violating love for them.

Interesting, isn't it? The things that naturally most outrage you, those things that most universally upset human beings everywhere, are the very things that the Bible labels "sin." We aren't often taught that "sin" is what you *ought* to get upset about—what you often hate automatically—because it's what God always gets upset about. You can see how far we've come from the bizarre notion of a prying, tyrannical God who requires us to give up all freedom and submit to his every whim, who fills us with guilt for no good reason and then punishes us mercilessly.

The God portrayed in the Bible is no killjoy. Love makes joy. But he is rightly hostile to evils because true wrongs hurt people and kill joy. The real God only asks us to give up acting like a traitor toward him and hurting people. His desire is simply that we would love well instead of lie, hurt, and destroy. God's anger (mirrored by your anger, when it functions accurately and constructively) is aroused toward only one thing: what is objectively, truly, and always wrong. In other words, sin.

God is slow to anger and full of undeserved kindnesses. He is like a parent who hangs in there, persistently loving a wayward child. He gets angry—really angry—at true evils. He shows further, spectacular kindnesses to people willing to deal with what's wrong.

In this chapter we've introduced two of the most unpopular and misunderstood concepts in our world: the wrath of God and sin. I hope these words can begin to serve you in a fresh way. They are extremely important things. When these concepts are unfairly portrayed, they don't serve you well. But when you understand them truly, they open doors to sanity. You can never really understand yourself (or God, or other people) unless you understand both sin and the wrath of God. They are intrinsic to your humanity and to what plays out on the stage of reality.

» » »

## Making It Your Own

1. You are likely to have multiple "But-What-Abouts" after you read this chapter. List a few of them here.

2. Think about the list of things that make God angry. Which of those things make you good and angry? Which of them are you more likely to ignore or excuse?

3. How does the description of God being good and angry challenge your thinking about your anger? How does it challenge your thinking about God's anger?

4. Would you want to live in a world where God never got angry? Where you never got angry? Why or why not?

Chapter 10

# The Best Anger, the Best Love

Many people view God as infinitely malleable, someone/something to whom each of us is free to attach our own opinions, as if God's character were decided from the bottom up. But God is portrayed in the Bible as a person. He expresses all the characteristics of personality. He notices people and evaluates what he sees. He plans and acts purposefully. He feels, thinks, relates, and remembers. At every turn, this person reveals his likes and dislikes—or better his loves and hates. Those words capture how intensely his pleasure and displeasure operate. *Recent image: God is a vulture equip ist*

This God inspired songs of love and lament. He said that people can actually know him. And he sent his one and only Son, Jesus, so that we could see exactly how God in the flesh uses anger. Jesus did not live a calm life. He cared too much. Yet he was not a tense person. He was not irritable, anxious, or driven. But he was not detached, cool, or aloof, either. He was no stoic or Buddhist. He plunged into the storms of human sufferings and sins. He felt keenly. At his friend Lazarus's tomb, in the presence of death and human woe, he both bristled with anger and wept with sorrow.

In the life, death, and resurrection of Jesus we learn a surprising truth about God's anger: God's anger is spectacularly unfair. Stay with me here. We usually call something "unfair" when we feel that we got a raw deal, that we got cheated out of something we deserve in all fairness. But what about when we get better than we deserve? It's a reverse "unfairness," a generosity that goes far beyond what would be fair. And, strangely enough, we find that hard to live with too.

To illustrate this principle, Jesus tells a story about a boss who hires people at different times during the day, right up to the last minute, the proverbial "eleventh hour" (a phrase that comes from this story). When it came time for the workers to receive their pay, those who came at the beginning of the day were astonished to discover that the latecomers got paid as much as they did. They went to the boss aggrieved, and he met their complaints with questions that made their pettiness apparent: "Did I not pay you what I agreed to pay you? Why, then, do you complain?" (Matthew 20:13–16, author paraphrase).

As much as we need it ourselves, grace can be a hard thing to swallow when it is extended to someone else. Can you relate to the all-day workers' distress? I can. And the anger that I feel—or *would* feel in their situation—reminds me that my anger is not as pure as God's anger. It reminds me how much I need the grace that I sometimes begrudge others.

The parable of the workers shows how hard it is for us to reconcile anger (which is so often fueled by self-righteousness) and love (which rejoices in another's good). That makes it hard for us to understand that God's anger and love are entirely consistent with each other. They are different expressions of his goodness and glory. As B. B. Warfield put it, "Jesus burned with anger against the wrongs he met with in his journey through human life, as truly as he melted with pity at the sight of the world's misery: and it was out of these two emotions that his actual mercy proceeded."[1] You can't understand God's love if you don't understand his anger. *Because* he loves, he's angry at anything that harms those he loves.

Notice the way God's children experience his anger. His anger is expressed *on their behalf* as supremely tender love! As we will see, the Bible is consistent about this truth. Yet anger by definition sets itself *against* things, with intent to destroy. So how can God's wrath become something God's children love and trust rather than something they fear or dislike? How is God's anger an expression of him being for us, rather than an expression of him being against us? The Good News is always presented in terms of how love and anger come to be resolved. God expresses his love for his people through four expressions of his anger.

## God's Anger Falls on Jesus

*First, in love, the anger that your sin deserves fell on Jesus, not on you.* Before you were born, God resolved to set you free from experiencing his wrath against your sins. In steadfast love, he freely offered his innocent Son to bear the wrath deserved by the guilty. God's anger punishes and destroys, giving our sin its due—but the blow was taken by Jesus, Lamb of God, Savior of sinners.

Because Jesus loves, he offered himself to bear the just fire of anger. The way of our deliverance is his pain, his glory, and finally our joy. God's loving anger is expressed in a way that brings us blessing. It is the basis of life from the dead—it assures us of true forgiveness. In this foundational act of self-giving love, we experience God's anger acting *for* us. In response, we confidently turn and believe.

## God's Anger Disarms the Power of Sin

*Second, in love, God's anger works to disarm the power of your sin.* His hatred of sin is again expressed *for your well-being.* In the present, on an ongoing basis, God deals with indwelling sinfulness.[2] The Holy Spirit pours out God's love in you as a burning fire against evil. He does not destroy you. He destroys sin and makes you new. In steadfast love he remakes us, not by tolerating our sin, but by hating our sin in ways we learn to love!

The process is not always pleasant. It often means suffering that catches our attention. It means listening to reproof and acknowledging failure and guilt. It means owning up to wrongs done. These things don't feel good. But deliverance, mercy, encouragement, and a clear conscience *do* feel good. They feel *very* good. God remakes us progressively into bearers of love, joy, and wisdom—bearers of his own image. Because he loves us, he's angry at our self-destructive sinfulness. God's loving anger on our behalf nourishes and encourages faith: it assures us that he will keep working both inside us and around us to set us free of indwelling evil (Hebrews 12:5–11).

In the new birth and sanctification, God's destructive power works within you against what is wrong with you. He is for you, making you new, teaching you to listen. He remakes you to be like Jesus. In the daily outworking of love, we experience God's anger working *for* us. In response, we take hope and began to learn the obedience of wisdom.

## God's Anger Delivers Us from the Pain of Others' Sins

*Third, God's anger will deliver you from the pain of other people's sins.* Because he loves us, the Lord is angry at people who seek to hurt us. In steadfast love, he will deliver us from our enemies. On the last day all causes of pain will be destroyed forever. At the same time, the Bible is clear that those who oppose God and hurt his people exist for a purpose: they are God's unwitting agents in the task of sanctification. They act for their own selfish reasons, but also accomplish God's purposes for good as he tests and transforms us through suffering. They are agents of God's loving discipline toward his people so that we might learn patience, faith, and love for enemies, courage, and every good fruit that can only be learned in tough times.

Our future blessedness is his glory and our joy. This delivering power of God for his glory and his people's rescue is the theme of many psalms. They connect the steadfast love and mercies of the Lord to this loving wrath by which he delivers his children from those who harm them.[3] "If God is for us, who can be against us?" (Romans 8:31).

God's loving anger on our behalf nourishes and encourages our faith. He will set us free from what hurts. God's beloved children hope and trust that at the return of Christ his anger will make things right (Romans 12:19). In the final act of love, we will experience God's anger acting *for* us. In response, we groan and eagerly wait.

## God's Anger Protects Us from Ourselves

*Fourth, God's anger serves as a warning and check to protect us from returning to a lifestyle of sin.* The Lord's fiery holiness does not slip into the background once we come to know that we are lovingly gathered into the free grace of Jesus. One of the ways our Father raises his children is by expressing constructive, restorative displeasure. This helps to form an accurate and active conscience. We feel pangs at our Lord's displeasure because we are awake to his love for us.

Understanding God's displeasure with respect to his beloved children is a delicate pastoral question. We are going to look at this more slowly because it is so easy to misunderstand. To be joined to Christ by mercy means you are no longer under wrath, but under grace. You are free of all condemnation. You are beloved in the Beloved. The constructive displeasure of mercy makes God's anger your friend.

It is our supreme joy to have passed from death to life, and be under grace rather than under wrath. But does this mean that God never gets angry at the children he loves? God is a good parent. The first three aspects of the constructive displeasure of mercy—patience, forgiveness, and love—are obvious to his children. But what about the fourth aspect, constructive anger? Throughout our lives, as beloved but imperfect children, we experience the constructive effects of his fatherly displeasure.

He gladly takes the time to patiently raise us: "Listen to me. Remember this. Trust me. Follow me."
He willingly warns us: "Guard your heart. Be careful with your life."
He intercepts us: "You can't do that."

He disciplines the ones he loves: "When you do that, your life does not go well."

He warmly restores us to intimacy with himself: "Come back to me, my child. I freely forgive you, and there is joy both in heaven and on earth."

Of course God gets angry when his family is foolish, false, and sinful. It's because he loves us and is committed to our long-term welfare.

We see this throughout Scripture, both in Old and New Testament. Timely fatherly displeasure takes many forms. We see it in the lives of Abraham, Isaac, Jacob, Moses, Job, David, Solomon, and throughout the history of Israel. We see it often in the way Jesus disciples his followers. The Lord is upset at wrong in the Gospels, through his apostles to the first churches, in his letters to the seven churches of Revelation, and throughout the entire history of the church. God is a good parent. We witness a reflection when we see how other good parents raise their children by creating an atmosphere of love that teaches right and wrong.

Let's consider several examples that come close to where we struggle and need the curb and check of love's fatherly displeasure.

First, when facing irrational hostility, you and I can be easily tempted to cower in fear. How does the Lord teach us not to be afraid of what another person might do? He is direct and counter-intuitive: "Do not fear those who kill the body but cannot kill the soul. Rather fear him who can destroy both soul and body in hell" (Matthew 10:28). Whoa. And lest you take that wrong, and become frightened of the Lord, he immediately reminds you that the life of a sparrow and the hairs on your head both matter to your loving Father. Fear God. But don't be afraid of him. Both proper fear and proper fearlessness realign our conscience.

On a different note, we can easily slide into becoming overly comfortable with God. We begin to slip. We trifle with him. We take him for granted. Our Father who art in heaven, yada, yada. How do we learn to worship with an appropriate reverence, a holy caution, a deep awe, a proper fear? "Our God is a consuming fire"

(Hebrews 12:29). Whoa. You don't trifle with fire. Again, lest we take it wrong, the same passage proclaims how the sprinkled blood of Jesus speaks mercy and joy. The Lord both sharpens and soothes the conscience.

And, it is a triumph of grace when you believe that God truly loves you, forgives you, accepts you, saves you. But then, fickle creatures that we are, we can easily slide into pride, arrogance, and feeling superior to those who do not believe. God pulls no punches when we drift toward self-righteousness, because he loves us and a timely warning helps keep us sane, he says, "They were broken off because of their unbelief, but you stand fast through faith. So do not become proud, but fear. . . . Note then the kindness and the severity of God" (Romans 11:20, 22). Again, lest we take it wrong, the entire letter to the Romans is a proclamation of the mercies of God to a world under just condemnation. So "stand fast through faith . . . and continue in his kindness"—again, that's Romans 11.

## These Realities Nourish Our Hearts

Our Father knows us. Each of these four aspects of God's anger is constrained by mercy to comfort a different aspect of our human struggle.

When your heart becomes fearful, and you wonder how God could ever love you, remember. Jesus took your sins upon himself. The innocent was slain in place of the guilty. When God considers your failings, he remembers his mercy.

When you feel discouraged and weak, that you have no strength to fight all that is proud, unruly, and forgetful inside you, remember. The Holy Spirit hates evil, loves good, and he will not quit working on the inside. He will complete the good work he began in you.

When you feel overwhelmed by all the heartache, unfairness, disappointment, callousness, and betrayal that you experience, remember. The Lord will destroy every cause of pain, stumbling, and tears. Because God loves those he has befriended, he will defend them from every enemy: death, sin, Satan, and unfriendly people.

When you are tempted to pack it in and give up, plunging back into the darkness, remember. The Lord is a holy fire, and he disciplines those he loves that we might share his holiness. "The righteous falls seven times and rises again" (Proverbs 24:16). He will not let you go fatally astray.

God's wrath is your hope. God's wrath is my hope. We don't often hear that, but it appears everywhere in the Bible. Wrath is our hope because love masters anger. God's loving anger resolves the entire problem of evil in a way that brings him inexpressible glory and brings us inexpressible blessing. The God who is love justly condemns evil, severs the power of remnant evil, brings relief from suffering, and protects us from ourselves.

Even though God's wrath is the hope of his children and the despair of his enemies, it is also true that those enemies who turn and believe the staggering message of how wrath is converted into grace through Jesus Christ are changed into friends. The truth is that you can't understand God's love if you don't understand his anger. This is the message of the book of Psalms, that royal road into the heart of redeemed humankind, with its otherwise inexplicable interweaving of joy and sorrow, hope and anguish, confidence and fear, contentment and anger. "Oh, the depth of the riches both of the wisdom and knowledge of God! How unsearchable are His judgments and unfathomable His ways! . . . To Him be the glory forever. Amen" (Romans 11:33, 36 NASB).

It is this God that we were created to be like. We are made in his image. That's why we have the capacity for moral judgment. We are made to be aroused to anger and to constructive action in the presence of moral evil. That's what God is like.

But we have fallen into sin. That's why our anger gets so messed up, so twisted, perverted, and misused. We play at being God and try to run the world, punishing evildoers on our own terms. We get mad at things that aren't evil (it's just that our almighty will was crossed). Then we ignore things that really are evil—our own temper and bitterness, for starters—remaining indifferent to suffering and oppression. Finally, when we do manage to get angry at a real evil, we blow it so out of proportion that we "return evil for evil." We become like the things we criticize so that even anger legitimately aroused gets expressed destructively.

That's not the end of the story, though. You and I are redeemable. By the grace of God we are utterly redeemable. Whatever is perverse and insulting to God, worthy of his anger, can be forgiven and changed. Our evaluative capacity—the conscience—can be rewired. We can and will learn to perceive good and evil in a different way, the way things really are. This restores us gradually to sanity, to the image of Christ.

Our responses can be changed. Hair-trigger irascibility becomes slow-to-anger. Hostility turns to active love for enemies. Long-standing bitterness softens into the ability to forgive our debtors. The God who is totally for us and who loves us too much to leave us in our sin—the all-powerful God of the universe—is in the business of the long, slow fixing. He is at work transforming his children so that our anger will be reflected in loving action. How does that happen? That's the topic of the next section of the book.

» » »

## Making It Your Own

1. How is God's anger against sin truly good news for you?

2. Which aspect of God's anger on your behalf is most meaningful to you today? Why?

3. Any "But-What-Abouts" from this chapter? Note them here.

# SECTION 3

# HOW TO CHANGE

This book began with our experience of anger and has carefully drawn a picture of how we are meant to understand that experience. We have seen that a great divide between darkness and light runs through the heart of anger. The problem of good and evil—the deepest problem of being human—churns with your anger and mine.

This brings us to the practical question, how do you change? How does darkness become light? How do distorted humans become what they are meant to be? This section comes at the practical question from three angles. First, we will listen to a passage of Scripture. We will hear how God takes up our thorny struggle with anger. Second, we will consider how that same passage leads us into a lifestyle of growing faith and love. Third, we will walk through a case study of how we change, breaking the change process into eight steps.

CHAPTER 11

# A Mirror on Your Anger

You have probably had the experience of getting disoriented when trying to find your way in a strange city. You miss a turn and find yourself completely lost. It's easier now with a GPS in your hand or car, but even that can send you down the wrong road. Compare that experience with missing a turn when driving in your own neighborhood. When you are *oriented* it's easy to double back. You can even take a route you've never driven before. When you basically know where you are and the direction you want to head, you come out OK. But when you're *disoriented*, you don't know left or right, backward or forward, which way to turn.

When we get angry, our experience can resemble being lost in a strange neighborhood. We get disoriented by our experience of anger. But the difference is that we don't usually realize how lost we are. When we're self-righteous, we *feel* oriented, even when we're completely lost. When we play the terrorist or vigilante, the betrayed lover out to get even or the kid throwing a tantrum, we *feel* like we have a clear idea of what happened and what needs to be done now. But we're deluded. Anger deludes all of us. It is a brief (or lifelong) madness.

Our bad angers shout out, "My kingdom come! My will be done! Judgment and wrath upon all who transgress against Me!" How does such madness become sane? How do you change something so deep-seated? How can something so hot-headed, so consuming, so willful be softened? How can something so instinctual, habitual, and automatic ever change? How can we be turned upside-down and become right-side up? How can this inflated sense of self ever shrink, becoming the true size of a human being? We must be *reoriented*.

To be made new means dying to what is old . . . to be made new means awakening to new life. We might say it this way: you and I must become Christians with respect to our angers. We must learn to stop complaining, criticizing, arguing, and being bitter and hostile. To do that we need the mercies of Christ—and Christ freely gives himself to the needy. Because of our tendency to flip out and revert to old ways, we need to enter lifelong rehab. The Christian life begins with an awakening and continues with a reorientation process. It presses forward until you see Jesus face-to-face. You and I are in process.

I know many people who have relearned to do anger, who have had their anger significantly transformed. Each of them bears witness to the active hand of God. It takes grace. And each of them bears witness to the diligence of humility. It takes grit. You must honestly and patiently wrestle with yourself. You must consciously choose to become a different kind of person. You must work it out over a lifetime. None of us will be perfect in this life. But each of us can grow. Any headway you make in the reorientation of your anger is worth more than any amount of money: "nothing you desire can compare" (Proverbs 3:13–15).

The goal is to keep changing in the right direction. Some five hundred years ago, the honest, wise, and very temperamental Martin Luther described matters this way:

This life, therefore, is not righteousness
but growth in righteousness,
not health but healing,
not being but becoming,
not rest but exercise.
We are not yet what we shall be,
but we are growing toward it;

the process is not yet finished
but it is going on;
This is not the end but it is the road;
all does not yet gleam in glory
but all is being purified.[1]

Notice that there is no quick and final fix yet. Instead of one and done, there is a lifelong, intentional process. There are lots of works-in-progress, lots of going somewhere, but not there yet. Notice all the "-ing" in what he describes: heal*ing*, becom*ing*, grow*ing*, go*ing*.

Notice also that it's not an aimless process, change for its own sake, an end in itself. Some people talk as if the path itself were the destination. They say, "It's how you're going, not where you're going. It's the journey, not the arriving." That's pious nonsense. Direction is everything. What use is it if I run energetically and skillfully in the wrong direction? You can run for miles parallel to the beach (or away from the beach) and *never* arrive at the ocean! Contrary to fantasies of directionless change, this change process has a shining and desirable destination, to become a certain kind of person.

The man who wrote the lines above was a German monk. He had struggled long with his volatile temper—and with his fears, lusts, depression, and guilt. Through it, he learned how the inner struggle works and works out. He learned how to get somewhere, not simply to flounder. He learned how to go somewhere good, not any-old-where. You can learn too.

War-making is a prime trait of sinners. It's the image of Satan: liar, murderer, divider, aggressor. Peacemaking is about God in Christ and how human beings are renewed in his image. The Lord is the supreme Peacemaker. Even in his common grace, God inhibits the outworking of evil's logic, often preventing human life from dis-integrating into anarchy and barbarity. Those forms of partial peace negotiated and sustained by diplomats, mediators, counselors, and other constructive people are gifts of common grace.

God's special grace even more profoundly inspires you to make peace. Warlike humans surrender to Christ. He made peace once for all between us and God. He continues to make peace, teaching us to do the same with each other. He will make peace, finally and forever.

This chapter will look at the Scriptures, and several key truths the Lord teaches us about how war becomes peace. This involves asking the questions, When God looks at your conflicts, what does he see? And how does God make right what is wrong? The Scriptures reveal God's gaze, the criteria by which he continually evaluates human life, and they also reveal the means by which human problems are redeemed.

## Looking into Scripture's Mirror

The Bible is packed with stories and teachings about anger, conflict, and alienation—and how to solve such problems. Anything the Bible discusses frequently must be a universal struggle. We each put our own spin on sin, but the basic sins indwell us all. For example, Titus 3:3 (NASB) offers this general assessment of the angry human race outside Christ's rule: "Spending our life in malice and envy, hateful, hating one another." Not a pretty picture. Some people are more civilized about it, some less, but we all look out for Number One in some fundamental way, and we collide with others looking out for the same thing.

Consider the representative "works of the flesh" that Paul lists in Galatians 5:19–21 (NASB). More than half the items describe some aspect of conflict: "enmities, strife, jealousy, outbursts of anger, disputes, dissensions, factions, envying." Consider also 1 Corinthians 10:13, "No temptation has overtaken you that is not common to man." When it comes to interpersonal conflict, all of us could introduce ourselves like participants in an AA meeting: "My name is _____ and I get irritated. I get into conflicts. I rehearse grievances."

There is no better place to look in Scripture to understand our anger, understand God, and grow in our relationships than James 4:1–12. No more accurate and profound analysis of the dynamics of conflict has ever been written. No more hopeful and condensed description of the dynamics of peace could be written. No more powerful promise of aid has ever been given. James places all anger in the light of the piercing gaze of God, and promises grace upon grace.

### Why Do You Fight?

> What causes fights and quarrels among you? Don't they come from your desires that battle within you? You desire but do not have, so you kill. You covet but you cannot get what you want, so you quarrel and fight. You do not have because you do not ask God. When you ask, you do not receive, because you ask with wrong motives, that you may spend what you get on your pleasures. (James 4:1–3 NIV)

James poses the question, "What causes fights and quarrels among you?" So *why do* you fight? Notice that James does *not* say, You are fighting because the other person is a blockhead; because your hormones are raging; because a demon of anger took up residence; because humans have an aggression gene hardwired in by our evolutionary history; because your father used to react in the same way; because core needs are not being met; because you woke up on the wrong side of the bed and had a bad day at work. Instead, James says, you fight because of "your desires that battle within you." You want something but don't get it. The biblical analysis is straightforward and cuts to the core. *You* fight for one reason: because you aren't getting what you want. And those desires dig in. You fight because you want what pleases you, and what you expect and demand is being frustrated.

The world gropes after this truth and, at the same time, runs from it. Any thoughtful person can point out how people get into conflicts because of crossed "expectations." It is not difficult to get people to articulate what their (perhaps previously unspoken) expectations really are. People can even evaluate and alter some of those expectations, thus creating a more harmonious climate. But the core problem of self-centered craving is not really addressed. We replace blatantly selfish expectations with subtle expectations. And the conflicts that cry out for a repentant heart before God are dealt with by ignoring the anti-God obsession that operates within all "expectations" and "felt needs."

Some find the Bible too obvious and simplistic. "Of course" people get angry when they don't get what they want; there must be something "deeper" to really explain problems. But they miss a deeper thing: The expectations that lead to conflict reveal something fundamental about where the combatants stand not just with each other, but with respect to God himself. In our demands we stand for ourselves and against God at the deepest level: "My kingdom come. My will be done."

Nothing lies deeper than the lusts that lead to conflict. Our cravings rule our lives. They directly compete with God himself for lordship. No problem is more profound and more pervasive. James 4:1 says that such desires "battle" within us. This does not mean that desires battle *against* us or *with* each other. These are *our* desires, expressing who we are.

The metaphor envisions siege warfare, an army digging in around the city. Our desires become entrenched . . . hence we fight and wage war. We *would* act as peacemakers if we obeyed the Lord instead of asserting our desires. But where you find quarrels and fights, you are witnessing people obeying the desires of a different lord.

## Who Are You When You Judge?

Brothers and sisters, do not slander one another. Anyone who speaks against a brother or sister or judges them speaks against the law and judges it. When you judge the law, you are not keeping it, but sitting in judgment on it. There is only one Lawgiver and Judge, the one who is able to save and destroy. But you— who are you to judge your neighbor? (James 4:11–12 NIV)

Who *are* you when you judge? None other than a God wannabe. We judge others—criticize, nitpick, nag, attack, condemn—because we literally usurp God's throne. In this we become devils to each other, acting as accusers. When you and I fight, our minds become filled with accusations: your wrongs and my rights preoccupy me. We play the self-righteous judge in the mini-kingdoms we establish: "You are so stupid. You've gotten in my way. You don't get it. You are a hindrance to my agenda."

What is an argument? In an argument, you offend *me* by crossing my will. I respond by pointedly confessing *your* offenses to you! At the same time, I explain to you how all my failings are really your fault. If only you were different, I wouldn't be the way I am. You do the same to me, pointedly confessing my sins to me and excusing your own. Nowhere in the heat of conflict does anyone confess his *own* sins, except as a way to buy time for a counterattack: "Yeah, I was wrong to do that, but . . ."

The log remains firmly planted in the eye (Matthew 7:1–5) as each party plays lawgiver and judge. But there is one Lawgiver and Judge, he who is able to save and to destroy. Who are you that you judge your neighbor? Here we see that a far more profound conflict burns at the heart of interpersonal conflict. Presumption, pride, demand, and self-will stand at odds with the one true God.

James 4:1 and 4:12 sound the two key themes that lie at the heart of conflict: grasping demand and self-exaltation. Each of us says, in effect, "My will be done—and damn you if you cross me." To find God's solution to conflicts, you must ask and answer the questions, What do I want? and How am I playing God in asserting my will? Such a profound and explicit analysis of the vertical dimension in interpersonal conflict will provide the key to begin to unlock anger. As long as we remain only in the horizontal dimension, there will be no genuine and lasting peace.

This is the reason that secular forms of peacemaking cannot avoid shallowness. They often have some good strategies, such as the following:

- Clarify your expectations
- Listen well and repeat back what you've heard
- Phrase your concerns and objections in non-condemnatory ways
- Count to ten before voicing anger
- Communicate respect for persons amid disagreement over issues
- Watch your body language

But without the vertical dimension, at best one makes compromises born of a somewhat more enlightened and mutual self-interest. Humility before the living God and love for neighbor are impossible. But where conviction of sin before God occurs, genuine peacemaking becomes not only possible, but logical. Yes, the other person may have started it. What he said and did to you may indeed be worse than what you said and did back. But when God holds up a mirror, he shows you *your* participation in the conflict, what you bring to the conflict—your pride, god-playing, and willfulness. God's perspective reveals how the colliding wills of two petty wannabe gods lie at the heart of those quarrels and fights.

## But He Gives More Grace

My wife Nan and I are both fairly mild-mannered people. So it might be tempting for us to believe that we never play at wanting to be God. Sadly, our conflicts tell a different story.

One of the first conflicts we experienced actually involved four small arguments in a row. That is significant in itself. You will find that many arguments are patterned. They are repeatedly triggered by the same sort of situation, and they play out the same themes. It's as if the two parties follow a script and act on cue. In our case, things got tense between Nan and me on four successive Sunday evenings in June. We had been married less than a year, and I was working as a summer intern in our church. Let me set the stage, first from my vantage point, and then from Nan's.

For me, Saturday was a busy, high-pressure day. I was focused on preparing for Sunday's events. Many activities would come to a head throughout that day. Sunday morning I got up early to finish preparing to preach, teach, or lead worship. The day was intense, filled with many responsibilities and with people, people, people. I'd talk with people, listen attentively, express care and concern, try to help, pray. I'd counsel both informally and formally.

In the afternoon we usually had people over. I often had to preach in the evening or lead worship, so further preparations—both finalizing content and collecting my soul—would fill the late afternoon. After the last conversation had ended, Nan and I would get home about eight o'clock Sunday night. I had one thing on my mind: *peace and quiet*—to savor the sports page, to sip a tall glass of iced guava juice, to nibble my way through a handful of Fig Newtons. I was ready to close up shop on relating to any fellow human beings.

Meanwhile, what was Nan experiencing? For the previous two days she had supported her husband in all the things he had to do. She had prayed for each of my responsibilities, and had borne with my preoccupation. She had watched me talk with other people, offering them a seemingly endless supply of hospitality, patience, attentiveness, and biblical input in response to their needs and concerns. She also had been active in hospitality or teaching Sunday school.

She was excited that now we finally had an opportunity to be together, an opportunity to talk intimately and personally, an opportunity to look at the week ahead and do some planning and praying. Come Sunday night at eight o'clock, Nan had one thing on her mind: *personal connecting*. She wanted a sympathetic and listening ear, someone to hear how *her* weekend had gone, to bear *her* burdens and share *her* joys, to walk with into the next week.

Do you get the picture? There's one train track, but two trains heading in opposite directions. The northbound and the southbound trains are due to collide at precisely eight o'clock Sunday evening when we arrive back home! You can see exactly what's going on in terms of James 3—4. The Pastor and Pastor's wife are not pretty pictures at this moment.

What caused the quarrel, the unhappy bickering, the self-pitying sense of not being understood and loved, and the self-righteous sense of offense? Is it not your pleasures, your cravings, the expectations that have dug in deep in your soul? I was ruled by my desire for pleasurable rest and relaxation. Nan was ruled by her desire for intimacy. The all-too-predictable result? A weekly quarrel.

A But-What-About question immediately rises up in most minds—particularly participants in the conflict. What's wrong with what we each wanted? Isn't rest one of the commandments of God? What's wrong with wanting to enjoy the good gifts of food, drink, and leisure at the end of a long day and before the week that lies ahead? Isn't Sabbath refreshment, laying burdens down, one of God's good blessings? From Nan's side, isn't intimacy, a husband's nourishing and cherishing his wife, the mutuality of bearing burdens and sharing joys, one of the commandments of God? What's wrong with wanting your husband to care about you too, along with all the other people he talked with at church? Isn't giving and receiving love one of God's good blessings?

The truth is that there is nothing wrong with those things—in their proper place. But they have gotten out of proportion, as demonstrated by the strife that results. How do we put them in their place? How does real change happen in our hearts and in our relationships? In the next chapter we will look closely at the tools God gives sinners so that they can pursue change.

» » »

## Making It Your Own

1. What tips and strategies have you found somewhat helpful in managing your anger?

2. How does recognizing the deep heart of conflict change how you think about anger?

3. What is the significance to you of "God gives more grace"?

4. After you read the story about Nan and me, what was your first reaction? Did our "small" conflict feel familiar to you? Do you have similar stories to tell about conflict in your relationships? Describe one.

CHAPTER 12

# He Gives More Grace

What's wrong with what I want? What's wrong with what you want in your conflicts (both big and small)? As we answer that question, we will get to the heart of our conflicts and also get direction on how change can happen.

Scripture, the Holy Spirit's MRI of the heart, makes clear that it's not the (good) desires that are the problem. It's when such desires *rule* that they produce sin, not love. When God sees into the heart of conflict, he sees the private kingdoms we each create. We each ascend to the throne, converting desires for blessings into the will of a god: I crave, I need, I must have.

We each had fallen prey to sin's insanity and self-defeating futility. I was willing to quarrel in order to get peace and quiet! Nan was willing to quarrel in order to get intimacy! There is nothing *per se* wrong with wanting either rest or intimacy. But when I *want it too much*, when it rules me, I sin against the Ruler of heaven and earth. When expectations dig in, we inevitably sin against each other too. We think, *I've gotta have it! It's mine! I demand my rights. I need to meet my needs. You're getting in the way of my precious, cherished longings! You're messing with my program to control reality. You're not meeting my expectations.*

Take a moment and consider the desires at work when you get irritated or angry. What do you want? How do you organize your life around what you want? Are you playing God? Those are not questions meant to send you on some introspective idol-hunt or an archaeological investigation into shaping influences from your past. Ask the questions straightforwardly. They have an objective, present-time answer. You aren't probing for a subjective experience, a feeling, or an elusive moment of insight. Look for something tangible: "What exactly do you *want right now* that makes you warlike, when Christ's rule would make you peaceable?"

Answer honestly and you will have identified *why* you participate in sinful conflict. There are no deeper reasons for your sinful anger. Violation of the "first great commandment" is the deepest motive of all. In those moments of conflict I *loved* rest more than I loved the living God; Nan *loved* personal connecting more than she loved the living God. My outward sins in the situation included a grumbling attitude and critical words, but those actions erupted from the craving for down-time. Nan's outward sins included a grumbling attitude and critical words, but those sins poured out of the craving for marital intimacy. For both of us—as for all of us—the horizontal sins register and express the vertical sins.

Those vertical sins are so serious that they merit the blunt labels the Spirit uses in James 3:13—4:12: bad zeal and selfish ambition, pleasures, lusts, and envy, adultery against God (a metaphor for idolatry), love of the world, pride, double-mindedness, and playing God. We are meant to live with God on the throne, with a wide-open heart to him and others. But a contentious, judgmental person has shriveled up inside, shutting down to both God and neighbor. On the outside, a contentious person speaks rotten words that tear down rather than build up and condemn rather than give grace (Ephesians 4:29). On the inside, a person swept up in sinful anger has become demonic and diabolical—in the truest sense—an image-bearer of the hostile critic of God's people (James 3:15; 4:7). God intends a different image, that we become bearers of mercy, redemption, and aid to others, even—particularly—in their sins.

What happens when war-makers come to see the significance and scope of this vertical dimension of conflict? We are brought up short. We are humbled for specific sins before the face of God. The Searcher of hearts catches us by the collar and makes us look in the mirror. No wriggling away.

Imagine standing at the rim of the Grand Canyon from predawn darkness until the full light of day. At first you peer down into inky darkness, but as the sky slowly brightens, impenetrable darkness gradually gives way to gray. You begin to discern the shapes and contours of the abyss below. You see dimly what was right in front of you all along. That's what it's like to identify by name the specific lusts that characteristically produce your battles. Finally, as the sun breaks forth, the rocks begin to glow with every color of fire. The canyon blazes, and you see everything in vivid detail. That's specific conviction of what is true: "My anger at you—not only my cutting and defensive words, but the dismissive attitude, the negative, damning spin I put on everything you did, the positive, justifying spin I put on my own performance, the evasions, the self-righteous and self-pitying emotions and thoughts, all these and more—expresses my diabolical pride against God and my restless demand for what I want."

## He Gives More Grace

What happens next? Here's how James puts it:

> But he gives us more grace. That is why Scripture says:
> "God opposes the proud, but shows favor to the humble."
> Submit yourselves, then, to God. Resist the devil, and he will flee from you. Come near to God and he will come near to you. Wash your hands, you sinners, and purify your hearts, you double-minded. Grieve, mourn and wail. Change your laughter to mourning and your joy to gloom. Humble yourselves before the Lord, and he will lift you up. (James 4:6–10 NIV)

There is grace for the humble. Grace for those who ask for it. Instead of confessing others' sins, you can confess your own. Instead of proudly proclaiming your own rightness, you can confess your many sins, failings, and weaknesses and ask for grace. Instead of railing against God when you don't get what you want, you can submit yourself to God and draw near to him.

The wonderful result is that God himself will lift you up. God himself will show favor. He will begin to change you at the deepest level so that what you want reflects the rich, good life that God desires to give you. Then you will be a carrier of peace to the rest of the world. The peace of heaven will rest on your relationships. James explains that heavenly peace this way:

> But the wisdom that comes from heaven is first of all pure; then peace-loving, considerate, submissive, full of mercy and good fruit, impartial and sincere. Peacemakers who sow in peace reap a harvest of righteousness. (James 3:17–18 NIV)

What a change it is to experience God lifting you up and giving you his peace! What an amazing thing to be able to share the peace of Christ with others. How does that change happen? Gradually and over time, but it does happen.

Every facet of the grace of God is tailored to make us new when we are angry—critical, fearful, and proud. In place of living deformed lives, we find the "double cure" for sin's guilt and power[1]— those who seek Jesus find true forgiveness. In Jesus, those who ask receive the Spirit from our generous Father. We will be reformed into the image of the Son who lived and died for us that we might live for him.

What must you do? Angry people must turn and seek God. James 4:6–10 captures this relational reality called repentant faith. We turn in need to the Person willing and able to help. The Lord offers a radically "vertical" solution for the radically vertical problem of the heart. It is striking how God-centered this solution is. Submit to God and resist the devil. Draw near to God. The proud devil flees as God draws near to you. Cleanse your hands from those outward expressions of sin: the chaos and every evil practice, the quarrels and conflicts, the speaking against one another. Purify your heart from those inward defections: the double-minded desires that might profess God but serve my gods. Grieve. Humble yourself in the presence of the Lord.

Notice how *present* God is. Notice how *relational* the solution is. We seek and find Someone moves toward us. Someone who will be gracious. Someone whose power freely helps us. To really solve the heart of conflict you must seek God's mercy. Our conflicts are fueled by usurping God's place. The grace of Jesus Christ forgives and reinstates God's rule in our hearts.

James's solution cuts to the core of what's going on in conflict. Solving the spiritual core gives the recipient of grace the power and humility to pursue many different strategies that lead to genuine peace. Courage, willingness to forgive, genuine love (even for enemies), patience over the long haul—these are matters of character, not mere strategies. Constructive strategies flow from a character transformed by our humbling need for the mercies of God.

## From Anger to Peaceable Wisdom

What does this look like interpersonally? Formerly angry people are enabled by God to give love and to make true peace. If you once attacked people, you learn to interact constructively. James 3:17–18 describes it compactly. God the gracious Giver gives "wisdom from above" (cf., 1:5, 17; 4:6). It is *wisdom*: practical, specific, walked out, talked out. It is a way of life, the opposite in every respect to the words, tone, thoughts, actions, and attitudes of sinful anger. And it is *from above*, the gift of God through the Lord Jesus Christ. He alone gives the goods that truly solve interpersonal conflict. If you lack wisdom—and quarrels and conflicts are prime examples of folly—ask God (James 1:5).

The wisdom he gives is first *pure*. Angry people churn out mental, emotional, and verbal pollution. They vent ugly things. Their hypocrisy condemns others' failings while they themselves plunge headlong into spectacular sins. Contentious believers have hearts that are dangerously divided—impure. Repentant faith purifies our hearts. We begin to live a life that is pure. Simple. Straight. Pursuing the good and true. Committed to others' welfare, not calculating self-interest or scoring points.

Godly wisdom is first pure, and then peaceable, gentle, reasonable, full of mercy and good fruits, without partiality, without hypocrisy (James 3:17). Reread that sentence slowly because it is a stream of living water. Jesus is like this. We can become more like this. *God of mercy, make it so.*

*Peaceable* people lay aside warlike traits: defensiveness, aggression, criticism, self-justification, scoring points, touchiness to offenses. These moral weeds—the "filthiness and rampant wickedness" that comes from the anger of man (James 1:20–21)—get plucked up by the roots and begin to wilt. Sweet fruit begins to grow as the Word of God and other good gifts take root: teachableness, forbearance, kindness, contentment, and gratitude for the inexpressible gift, an outlook of charity rather than peevishness. *God of peace, make me peaceable.*

The English language has no full-orbed equivalent for the word translated as *gentleness.* Jesus exhibited this trait so remarkably that its fragrance and coloration marked his entire life. Here walked the Lord of glory among his own people. Every human being that Jesus met owed him life and utter loyalty. This is the LORD, to whom temple sacrifices were offered in repentance and gratitude. Yet most of these people ignored Jesus, misunderstood him, tried to use him, reviled him, and plotted against him. Even his own intimate followers, who basically loved him, repeatedly proved themselves dense as stones. How did he put up with it for thirty-three years? Gentleness. He was utterly mastered by merciful purposes.

Jesus dealt gently with the ignorant and misguided, even when he suffered at their hands. Such meekness is incalculably powerful. It is a virtue almost beyond our imagination, the ability to endure injury with patience and without resentment. I have known several people who demonstrated the firstfruits of this virtue. Their lives showed hints of radiance, a glimpse of the unveiled glory of Jesus, the loveliest thing I've ever seen. They were purposefully constructive in the most difficult circumstances.

We can understand to a degree that Jesus was compassionate toward sufferers. But when we consider that the Christ's master purpose was self-sacrificing mercy for his enemies, here the gentleness of Jesus exceeds comprehension. George MacDonald captured the essence of such gentleness this way: "It's a painful thing to be misjudged. But it's no more than God puts up with every hour of the day. But he is patient. So long as he knows he's in the right, he lets folk think what they like—'til he has time to make them know better. Lord, make my heart clean within me, and then I'll care little for any judgment but yours!"[2]

It is unfortunate that "gentle Jesus, meek and mild" has become a picture of someone weak and ineffectual, a sentimental, pablum savior, good for children, but not good enough for grown-ups. May the God of the Lord Jesus Christ give us his true gentleness. Such strength is a regal attribute. *Gentle Master, gentle me.*

The wisdom from above is also *reasonable.* It has never ceased to amaze me how reasonable Nan starts to sound once both she and I begin to repent of sinful anger. People in conflict have distorted hearing and speaking. We tune in to the same wavelength we broadcast on. I'll listen for and speak whatever proves you wrong and proves me right. It's the wrong channel. Angry people are unreasonable. We don't talk sense when we are contentious. But peaceable people send and receive on a different wavelength. They listen for what makes peace. They speak what makes for growing in the grace and knowledge of the Lord Jesus Christ. Wisdom makes sense. It's accurate, constructive, winsome—even when it says tough things. And when you say true and constructive things, you are far more likely to get a fair hearing. No guarantees, of course, but reasonable words are hearable. *Wonderful Counselor, make me reasonable.*

Naturally those who repent of an angry critical spirit become *full of mercy.* If I've found the mercy of Jesus overflowing toward me for spectacular and fatal sins of pride, demand, and anger, it's only natural for me to overflow at least a little with the same mercy toward others for their lesser sins against me. The more deeply you get to the heart of your participation in conflict, the more you will understand with joy the mercy of God to you. And you'll become correspondingly merciful and patient toward others in their sins.

Critical, feisty, irritable people don't understand much about God's mercy. They might mouth the words, but their actions reveal that they still serve lusts and fears. And others will pay the price for perceived transgressions. It has been revealing and humbling for me to ask myself, "Who am I full of mercy toward, and who am I merciless toward?" I have to give a mixed answer. Persons ABC are on my easy-to-show-mercy list, and persons XYZ are on my tend-to-be-merciless list. The difference between the two lists has little to do with the people's particular strengths and failings. It boils down to my expectations, to whether I view that person through the lens of the Redeemer's merciful agenda or through the lens of my own instant and insistent demands. *Father of mercies, make me merciful.*

You become *full of good fruits* as you learn to make peace, not war. The good fruits of peacemaking are as diverse as the evil works of war-making. Scripture gives no exhaustive list of good fruits. No list could ever capture the many creative, timely, and appropriate things that constructive people do and say as they learn to make peace:

- Keep your mouth shut, when you used to blurt out a reaction.
- Listen, when you used to be busy crafting a comeback.
- Speak up courageously, when you used to get intimidated.
- Embed any specific criticism of another in both appropriate commendation and Christ-centered optimism.
- Treat people fairly, representing them accurately and recognizably; no gross caricatures.

- Speak accurately and abandon prejudicial language: "always" and "never" are rarely true and are invariably more destructive than constructive.
- Speak calmly, rather than with gusts of inflammatory emotion.
- Speak frankly, rather than inhibited by timidity.
- Raise an issue you used to swallow.
- Overlook an offense you used to explode over.
- Solve the problem, rather than attacking the person.
- Expect to see Christ at work, rather than despairing or panicking when troubles come.
- Replace harsh words that stir up anger with gentle answers.

When you get the log out of your own eye, you really can see clearly to help take the speck out of your brother's eye. Odds are that he'll trust you as you do it and he'll love you for it. The cornucopia overflows. *Fruitful Spirit, bring forth your fruit in me.*

James's comment that peacemakers are *without partiality* is particularly striking. It points out something rarely mentioned. I've noticed that when people genuinely repent of sinful anger, two amazing things happen: They become able to discuss their own sins accurately—after all, such sins now exist in the light of Christ's grace and will be progressively dismantled by grace. Simultaneously, they become able to talk about other people's sins charitably. There are no more axes to grind, but an emerging desire for the well-being of the other in the hand of the merciful Redeemer. Impartial people become able to sort out who contributed what to the overall problem. Such even-handedness stands in marked contrast with the polarization of conflict.

I recently witnessed a wife discussing her own sins without defensiveness, and the sins of her husband without accusation. Simply, utterly amazing! The marriage had been in crisis. They had been at each other's throats. Hostility, disappointment, defensiveness, and self-pity had ruled. But as she dealt with herself before God, the prejudice and bigotry of anger vanished. She was free to get about the business of being a constructive help in the process, rather than a destructive hindrance. *O God, who is never unfair, make me impartial and even-handed.*

Finally, peacemakers are *without hypocrisy.* You don't stir up a whole evening of trouble and misery to get a few moments of peace and quiet! You don't stir up an evening of hostility to get some loving attention! You don't judge others for the Little League sins against you, thereby committing Major League sin against God.

People in conflict are hypocrites. They dish out global condemnation, while feeling outrage whenever they are mistakenly criticized regarding some tiny detail of a story. They grouse about a spouse spending twenty dollars on some perceived frivolity, while not thinking twice about spending five hundred dollars on their own hobbies. They damn others as theological idiots and biblical ignoramuses, while they are loveless and self-righteous. They defend the God of mercy mercilessly. They harshly accuse others of harshness. They get angry at angry people. They proudly judge proud people. They gossip about gossips. May God be merciful to us all. *O God, who is true, make me true to you.*

## Real Change in Real Life

Just as God's diagnosis maps onto real life, so we live out the cure in real life and real time. After Nan and I dealt with our Sunday-evening conflicts—after our "sunrise on the Grand Canyon"—we talked differently than we had talked before. Words came clothed in a different tone of voice. They carried a different attitude and intention. No longer adversaries and accusers, we began to talk honestly about our own failings. We began to love the love of Jesus, to pray for each other, and to worship the merciful One. There are three in our marriage, and one of us is perfect, good, and merciful. He's at work. Wisdom is feet-on-the-ground, every-word-out-of-your-mouth practical. We were enabled to make practical, problem-solving decisions.

There is nothing so unromantic as love.[3] Romantic feelings of attraction and pleasure will sometimes be associated with love, but the essence of love is different: a whole-hearted commitment to act for another's welfare. As we solved our Sunday night bickering, Nan actually *wanted* to give me rest, and I actually *wanted* to spend time with her and give her personal attention. We decided, as a matter of policy, to define Sunday night as a time of private rest and to take Monday morning as a time of extended communication. Interestingly, during the rest of the summer, we ended up informally connecting on about half the Sunday evenings anyway. Somehow when the lust for rest and relaxation was dethroned, I didn't "need" private peace and quiet so much. And, not surprisingly, when the lust for intimacy was dethroned, a lot more intimacy just seemed to happen. Those typical surprises occur when people get to the heart of conflict and find needed grace.

Does this mean we never bickered again? Would that it were so! But during that summer more than thirty-five years ago, Nan and I were given a road map to the fountain of life and were enabled to find grace. We gained an enduring understanding of our characteristic sin patterns and tasted the joys of repentance and godliness. God gives more grace.

## Walking by Faith

In James 3—4 the Holy Spirit repeatedly calls us to stand before the mirror and to see what is true. He repeatedly calls us to stand in the light of God who does what he promises.

> "He gives more grace. God opposes the proud, but gives grace to the humble."

Let those words be stamped on your heart. Faith takes God at his word. Imagine yourself scraping bottom in your checking account. A wave of bills arrives in the mail and must be paid. That night your soul flutters with anxiety. You lie awake with your mind running in circles, calculating and recalculating, planning and worrying. The next morning, out of the blue, your bank calls and says, "Someone just wired $10,000 into your account. The money's available, so live accordingly... Yes, it's in *your* account... No, there's been no mistake." Would you keep worrying? Or would you be filled with gratitude and pay your bills with a glad heart?

Faith lives as though what God says is true.[4] God *does* give more grace to the humble. Humble yourself. God *does* oppose proud warmakers. Come out with your hands up and surrender. He *truly* forgives those who open their eyes to their sins. Stop, open your eyes, and confess. He sealed his promise in the blood of Jesus. Count on it. He *actually* gives the Holy Spirit to his children who ask—so ask.

"If any of you lacks wisdom, let him ask of God, who gives to all generously and without reproach" (James 1:5 NASB). Ask unafraid, knowing your need. "You do not have because you do not ask. You ask and do not receive, because you ask . . . so that you may spend it on your pleasures" (James 4:2–3 NASB). Ask, repenting of your lusts. God himself will empower your change. He will give you wisdom to walk in the image of Jesus Christ.

The humble faith that makes for peace is just as objective as the proud craving that makes for conflicts. Many people view faith as their *feelings* of trust, confidence, peacefulness, contentment, happiness. Many people view prayer as an *experience* of certain religiously colored emotions: fervency or stillness, joy or familiar comfort. Such feelings are sometimes associated with faith and prayer, but the Psalms illustrate how the faith that talks to God can express itself in many different feeling states, some pleasant, some rather unpleasant. And we should never forget that many forms of falsehood may feel peaceful or fervent or confident. The state of your emotions is no accurate register of whether you are actually relying on God.

The essence of living faith is something different than any particular experience. Seek the true God who speaks truth and offers true help. Faith takes God at his word and acts on it. There is nothing as un-experiential, un-mystical, and unsentimental as faith. But robust, straightforward, simple faith is powerful. Relate your life to God in Christ, and he will rearrange your life. Take God at his word. To get to the heart of conflict you must seek God. And if you seek, you will find. And you'll change, because living faith can never prove fruitless: "the seed whose fruit is righteousness is sown in peace by those who make peace" (James 3:18 NASB).

On the day we see Christ, all who are in him will be like him. From that day on there will be no more causes of stumbling, no more "quarrels and conflicts." The process of getting to the heart of conflict will one day be finished. Simple and pure devotion will replace double-mindedness forever.

» » »

## Making It Your Own

One practical aspect of Scripture is that God often gives us open-ended "categories." These invite us to insert our own particular details. We are invited to personalize the things said.

1. When James 1:2 says, *Count it all joy when you meet trials of various kinds*, we are invited to insert the particular troubles and hardships that we face. What are the trials in which you find yourself tempted to complaining, or bitterness, or anger?

2. James 3:16 vividly describes the inner disorientation that leads to the outer chaos of bad anger (and other sins too). *Jealousy and selfish ambition* describe inner attitudes. *Jealousy* literally means "bad zeal," wanting, seeking, and living for the wrong things. Selfish ambition means lifting me up, aspiring to play god, seeking to control the world. When your anger runs off the rails, what demands and forms of self-exaltation are at work?

3. The *disorder and every evil practice* that James 3:16 flags includes all forms of bad anger, whatever creates turmoil, breaks relationships, and sets people against each other. James 4:1–2 and 4:11–12 fill this out specifically with regard to anger: fighting,

quarreling, literal and figurative murdering, speaking against others, judging others. How exactly does your bad anger demonstrate such chaos and interpersonal destructiveness?

4. James 4:6 says that God gives *more grace*. Grace has many components: mercy, forgiveness, protection, strength, encouragement, and so forth. Every component involves God giving you himself. The Father takes you as his own child and teaches you to know him. The Son died for you and now shepherds you and protects you. The Holy Spirit awakens and energizes you. What does God promise that you need from him?

5. James 4:6–10 describes many qualities of an honest, fruitful relationship with God: submitting to God, drawing near to him, cleansing our hands (the things we do and say), purifying our hearts (the things that rule us, the things that we want), mourning our sins, humbling ourselves before him. These are all related, but pick one to act on right now and reach out to God.

6. James 3:13 and 3:17–18 describe *good conduct* and the *wisdom from above* as peaceable and constructive. What particular aspect of this do you most need to cultivate in your relationships right now? What will it look like for you to do this?

CHAPTER 13

# Eight Questions:
# Taking Your Anger Apart
# to Put You Back Together

The last two chapters got you oriented to Scripture. They started moving you to personalize God's outlook and gave you ways to understand your struggles with anger. In this chapter we will get even more specific. I will give you a vivid snapshot of a typical moment of irritation. Then I will give you eight questions to help you make sense of any incident of anger, whether mild and momentary, or intense and longstanding. Think of these questions as helping you push the pause button and then advance the video frame by frame. They help you sort out exactly what is going on in tumultuous, confusing moments. But first, the story follows:

Imagine you have to get to a very important appointment. Perhaps you've been sick for several months with a mysterious ailment and a top specialist squeezed in an appointment for you as a favor to your family doctor. Or perhaps you're making a major sales presentation. You've been working on this for six months, and today's the day. Perhaps an old friend finally agreed to get together for lunch after years of alienation. Imagine one of these scenarios, or pick your own similar situation to make it vivid and personal.

Your appointment is for noon, but you're running a little late. It's now 11:55 a.m., and you're still ten minutes away. So you're hurrying, pushing the speed limit to make up time. All of a sudden, a line of taillights stretches out ahead as far as you can see. Traffic comes to a paralyzed halt. You sit. You pull out your cell phone to make a call. The battery is dead. The minutes are ticking away. You're incommunicado. The traffic shows no immediate signs of un-snarling. How do you react?

One common response? You snarl, and your anger shows no im-mediate signs of unsnarling! It might be only a spasm of irritation and disgust. It might rocket into full-blown road rage. But either way you feel some degree of rapidly mounting frustration. Who are you mad at? The idiot driver who caused an accident? The bozos in the Department of Transportation who decided to do midday con-struction? All those other drivers who decided to clutter up your road and get in the way of your plans? Are you mad at your sickness? At the sales rat race? At your hypersensitive friend? At yourself? At the Fates, always conspiring to mess up your life? At God, who runs such a frustrating universe?

When you've got to get somewhere, but get stuck in traffic, you're handed a great opportunity to learn the ABCs of anger. You'll also learn the ABCs of many other basic life struggles. When you're idling in traffic while an important meeting slips away, anger rarely stands alone. You might feel lots of other things at the same time. Often all the "bad" feelings come rolled into one seething ball of miseries. For example, in addition to anger, perhaps you're anxious. Stewing on the highway, you worry, envisioning many dire consequences. Maybe it's cancer and I'll die? Will I lose the sale . . . my job . . . my house? What if my ex-friend gets huffy because I'm late for lunch, writes me off yet again, and talks about me to all our friends?

Or you might feel extremely helpless and very unhappy. A pain-ful anguish grips you. Such feelings are a small taste of the stubborn darkness that gets called "depression" when it takes over. Maybe you feel guilty, flooded with "if onlys." If only I'd left some buf-fer time. If only I'd listened to the traffic report on the radio. If only I'd plugged in my cell phone last night. If only I didn't always procrastinate.

Perhaps you feel a sudden deep need for something to make you feel better, to make you forget your problems. You restlessly surf around the radio dial, hoping to find something to drown your sor-rows. You gobble a bag of peanut M&Ms in about eight seconds. And then another bag of M&Ms. All in all, stuck in traffic, you are definitely not a happy camper.

We each fill in our own details. I, for instance, am a fan of pea-nut M&Ms, though I am not much prone to the "if onlys." Your details are probably different from mine. But are you with me in relating to this kind of experience? If you can't identify at all, have you checked your vital signs lately? Such reactions are basic human nature in facing life's petty frustrations.

This chapter will walk you through eight questions that will help you turn an anger incident into something positive—eight ques-tions to ask yourself while you sit in traffic, so to speak. The first four questions help you to take apart and make sense of your anger. The second four lead you to find help, moving you in a construc-tive direction. Working through these eight questions will help you understand yourself. They will help you find God in the midst of your angry moment. They will also make you more helpful to other people. When you've really learned something well, you've got some-thing good to give away to others.[1]

These eight questions aren't magic. They don't capture all the flexibility of real-life wisdom. But they are the building blocks. Think of them like the notes on the music scale. Working through these eight questions is like practicing scales and arpeggios. It's not yet Louis Armstrong's trumpet solo "West End Blues." It's not Yo-Yo Ma playing Bach's "Cello Suite No. 1." This is do-re-mi. But you learn to play skillfully by mastering the basics. In that spirit, here are some questions to ask about a situation that angers you.

## Dismantling Your Anger

### Question 1: What is my situation?

This first question is the easiest one. When did you get angry? What was going on? What aroused your irritation? Who were you mad at? What situation, event, or person made you angry? Anger is provoked. Anger has an occasion. Anger is *about* something. Anger flares up for some reason, in some specific time and place. So this first question asks what was happening *to* you in this traffic jam. Here are some of the significant factors:

- The appointment is important with respect to your health, your finances, your relationships.
- It's 11:55, the appointment is at 12:00, and you're still ten minutes away.
- The traffic jam obstructed and then imploded your plans.
- The highway department, or a fender-bender, or heavy traffic caused this particular tie-up.
- Your cell phone is dead, leaving you unable to communicate.
- The person waiting for you will probably react in an unfavorable way. You could lose your health, money, or a friend.

Notice that none of these describes *you*, the person who reacts— who *must* react in some way or other because you are a human being, not a stone. All of them name the significant things happening to you in your world. They answer the when, where, at what, and with whom of your experience of anger. They locate you.

### Question 2: How do I react?

This question is also relatively easy to answer. It ferrets out the many ways that we express anger (or other close cousins in the displeasure family).

What happens in your thought life? Perhaps there's an inward "Aargh!" You mentally curse the transportation department or other drivers. You confess their many sins to yourself! You prosecute their crimes in the courtroom of your mind! Or perhaps you play out anxious mental scenarios of how the person you're meeting might react. Probably you script out and rehearse what you'll say, how you'll explain and make excuses for leaving them in the lurch. You replay times when this sort of thing happened in the past. Or the voice of self-recrimination grabs the microphone of your thoughts: *Why didn't I leave earlier, or take a different route, or listen to the traffic report on the radio, or remember to charge my phone? What if the person I'm supposed to meet gets disgusted with me?* Perhaps you think a profanity or an obscenity, invoking God's wrath or some bodily function in service to your frustrations. Perhaps in the theater of your mind you play videotapes of your upcoming funeral—turns out it was colon cancer after all. Perhaps in the next ten minutes you calculate and recalculate your net worth and current income six different times. Our minds get very busy when we are angry.

How about the physiological aspect? A general nervous tension pervades your body. Blood surges to the extremities, priming you for action. Adrenaline squirts into the bloodstream. Muscles tighten in your neck and shoulders. Your stomach churns. Your breathing becomes more rapid and irregular. You start to perspire slightly. When we are angry, our bodies race into action.

What about your emotions? You feel peeved, irked, ticked off, hot and bothered. (We have so many great words to describe feeling that way!) The longer you sit, the more your blood boils and steam comes out your ears. (So many great metaphors.) Perhaps you feel uncontrollably hungry for candy. Perhaps you feel desperate fear at the possibility of colon cancer. Our emotions become all-consuming.

Actions? Anger says and does things. Perhaps you press up almost to the bumper ahead. Don't let anyone merge from the sides. Don't make eye contact. Keep your eyes rigidly forward. You groan and sigh. You vent your disgust verbally: "I can't believe it! This is ridiculous! Of all the . . ." You flip the radio on and off aggressively, getting impatient whenever an ad breaks in. When you finally arrive at the appointment an hour late, perhaps you pour out a semi-coherent outburst of anger and excuses. We do and say many things to express and vent the destructive energies of anger.

This stew of anger (mingled with some fear and some comfort) is a classic human reaction.

### Question 3: What are my motives?

Now ask, *Why* do you get angry? This is the million-dollar question. Depending on how you answer it, you'll either stay mad, or you'll talk yourself down into an artificial calm, or you'll learn to find God and respond constructively. The easy answer is to point the finger at the situation: "I get angry *because* of all those bad things in Question 1." That sounds plausible. No traffic jam, no anger. No missed appointment, no anger. No loss of life's good things, no anger. But it's the wrong answer. Question 1 answers important questions: when, where, with whom, and at what. But Question 3 answers *why* you get angry. And it doesn't look at your circumstances. It looks at *you*.

We fuss and fume for reasons having to do with who we are. Our *motives* decide which direction we will head. Our *expectations* get us moving. So what controls you? What directs you? What energizes you? You can get at this by asking simple questions and giving honest answers. Read these slowly, thinking your way back through the stuck-in-traffic story.

- In this moment of anger, what do you want? "I want _____ ." When that particular desire gets frustrated, you get fried. Your outburst is a revelation of your most urgent desires.
- What do you believe you need and you can't live without? "I need _____ ." If you absolutely must have something, you'll blow a gasket when you can't get it.
- What do you most fear? "I fear _____." Is it poverty? Sickness? Loss of reputation? Being out of control? A tantrum

of anger, anxiety, or escapism bears loud witness to what you fear.

- In this situation—11:55 a.m. with you about to miss an appointment—what do you most love? "I love _____ with all my heart right now." Your anger reveals right now, in the moment, what you cherish.

- What is the centerpiece of your hopes and dreams? "Life will be a joy if only _____." We usually think of our hopes and dreams in theory, in generalities, in the ideal. But our anger shows exactly which hopes are now walking in the real world.

All these answers are different ways of saying that the anger arises from desires and beliefs that master you and define you. Your anger reaction is not caused by the situation alone. It is caused by what you most deeply believe and most passionately cherish—right now, when you find yourself in this situation. The situation triggers you and tips your hand. It forces you to reveal who you really are. It pushes your buttons. Your buttons say something very significant about what rules you. No traffic, no anger, no revelation of your pride.

This is the opposite of how we tend to think in the heat of the moment. We think, "I'm angry *because of* the traffic, the cell phone, the trashed appointment." We point fingers. We look outside for the cause, when the real cause is inside.

Here's an easy way to prove that this is so. Imagine that you had actually wanted to *avoid* the appointment. What if you didn't really want to go to the doctor, but your spouse made the appointment and nagged you into going? What if you were ill-prepared for the sales call and would love a good excuse to buy more time? What if the estranged friend had set up the luncheon to reconcile, and you'd rather nurse your hurt feelings? In these cases you might be chortling with joy at being stuck in that exact same traffic jam.

Imagine *that*—a heaven-sent excuse! No one can blame me for skipping! The exact situation that usually feels frustrating now feels liberating.

"Anger problems" are obvious. Countless people have sought counseling or been sent to counseling because their anger was destructive. But I've never known anyone who sought counseling for a "happiness problem." It's not an uncommon problem, but we almost never notice it or want help for it. We rejoice when we get what our hearts crave, however misguided or even evil our desires.[2] The traffic jam is significant as the occasion of anger, but it is not the final cause.

What motives caused that tantrum in the traffic jam? Here are six possible rulers of the heart. Try these on for size, and personalize it for yourself.

1.  I want to get where I want to go when I want to get there.
2.  I care what people think of me. I need the love and respect of the person I'm meeting.
3.  I want and need the money this sales call was likely to produce.
4.  I believe that my access to medicine will save my life. I want the cure that doctor is sure to provide.
5.  I need to be in control of my world, and to prove I'm in control and competent.
6.  I need some break, escape, or comfort to calm me down when I'm upset.

These sorts of things answer the *Why?* of your temper. You should say, "The traffic jam caused me to blow up *because* I want _____." Fill in the blank with something about yourself. Do any of these cravings ("I want") and beliefs ("I think I need") fit the pattern that underlies your typical outbursts of irritation?

Such misguided motives are simply the ABCs of human nature. For example, take "I want what I want when I want it. I need to be in control." What is the real name for that? It's simply unvarnished *pride*, acting as if I am God, as if the universe revolves around me and my desires. With good reason, pride is the first of the classic seven deadly sins. Most people think of pride as "thinking you're superior to other people." That's part of it, but the deeper meaning is simply thinking that life is all about me. Most temper tantrums in traffic, most road rage, most tense irritation have pride as the straightforward cause. A temper tantrum in traffic plays out big, bad things in a small corner of life.

How about "I need other people's approval and love, and to keep up a good reputation in their eyes"? That's called *fear of man* in the Bible. It describes our tendency to put other people's opinions in the place of God. When the eyes of others replace the eyes of God, it creates a blinding obsession with image and being loved. It creates a blinding fear of rejection. The particular preoccupations, anxieties, and angers that arise when you are stuck in traffic often point directly back to this motive.

How about "I want and need money; it's the source of my identity and security"? Jesus called that motive *love of money*, a prime hijacker of our affections. Why during a traffic jam would someone recalculate income and net worth over and over, while tensed up with angry anxiety? It says something profound about what that person most deeply loves.

What about the desire for health? Anger and its unhappy cousins reveal the structure of a person's most profound and profoundly deviant faith commitments: "Modern medicine is the cure-all. My greatest need is for good health. As long as you have your health, everything's OK." Modern culture assumes this. Many people live as if it's so. But is this even remotely true? The mortality rate for patients in whatever state of health or sickness continues to be 100 percent, as always. Living for your health is always a losing bet in the long run.

Perhaps my greatest need at 11:55 a.m., stalled on the highway, fretful and fuming, is to get a grip on my deviant faith. Those various bad reactions—chaos and every evil—reveal the blind obsessions

I have and the faith I put in myself and other humans as ways to get what I want. But the truth is that, at that moment, no matter what pressure I am facing, my greatest need is for his mercies.

When a tantrum in traffic brings you up short and makes you know yourself better, it opens the door for a profound transformation in what you live for. Imagine that—a small incident while trying to get to your appointment can change your life. Questions 1 and 2 are easy and obvious: something happens, I get mad. Question 3 starts to rewrite the script. It looks behind the scenes. It changes the meaning of anger. It redefines the real cause. It begins to awaken you to reality.

Question 4 bounces us back out to notice again the wider context within which anger operates, examining not so much the way the world arouses our anger, but the ways our anger impacts the world.

## Question 4: What are the consequences?

Anger has consequences. It creates feedback loops, vicious circles. The Bible uses a vivid metaphor: you reap what you sow. Put marigold seeds in the ground, and guess what springs up in a blaze of gold? Mow one dandelion when the white ball of seeds is full, and next year you'll have a thousand dandelions dotting your yard. Sow an outburst of anger in traffic, and what will you reap? Bad attitudes are highly contagious. Perhaps my aggressive, dog-eat-dog, me-first attitude provokes others around me to do more of the same. Perhaps as drivers aggressively edge forward to merge, I grind my bumper into the fender of the car squeezing in from the right, getting an earful of hostility and the unhappy prospect of paying the $250 deductible on my collision insurance. So I'm out money (ironic, if I live for money). Perhaps I reap emotional and physical consequences: guilt, increasing stress and tension, stomachache and headache. Studies seem to show that angry people have a higher incidence of heart disease and Alzheimer's. So I'm out health (ironic, if I trust in doctors).

Perhaps my temper continually hurts the people around me, so I'm out relationships (ironic, if I live to be liked).

The consequences might even prove fatal. Several years ago on a highway here in Philadelphia, traffic was inching along on a hot summer day when one car cut off another. The man who was cut off made an obscene gesture and shouted profanities. The driver of the first car pulled out a gun and fired, killing the second man's wife.

The consequences are unpredictable. But we live in a universe where everything we do has consequences, whether subtle or obvious. Perhaps when you finally arrive at the sales appointment you're so hot, bothered, flustered, and full of excuses that you make a terrible impression and lose the sale. Maybe the consequences of your blowup at noon are as simple as a being out of sorts the rest of the day—and nothing goes right.

These first four questions climb inside the everyday, vicious circle of anger. We've slowed down the video. We've asked questions about what happened and separated out the component parts. We've identified the specific provocations. We've named the thick stew of reactions. We've taken the courageous, clear-eyed step of facing underlying motives. And we've taken seriously the significance of our actions by attending to the consequences.

We've glimpsed, even in a traffic jam, the vicious circle that biblical shorthand labels as "temptation, sin, lusts of the flesh, and misery." Those Bible words often get so clogged with religiosity that the realities they describe get lost. But these first four matter-of-fact, eyes-open, feet-on-the-ground questions are asking about issues that are front and center in the Bible. What is the word for being stuck in traffic while something very important is getting shot down in flames? That's a painful temptation. To be filled with bitterness and hostility, to do destructive things, to feel destructive feelings, to think destructive thoughts? That's grievous sin. Why do I react this way? Living for "*my* will be done" is a lust for my own will to rule all. This is a serious defection from what a human being is meant to be. And all the bad things that happen next? I reap what I sow in miseries of various kinds.

The first four questions explore the problem. The next four questions bring hope and move toward resolution. The God who talks about what happens in traffic jams has been peering into this situation, teaching us how to understand what's going on. The God who cares to help us enters into our plight. He speaks and acts into the immediate problems we face when stuck on the road and fuming. We could even say that, understood the right way, the whole Bible from Genesis to Revelation is "about" what's going on when you get stuck in traffic. It's about how to make right what goes so wrong.

So the fifth question talks about God and the difference he makes.

### Question 5: What is true?

What does the Bible say about being stuck in a traffic jam and reacting poorly? The details aren't in the Bible, but God's words speak directly into this very situation.

Consider Psalm 23, probably the best-known, best-loved passage in the Bible. It was written 3,000 years ago. A man who knew many troubles and frustrations poured out his heart. He puts what is most meaningful to him into exquisitely simple words. He was a remarkably honest human with an extremely unusual way of looking at the world. Even people who say they don't believe in God have been known to find David's words strangely comforting. Listen to them again.

> The LORD is my shepherd; I shall not want.
> He makes me lie down in green pastures.
> He leads me beside still waters.
> He restores my soul.
> He leads me in paths of righteousness for his name's sake.
> Even though I walk through the valley of the shadow of death,
> I fear no evil, for you are with me;

Your rod and your staff, they comfort me.
You prepare a table before me in the presence of my enemies;
You anoint my head with oil;
My cup overflows.
Surely goodness and mercy shall follow me all the days of my
    life,
And I shall dwell in the house of the LORD forever.

What does this have to do with your irritation in traffic? David never experienced gridlock, but he did experience the exact same *kind* of thing: life's threats and frustrations that often trigger anger. How does Psalm 23 speak into a traffic jam?

*The* LORD *is my shepherd; I shall not want.* Stuck in my car, incommunicado, frustrated, I feel all alone in a threatening world. No one's looking out for me. I may lose health, money, friendship, or reputation. No wonder I'm irritated, anxious, and tense. But David says, "I'm not alone. I lack nothing good. Someone is watching over me. Someone is taking care of me." That recognition of a loving, powerful personality on the scene radically changes *everything.* A tantrum is governed by rules: perceived threat, frustration, loss, aloneness. But perceived friendship and hands-on care changes the rules. Faith awakens, takes a deep breath, and calms down.

*He makes me lie down in green pastures. He leads me beside still waters.* How forcefully good is this? Someone is *making me* lie down in a rich, nourishing place. Someone is *leading me* to a safe, satisfying place. Don't imagine lush meadows and gushing streams; imagine a flourishing oasis in a barren desert. David is talking about coming to a very good place in the middle of a tough place. Can this also prove true for you at 11:55 a.m., bottled up on the highway, your plans draining away? Can someone get you to a good place right now? David has a rich sense that God's hand is working good in his life today. The reality of being cared for outweighs the hardships of the moment.

*He restores my soul.* This describes being turned around inside and out. He turns *me* from a bad place to a good place. He brings me from a destructive place to a constructive place. He brings me back to life. It's easy to see how this applies to the firestorms of anger and anxiety. He restores my soul, quenching my upset, refreshing me, giving me himself.

*He leads me in paths of righteousness for his name's sake.* This is perhaps the most astonishing line of all, for two reasons. First, this recognizes that God leads me in "paths of righteousness." That describes walking through life on a path in which everything wrong is being made right. Everything wrong about me—anger, bitterness, fear, anguish, escapism—is being straightened out. Everything wrong with the world I live in—loss of money, health, friendship, reputation—is being reversed.

Second, God does these things for me because of who *he* is. That's what the phrase "for his name's sake" means. God stakes *himself* on bringing me through life's troubles into a good life. He does it for *his* reasons. This is not a magic immunity against troubles. It doesn't mean I won't end up with colon cancer. I might lose the sale. I might face an irreparable breach in an old friendship. The battle with my temper is not necessarily easy. But it does mean that all troubles along the way will come out joyful in the end. It may not feel like it right away, but *this* is the path. Right now, here on the highway, stuck in traffic, hopelessly late, he is making me into a man of peace not war.

*Even though I walk through the valley of the shadow of death, I fear no evil, for you are with me.* This gets to the bottom of things, whether you're stuck in a literal or a figurative traffic jam. A "shadow of death" is something bad that gives a foretaste of ultimate loss. That is *exactly* what's happening to you at 11:55 a.m. Is it colon cancer? A financial hit? Loss of the possibility of a loving relationship? Those losses taste of death. These things are "evils," bad experiences that people rightly fear. Your anger may get way out of line, but it's not crazy. Much of the anger and anxiety that boils up in that traffic jam comes because you fear the possibility of some real evil. But if someone truly good is with you, then "fear no evil."

*Your rod and your staff, they comfort me.* These are a shepherd's tools for lifting a sheep out of trouble and for fighting off predators. If someone else cares about my welfare, and will protect me from both myself and others, then I've got a real reason to be comforted. A powerful friend is watching me in the darkest valley—and the most impenetrable traffic jam.

*Surely goodness and mercy shall follow me all the days of my life, and I shall dwell in the house of the LORD forever.* This is astonishing. In traffic, obvious obstacles stand in my way, and I'm easily irritated by them all. But if the good Shepherd's loving-kindness tracks me down and finds me, then I'm glad beyond telling. Which will it be? "I'm sitting in traffic for the next hour fuming" or "I am living where the Lord himself lives, right here, now, and forever"? A traffic jam is embittering if you are all alone with your desires and fears. If you are at home with the Lord who loves you forever, who will bring you safely to the house of the Lord, then your joy is anchored in something bigger.

Many other themes and truths from God will prove significant for you in unraveling your temper and rebuilding your joy. But you won't go wrong if you start with Psalm 23. Make it your own. The dark turbulence and anxious hostility of angry fears cannot coexist with Jesus, our good Shepherd, who elicits such bright trust. Psalm 23 is very specific, and we live on specifics.

I will mention three more general truths. They will help you to appreciate *why* Psalm 23 speaks so personally to you. Reckoning with these things will help you take advantage of other specific truths. They help you know what you are looking for when you are looking for help.

First, God is present, personal, and active. Take that sentence slowly. God is present, not far away. He is personal, not just an idea. He is active, not hands off. This reality breathes through every sentence in Psalm 23. I'm not talking about abstract theological theory.

I'm not talking about religious rituals and devotional practices. I'm not talking about trying harder to be a good person or trying to talk yourself into feeling better. I'm talking about the Person at the center of it all. This world, including your missed appointment, belongs to Jesus Christ. He is King of kings. He is in control of this and every other situation. He is doing something in real time (now), in real places (here where you sit in your car). He has something to say to *you* about how you're reacting and why. He has something to communicate to you about who he is, and how he is relevant. The frustrating situations described in Question 1 are not accidents. I was never meant to control the world, but that does not mean the world is random, purposeless, and out of control. The Lord Jesus is my Shepherd, I shall not want.

Second, Jesus summarized the Bible's goal in this way: "You shall love the Lord your God with all your heart and with all your soul and with all your strength, and with all your mind, and your neighbor as yourself" (Luke 10:27). God's law is a picture of how a human being becomes truly human (Galatians 5:6; 1 Timothy 1:5).

It's the way life is meant to be. The God of the universe calls us to love him with utter devotion. When I forget my Shepherd, I orient my life around another god and love some good gift more than the Giver. God, who made people in his image, calls us to love each other with the same fierce concern that we look out for our own interests. When I forget, I get frustrated and hostile, or fearful and withdrawn. When I remember, I get fiercely caring. Will I love my self-interest and become wholly indifferent to the interests of my neighbors whose cars surround me? I am commanded to the sanity of love, and it lays my heart bare.

I was driving down the road minding my own business (more than I knew!). Everything ground to a halt. And I fumed. And those other cars became my competitors, my enemies, anonymous opponents, depersonalized. As I look in God's brilliant mirror, I come to realize that right now at 11:55 a.m. here on this highway, I have no love for the God whose world this is. I have no love for others. I am a traitor to what is true. He arrests me.

The law of love is a mirror showing us who we are. It is also a lamp, lighting the way to where we ought to be. Right now, here in traffic, it is possible to love the Lord who is your Shepherd. He guides you to treat others differently. Do you see in that car next to you? There sits a person, just like you. Could you consider the interests of these other people, each one heading to some appointment? And how about those people who will be disappointed and inconvenienced because you don't show up? What will you say when you finally arrive at your appointment? Will you make excuses and vent, or will you consider their interests?

I *could* wait out this traffic jam with patience. It's no accident "Love is patient" comes first in 1 Corinthians 13. Patience isn't very dramatic, but it counts. "Love is kind" comes next in 1 Corinthians 13. As the traffic merges, I could let someone in. How much more practical can it get? Maybe I could even let in two cars. And when I get off the highway, courtesy will make a phone call as soon as possible to let the waiting person know the situation. I could express my heartfelt apology without any of the emotional dishevelment, the groveling, or the excuse-making that so vividly display how our hearts are still not right. I could get down to business in a constructive way. Make the sales presentation? Arrange a new doctor's appointment? Find out how my friend is doing?

But how can I ever do any of these wonderfully sane, constructive things mentioned in the last paragraph? I cannot do it without help. That's the third crucial truth. We saw everywhere in Psalm 23 that Someone else is at work in me, and at work for me. The Lord of life, the good Shepherd, must love me and take me by the hand. The God who is God comes in person. I'm not hung out to dry on a highway choked with cars, merely exhorted to demonstrate greater self-control and take the high moral ground. Remember, I have been convicted of violating nothing less than the first and second great commandments in this "small" incident on the highway. Questions 2 and 3 uncovered enmity and treason. When I'm seeing straight, I realize that these are sins, interpersonal offenses, death penalty crimes coming out in everyday ways. I don't just need "anger management" strategies; I need mercy.

Out on that highway in mid-tantrum, I felt all alone, frustrated, angry. My anger didn't *seem* to be against God. I probably didn't give him a thought. But pride, fear of man, obsession with money, and faith in medicine shouts against God. Mid-tantrum, there was no one to help me. But the good Shepherd comes as the Lamb of God. He dies for just such sins, to forgive me in real time, in a traffic jam. My first need—even before patience and genuine kindness can begin to replace irascibility—is my need for mercy.

When your eyes are wide open to who you are and how much you need help, then everywhere you turn in the Bible you find "gospel." You find the Redeemer you need and who will meet you in your exact need. You find good news in word and deed: God comes in person to save us from ourselves. Jesus Christ shows up in traffic jams, the Word made flesh, full of grace and truth. The mirror of love showed me what I was doing and brought me up short. The lamp showed me what ought to be. The gift of God in person builds a bridge between the two and begins to make what is into what ought to be.

So how do you walk across that bridge from death to life, from anger to mercy?

## Question 6: How do I turn to God for help?

Question 5 laid out the worldview within which anger problems find hope. God is revealed. The escape route from our foolishness into a living wisdom is made clear. But mere analysis, even the clearest thinking (something Questions 1–5 seek to bring about) won't change me. Question 6 gets me moving. Question 6 is not really a question—it's an action step. Do it. Turn to him. Ask for help. Seek mercy. Knock on the door. Humble yourself. Transact with God.

Meet him. Need him. Trust him. Talk it all out with him by filling in these blanks with the relevant particulars:

You are _____.

I'm facing _____.

You promise _____.

I've done wrong by _____.

I've been misruled by my love of _____.

Please forgive me for _____.

I love you because _____.

Please help me to _____.

Thank you for _____.

I rejoice that you _____.

Angry people always talk to the wrong person. They talk to themselves, rehearsing the failings of others. They talk to the people they're mad at, reaming them out for real and imaginary failings. They talk to people who aren't even involved, gossiping and slandering. But chaotic, sinful, headstrong anger starts to dissolve when you begin to talk to the right person—to your good Shepherd, who sees, hears, and is mercifully involved in your life.

To apply the truths of Question 5 is to start talking. Have you ever noticed that Psalm 23 is mostly conversation? David starts out

I absolutely must preach this!

talking about what God means to him. But he doesn't get far before he starts talking *to* the God he needs and loves: "I will fear no evil, for *you* are with me."

Do it. God begins the conversation with you by giving you Psalm 23. Speak up.

## Question 7: How could I respond constructively in this situation?

Repentance and faith lead to concrete changes in behavior, emotion, and thoughts. Active love and obedience are just as specific as the sins described in Question 2. At the simplest level, you might take a deep breath and relax, trusting that God is indeed in control. But God has other fruits in mind too. You become a charitable, courteous driver. Let a couple of cars in. What does it matter if you're two more car lengths behind? This traffic jam is no longer a dog-eat-dog battle. You verbalize thanks to God. You plan what you will say to the person you've stood up: not anxious excuse-making or blustering irritation, but the simple facts and a concern for that person's welfare.

What a joy to be free of the emotional chaos of sin. Instead of that hot stew of anger, anxiety, confusion, and disgruntlement, you're peaceful. You taste a bit of the "peace which passes understanding" and "secret of contentment" that comes from living in the light of mercy. Question 7 tackles every aspect of the situation described in Question 1 and walks out the will of God in detail in your world. You become a force for good.

## Question 8: What are the consequences of faith and obedience?

We've already mentioned some of the emotional benefits of faith and obedience. Physically you may have prevented a dented fender or even a killing in that traffic jam! Somebody else was kept from stumbling into sinful anger or murder on my account. And in my corner of the world, the half dozen drivers around me who experienced my courtesy and relaxed response may have calmed down too.

Here we come full circle and find that godliness, while not guaranteed to change the original situation, often has an effect for good on the world. Maybe I end up making the sale anyway because the manager is impressed by the calm, reasonable way I handled what might have been a nerve-racking situation. He'd seen too many other emotionally disheveled salesmen spouting excuses and coming on strong. Godliness intrigued and attracted him.

The possibilities for the many-sided blessings of God are endless. Instead of my day being ruined, God has extricated me from sin and misery. This could be one of the most significant days in my life from the standpoint of growing into the image of Christ. I've learned how life works in God's world. I've learned how grace works. I've learned profound lessons in a very tiny corner of life. And perhaps when I talk to a troubled, distraught friend that evening on the phone, I'm able to comfort those in any trouble with the comfort with which I was comforted by God in my trouble (2 Corinthians 1:4). I didn't suffer much—it was only a traffic jam, after all—and maybe my friend is suffering a great deal. But the dynamic of the human heart is identical. I will understand my friend's temptations to bitterness, anxiety, and discouragement because I've understood my own. And I've come to understand the way of escape. "Love to the loveless shown that they might lovely be."[3] Walking this through has not only blessed me, but makes me able to wisely help others.

A traffic jam. It's only a tiny case study. Some people might ask what this has to do with major troubles, major provocations to anger. In the way the Bible views life and comes at problems, it has everything to do with them. The same truths about God apply in the same way. Sure, many details will differ. And the Bible is frank: there are tears that won't be wiped away and enemies that won't be out of the way until the last day. Question 8 does not create heaven on earth. It does, however, help you get a taste of heaven—even though many enemies have not yet been put under Christ's feet. If on the day I see Christ I will be made completely like him, then in a small way I taste the joy of heaven in a traffic jam by being made a bit more like him.

These eight questions orient us to *Christian* reality—which is to say, they orient us to reality. They teach us about our world, ourselves, our God, and how to live. People God teaches how to handle traffic jams, he will teach how to handle other things.

>> >> >>

## Making It Your Own

1. Work through the eight questions in this chapter using the last time you got irritated for a case study.

2. Next time you get irritated, stop and work through these eight questions.

# TACKLING THE HARD CASES

We have come far. Our early exploration into how we experience anger led to gaining perspective and understanding. Understanding then led us toward action. We painted the change process in broad strokes, considering James 3—4 and then putting our eight questions to work. This final section will paint with a finer brush. We will look carefully at four key problems: extreme provocations to anger, everyday irritants, anger at yourself, and anger at God.

CHAPTER 14

# "I'll Never Get Over It"

Like fine china that doesn't get brought out for everyday use, the hardest things—the things we have the most right to be angry about—are often kept hidden away in a cabinet. Many people, perhaps even you, carry unspeakable things inside—things that make it hard to talk and hard to go forward. Perhaps you have heard someone say, or have said yourself some variation of these words:

> I'll never get over it. What happened to me was so wrong. It hurt so much. I've been scarred so deeply by sheer wrongness, betrayal, cruelty, and brutality. My reactions are confused and tangled. My anger is raging like a nuclear furnace inside me. It seems as permanent, destructive, and deep as the hurt.

You are right. You'll never get over it. Does my answer surprise you?

Perhaps you find it curiously liberating to say you'll never get over a particular hurt. That's right . . . of course. How freeing to admit the truth. A human being is not meant to deal with a terrible wrong by having it simply washed away. So you don't have to chase an impossibility. You don't have to try to anesthetize yourself with various substances and activities. You don't have to feel like a failure because you are not happy and smiley all the time. If you aren't expecting to find some magic that will leave you unmarked, then you can get down to working through your painful experience.

Perhaps, though, it's not a relief to hear that some experiences will never go away. Instead you feel even more hopeless. But there is hope. Yes, the experience will always be there, but you do not need to be forever defined by what happened. I hope this chapter will be a start, a small piece of help and hope that will give you direction out of your despair. The reasons for realistic hope run deeper than any hurt.

You won't forget, but you do not need to endlessly revisit what happened. You do not need to be imprisoned in your reactions. It's never easy, of course. By definition, to transmute a very deep furnace of pain and anger into something fruitful is hard. It is refreshing to admit, "That suffering will mark me. I will never 'get over it.'" Even a new sense of life purpose will in some way be shaped by what happened. In fact, you would be untrue to your humanity if you simply got over it. A significant experience will mark you for life; it should mark you.

But the pain and hatred and despair do not need to remain a running sore infected by rage, mistrust, and callousness. There is a way to go *through* it and come out in a good place. We can get a taste for how this works by looking at the lives of some who have also been terribly wronged.

Candy Lightner never got over the death of her thirteen-year-old daughter, who was run over by a drunk driver. But this irreversible suffering was somehow transmuted into a constructive mission. She founded Mothers Against Drunk Driving (MADD) in 1980.

Martin Luther King never got over a lifetime of experiencing racial prejudice. Such experiences are the crucible within which people easily respond to a terrible wrong with bitterness: "Because I've lived a nightmare, I have reasons to be full of hate. I don't care anymore." For King, it led to, "I have a dream," a purpose big enough to live for and big enough to die for. His whole life was marked by the experience. But he was not disfigured.

Aleksandr Solzhenitsyn never got over his tortures in Joseph Stalin's gulags. His degradation in the camps became the seedbed of his life work. Read Solzhenitsyn's *Gulag Archipelago*. You will witness a rare example of a man who did not become self-righteous and self-pitying as he catalogued evils.

Each of these people is only a pointer. Each provides a flawed example, their good insights and resolutions mixed with remaining contradictions. They are people like you and me.

When something is so wrong that you will never get over it, your reaction will either make you live or it will kill you. Great suffering puts a fork in the road, and you will choose. The choice is between the way of bitterness and the way of grace and mercy.

*Kyrie eleison*—"Lord, have mercy"—is the essential prayer of the needy man or woman who turns to God for help. "Blessed are the poor in spirit" is the first and foundational beatitude (Matthew 5:3). The sense of need for help from outside yourself is an essential step toward sanity. It is this that Jesus commends so often in a person who shows "faith," and thus asks him for help. Faith is not a leap into darkness and unreason in spite of cold hard facts. Faith is the honest and reasonable step in the direction of the person who can help you, given all the facts.

I hope you have already taken to heart, as you have read, the truth that God is also angry about what happened to you. He is angry at *all* injustice, *every* betrayal, *any time* wrongs are done to another. He knows exactly how you were wronged, and he stands against injustice. But God gets good and angry. His response to evil is to do the greatest good thing the world has ever seen. He sends his own Son as a man of sorrows who enters and knows our suffering. He sends his own Son as the Lamb of God to die for the sins of his people. God doesn't want you to "just get over it" or to gloss over what you have suffered as if it didn't really matter. He wants to help you become good and angry as well. He wants you to become merciful, purposeful, hopeful. That process takes time. It takes courage to face the evil done to you and to then turn toward your God, who suffered unimaginable evil on your behalf.

## Three Stories

In this section we will work through three stories. The first story is from the novel *Cry, the Beloved Country* by Alan Paton. It is a story about a man who had to deal with great wrong. The second story is about a woman who was terribly abused as a child. I got to know her when she sought my help. The last story is the one you will tell—it's your story—told through the lens of the eight questions from the last chapter.

These are deep matters so we need to take the time to think through them thoughtfully. Learning to live fruitfully in the face of great wrong will take a lifetime of going to God for mercy and help in your time of need. There is something deeply refreshing in being able to say that what is broken can't be fixed as good as new. The pain from what hurts so badly can't be taken completely away. But you can learn a reason to live that is better by far. We learn from stories—both told and lived. Here's your opportunity to begin your journey of fruitful living in the face of great wrong.

### An Aggrieved Father

*Cry, the Beloved Country* is one of the great novels in the twentieth century. Paton's story does a better job than any theoretical analysis for giving you a feel for how struggles with hard things work out either for good or for evil. It's show (not tell) for how the struggle with overwhelming evils can be transmuted into good.

The story is set in South Africa during the 1940s (just before apartheid became policy). Stephen Kumalo is a black, Anglican pastor in a small, impoverished village. His son had left home for Johannesburg, where he drifted into a life of petty crime. Kumalo goes to the city, seeking to rescue his son. But he finds him too late. The son has just been arrested for a murder committed in panic when the homeowner walked in on a burglary.

The various dark responses to suffering appear in many different ways, in many different characters, for many different reasons.

We might be tempted to think of "pain" as a reaction to an uncomfortable stimulus. We might be tempted to think of "anger" as a flare-up arising from a specific provocation. We might be tempted to think of "fear" as apprehension in the face of a particular threat. But in *Cry, the Beloved Country* the stimuli, provocations, and threats spread as wide and deep as life itself. The very conditions of existence are systematically humiliating.

Kumalo and others in the story live within unfairness, injustice, extreme poverty, systematic racism, powerlessness, and the wrecked lives of loved ones who had bad options and made bad choices. When evil is all-encompassing, no one particular incident is decisive for causing pain, provoking you to anger, arousing fear. Any one of a thousand daily incidents simply delivers one more slap to the face of a man who has been repeatedly beaten. How could anyone get over this?

Kumalo struggles. He sometimes loses it. But he does not get lost in it. Several things prove significant as he comes through evils without becoming crushed by sorrow and the sins of others against him (and even his own bad reactions to those great wrongs). There are three factors that are significant in his journey.

First, he is befriended by a fellow Anglican pastor, Msimangu. This friend acts with kindness, generosity, and tact. But when Kumalo says to him, "You are kind," his friend answers, "I am not kind. I am a selfish and sinful man, but God put his hand on me, that is all" (p. 55). Msimangu was an honest man who reckoned with his sinfulness, weakness, and selfishness—and God's mercy made him different.

Msimangu's hard-won goodness gives him the authority to voice a great moral challenge to any human being who has faced grave suffering. Black South African? Survivor of domestic violence? Bereaved parent? You? He puts it this way, "I have one great fear in my heart, that one day when they are turned toward loving, they will find that we are turned to hating" (p. 71). He did not mean that he was waiting for those in power to change or to suddenly admit that they were wrong. But because he knew the inworking power of God's mercy, he could be frank with Kumalo's anger and fear. Will you who are wronged, do wrong? Will you find yourself turned to hating, or will you find the strong mercy that turns you to loving?

Second, while in Johannesburg, Kumalo rented a room in the house of an elderly widow, Mrs. Lithebe. She was poor and had her own troubles. But on a number of occasions when his troubles were too great to bear, too great to solve, she showed him some simple generosity. When he thanked her she replied, "Why else do we live? For what else were we born?" (pp. 151, 227). If you have faced a great wrong—racism, rape, betrayal—there is no immediate solution by which you or any other human can make it better. But small, practical kindnesses count. In the end Kumalo became like Mrs. Lithebe. He too became simple in showing small kindnesses.

The more insoluble and heartbreaking a problem, the smaller the action that is called for in any particular moment. We are slow to grasp this. Great suffering produces great anger, great fear, and great despair in part because no great solution is possible. But small kindnesses matter a great deal. Mrs. Lithebe grasped something that victims need to receive and can learn to give. Small good deeds amid great evils are part of becoming free from the waste of our wraths and sorrows.

Third, Kumalo returns home to his village when there is no more hope for his son. On the night before his son is to be hanged for murder, Kumalo says to his wife, "I am going up into the mountain" (p. 305). He gets away, taking the time to reckon honestly with himself and God. At first, the memory of all that had happened and all that was about to happen overwhelmed him. But then he consciously "turned aside from such fruitless remembering" (p. 308). "Fruitless remembering"—that is a good way to describe one place it is easy to get stuck when you've been done deep wrong.

He uses an interesting phrase for the alternative: "He set himself to the order of his vigil" (p. 308). Kumalo does not stay in regret, self-torture, recrimination, and accusation. He consciously heads in a different direction according to a different purpose. His vigil begins with the confessing of his sins, then giving thanks for those who showed him kindness, and finally crying out for mercy—for his son, himself, his people, and his country.

On his mountain, Kumalo seizes hold of the one hope deeper than the deepest wreckage of hopes. He brings his cares to the One who cares for him. He lives out the rhythms of Christian faith: self-awareness before God, frank confession, honest gratitude, pointed intercession . . . going forth to live in the way of obedience.

Our culture usually portrays our response to great suffering as something with "how to" solutions. But the things that cause the deepest angers, fears, and despairs are betrayals at a depth that calls for a different way of thinking about solutions. We must learn to live honestly in the face of evils that don't necessarily go away. You must learn to honestly face down your own evil in the light of bigger mercies: "I am a selfish and sinful man, but God put his hands on me, that is all." When someone else did you wrong by acts of hate, will you turn to hating? Or will you become good and angry? By God's mercy will you grow in being merciful?

Like Kumalo, when hopes are crushed and dismembered, we too must learn the one hope that can never be destroyed. "In this is love, not that we have loved God but that he loved us and sent his Son to be the propitiation for our sins" (1 John 4:10). Those aren't words for religious people in religious contexts. They are words for real-time heartache and trouble. You are beloved. Those words are for you, today.

When the reality of who you are in Christ takes root, you can learn how to live well. You can stand with dignity in the face of wrong. "Beloved, if God so loved us, we also ought to love one another" (1 John 4:11). You can do small things gladly. You learn that you can make some difference. You never think you are better than any other human being. You never think your efforts will right all wrongs. But you learn not to hate.

## A Woman Abused as a Child

Many years ago I had the privilege of getting to know a woman who had suffered more terrible things than anyone I've ever known. Martina was in her mid-thirties when she and her husband sought counsel for conflicts they were having about how to raise their children. We addressed those conflicts, but her larger story made a profound impression on me. She had been sexually abused from infancy until she was rescued by the Department of Youth & Family Services (DYFS) in her teens. She had been used as a sexual receptacle by her father, uncle, brother, and strangers. Her entire life, from age three to fifteen, was an Auschwitz of sexualized violence. It was all she ever knew.

DYFS sought out foster care and placed Martina with a family who loved her. They were safe. They provided for her. They protected her. They set clear guidelines for what was right and wrong regarding how to treat others with respect, what words to use, how to deal with problems, and how to express sexuality.

Of course, healing and change were not accomplished in one moment. When Martina came to live with the family, she was prone to violent rages, spoke abusively, was inappropriately sexual, stole whatever she could get her hands on, trusted no one, obeyed no one, lied freely, and existed in a maelstrom of impulsive cravings and terrifying fears. In other words, she incarnated all that is not love, all that is destructive and self-destructive, all that needs effective mercy and help. Out of the maelstrom of these sufferings and her own chaos, and in the context of her foster parents' love (that clear-minded "constructive displeasure of mercy"), Martina came to know Jesus when she was nineteen years old.

Jesus is not just a pointer, like Solzhenitsyn or Martin Luther King, Jr. He is the one to whom the pointers point. His story shows incalculable wrong becoming transmuted into unfathomable good. He was not above it all. A man of sorrows, intimately acquainted with grief, enters the hard places. Jesus never got over his experience of evil. But Jesus was not defined by what he suffered. He did not explode with darkness when he was trapped by darkness. He took to heart Martina's experience of great evils; he also took to heart Martina's own wrongs. Before God, she realized that she had no hope but his mercy. So she turned toward Jesus and asked for mercy. And he freely gave her a new life.

Without being conscious of the phrase, or knowing what it might mean, Martina began to embody that essential wisdom that says, "The fear of the LORD is the beginning of knowledge" (Proverbs 1:7). To see oneself as before the eyes of the King of creation, to see one's need for the mercies of the Savior of sinful and suffering humankind, this is the dawning light of all true sanity. Martina became sane, and she began to untangle a deep, dark tangle. She began to grow, and to grow up, and to love.

Without knowing fully what it meant, she took to heart, "Do not repay anyone evil for evil" (Romans 12:17 NIV). That sentence does the moral calculus for a victim in such a realistic, clean manner. What happened to me was evil. What I'm doing back is evil. I don't have to try to stack them up next to each other quantitatively. I don't have to say "Your evil is worse, so I'm OK." I don't have to say "You started it, so it doesn't matter what I do." I don't have to say "I might do wrong, but it's all because of you." Martina had the worst start in life of anyone I've ever known. But it was a deep pleasure to witness the courage and clarity of faith to which she had gradually come.

It's perhaps most surprising that Martina did not end up a drug addict or a suicide victim. But given that she found the mercies of Christ, it is perhaps not so surprising that she eventually became a social worker with a particular affinity for abused children. As the victim of racism works for racial justice, as the mother whose child is killed fights to eliminate drunk driving, so Martina works to help kids who've been done staggering wrong. It is perhaps surprising that Martina eventually got married and has two children of her own. That didn't come easy, and is another of those paradoxical hard-won gifts of grace.

Did Martina "get over" her first fifteen years of life? No. Will she ever get over it? Not in this lifetime. That family-sized Auschwitz marks her to this day. In one sense it will mark her to all eternity: *this* is where the love of God delivered *this* woman, and her gratitude and joy will always stand out against that backdrop. Even now, her hard-won, grace-given strengths show the fingerprints of her sufferings. Her love is a particular kind of love, forged from the furnace of a particular kind of hate. And her remaining sins still reflect the damaging marks of her life experience. She tends to fearfulness ("I just want to disappear off the scene and not have to face hard things"), irritability ("Don't come near me"), and suspiciousness ("What will happen to me?"), especially around assertive men, even when they pose no real threat. In her marriage there has been a long slow process of disentangling sex from being a dreadful evil and remaking it as a simple good. She's come a ways; she's got a ways to go. Her husband is a tender man (with his faults, of course), and she's learned more trust while he's learned more patience.

What does Martina teach us? I might say many things. But I'll mention three things about her life that made a particular impression on me.

First, there is a place to cry out to God, "Where are you? Why is this happening to me? Why did it happen? Why am I still struggling? How long until you free me from this trouble? You have promised me good; what good can come of something so hard?" It makes all the difference in the world that such things are said with a grief that needs God, that believes he is good, that loves him. Some people say things like this as bitter accusations against God. But angry reasons not to trust are the opposite of anguished trust. Martina had not only read the Psalms, she had taken to heart their inner logic of honest faith. In the Psalms she read anguished prayers to God that expressed her own struggles. Words like "The plowers plowed upon my back; they lengthened their furrows" (Psalm 129:3 NASB) and "They attack, they lurk, they watch my steps, as they have waited to take my life" (Psalm 56:6 NASB). And she also found prayers of faith that she could echo in her suffering, "When I am afraid, I put my trust in you. In God, whose word I praise—in God I trust and am not afraid. What can mere mortals do to me?" (Psalm 56:3–4 NIV). Her faith was not necessarily tranquil—faith can't be tranquil when troubles squeeze in on us and erupt inside us. As in so many of the Psalms, God repeatedly met Martina's daily honesty with what she needed for that day.

Second, often when you are early in the process of coming to grips with the kinds of suffering that you don't get over, it is insulting when someone says, "God will bring some good out of this." It sounds as if your sufferings are being trivialized, glossed over so that we can all get on to talking about something more pleasant. But later in the process, this is one of the most precious truths of all. God *does* bring good out of evil. It is so, and it works out in real life. Why is Martina intuitively both kind and firm with children whose lives are in wreckage? Some people are nice and sympathetic (but ineffectual); others are clear-thinking and blunt (but unsympathetic). How is it that Martina is able to be both sympathetic and candid? Paul put the dynamic this way: God "comforts us in all our afflictions, so that we will be able to comfort those who are in any affliction, with the comfort with which we ourselves are comforted by God" (2 Corinthians 1:4). You can give away what you have received. And that is one of the ways that good comes out of evil, without ever insinuating that evil is anything but evil.

Third, Martina will be marked in some way by pain and struggle throughout her life. For example, she has no relatives she can call her own. Her foster parents are dead and it's not quite the same with her in-laws, as much as she appreciates them. Her children have only one set of grandparents. Sexual intimacy with her husband can be shadowed with darkness—when she is tired, if they've not been communicating well, when he's in a bit of a rush, if she's been doing some fruitless remembering. It gets tiresome always dealing with her temptation to flinch and withdraw when she's around confident or opinionated people. Those are some of her battles. Is she abnormal?

No. One of the fine promises of God that speaks most deeply to her is this hope: "He will wipe away every tear from their eyes; and there will no longer be any death; there will no longer be any mourning, or crying, or pain; the first things have passed away. And He who sits on the throne said, 'Behold, I am making all things new'" (Revelation 21:4–5 NASB). One of the effects of being marked by suffering is learning to value the future. Not all the crying or pain goes away now, but he will make all things new.

Have you been marked by something that feels like you'll never get over it? Has something ruined your life? Are you struggling with your own rage, despair, indifference, and escapism? Perhaps you are attempting to help someone else whose life seems in ruins, and they struggle in all these ways. Like Martina, take heart.

### Your Story

Now it's time to tell your story, but perhaps in a different way than you have ever told it before. The eight questions from the previous chapter are like a good map and compass. A map and compass don't get you from here to there. They orient you. The squiggly red line on a map looks nothing like the actual road you must drive. It doesn't show the sun glare or ice, the traffic tie-ups, or the fact that when the road goes over a mountain you must shift to low gear. A map can't tell how long it will take you to get from here to there. Conditions vary.

If you are haunted by old suffering, by a nuclear waste of wraths and sorrows, put these questions to work. You may have to drive very slowly. You may have to get out and walk—or crawl! Sometimes you may feel like giving up and crawling into a hole. You'll need to get others to walk with you, to help you find and keep perspective. We aren't made to do life alone. You need others, especially where pain runs deep and anger runs high. And, unlike dissecting a simple act of irritable complaining, your answers won't fit neatly within any lines I might insert in this book. You'll probably need another sheet of paper—you could write a book.

You'll probably want to read a book or two. You might want to take up Alan Paton's *Cry, the Beloved Country*. Notice how deep reasons for great anger and misery become changed by a deeper moral calculation, and by the transactions that find deeper mercy. You might want to ponder *When God Weeps* by Joni Eareckson Tada and Steve Estes. Joni's sufferings are likely quite different from yours, but the same human struggles take place, and she finds a God bigger than pain and loss. You might want to read Ed Welch's *Shame Interrupted*. Suffering such as we have been describing is humiliating. Bitterness and anger are not the only weighty struggles. The victim of grave evils often feels dirty, degraded, and exposed. "There must be something wrong with me. I feel inferior, tainted, shameful. I'm always standing on the outside, like I never belong, I'm never safe, I'm never acceptable." Ed ministers tenderly and wisely.

Let's revisit our eight questions, this time applying them not to an imaginary traffic jam, but to the big hurts that seem insurmountable. Remember that your story won't be told in a few minutes as you read through these eight questions. It will be a lifetime journey, as it was for Martina and is for all of us. These questions are just a starting point, a way to connect your story to the deep reality of God's love and mercy for you, even (and especially) in the face of something that was terribly wrong.

**1. *What happened to you?*** It needs to be stated. But don't let it turn into fruitless remembering. Instead, remember that you are seeking to go somewhere good. A whirlpool of excruciating details is an easy place to drown. It can be helpful to be matter-of-fact: this happened. You might want to use a psalm to help you express what seems inexpressible. Three psalms that can be fruitfully used by those who have been terribly hurt are Psalms 55, 56, and 57. Psalm 55 is about being betrayed by a close friend. Psalm 56 is about someone who feels imprisoned by people who hate him. Psalm 57 is about having a predator after you. You might want to make a photocopy or print out these psalms, then go through them with a marker and underline all the phrases in the psalms that give words to the kinds of things you also experienced.[1]

**2. How have you reacted?** There's a history to this. Once again let the psalmist give words to you. Take a different color marker and underline all of the phrases that express how you have felt as you experienced hurt. Look at phrases like, "I am distraught. . . . My heart is in anguish within me; the terrors of death have fallen on me. Fear and trembling have beset me; horror has overwhelmed me. I said, 'Oh that I had the wings of a dove! I would fly away and be at rest'" (Psalm 55:2, 4–6).[2] How does your experience map on to what the psalmist is describing? What would you add? Or subtract? Perhaps you feel completely crushed by what happened. You can't get it out of your mind. You have gone over and over what happened thousands of times. You can't forget. Maybe you have tried to anesthetize yourself with temporary feel-goods. Perhaps now you are also struggling with an addiction. Or maybe you have turned your suffering inward and are experiencing a dark cloud of depression and cynicism about yourself and others. The interplay between your suffering (Question 1) and your reaction to it (Question 2) is part of your unfolding life story. That story counts. Any positive step will be the next step in *this* story, not someone else's.

**3. What do you believe, want, and fear that fuels your reactions?** The first two questions are the more straightforward to answer because they read straight off the page of your life. The rest of the questions take more time—perhaps a lifetime—to answer fully. With this third question it's important to keep in mind that not all sufferers respond the same way because who *you* are stirs in the crucial ingredient. Seeing where you go right encourages you that the Lord is already at work in the midst of a terrible circumstance. And seeing where you go wrong is the start of seeing how you might be remade right.

Notice the exact beliefs, desires, and fears that hijack, obsess, and enslave you. Notice also that the motives that master you for ill

always have a peculiar blinding effect. Your universe shrivels to the
size of your experience of pain, your bad reactions, your instinctive
motives. You blank out to the God who is bigger than your sufferings. You blank out to Jesus Christ who enters your plight, who is
merciful both to your pain and to your wrong. You blank out to any
deeper purpose within all that has gone so wrong.

*4. What are the consequences, the vicious circles?* How does
wreckage of relationships and destruction of lives follow on the heels
of Questions 1, 2, and 3?

*5. What is true about the Father of mercies and God of all com-
fort, who comforts us in all our affliction?* (2 Corinthians 1:3–4)
What one truth that you know about God would truly make a difference if you could take it to heart? What is something that you
need to be true? Consider, for example, the truth of God's presence
from Psalm 23:4: "Even though I walk through the valley of the
shadow of death, I will fear no evil, for you are with me." You might
take out another different colored marker (that's the third color if
you are counting) and go through Psalms 55, 56, and 57 again. This
time underline what the psalmist says about God in the midst of suffering. Start with some of these phrases: "the Lord saves me," "he
hears my voice," "he ransoms me unharmed," "he will sustain me,"
(Psalm 55:16–18, author paraphrase). As these truths take root, how
does it rewrite the script of your life? How does this change your life
today?

*6. Honestly seek God. How do your deepest motives change?*
Consider Paul's words in 2 Corinthians 1:9–10 (NASB), "We had the
sentence of death within ourselves so that we would not trust in
ourselves, but in God who raises the dead; who delivered us from
so great a peril of death, and will deliver us, He on whom we have
set our hope. And He will yet deliver us." Notice how something
changes inside Paul in the context of great suffering. The inner

change connects him to his Savior. He even saw his suffering as purposeful, bringing about that change: I almost died, *so that* I would not trust in myself but in the one who raises the dead. The psalms give you many templates for honest dealing with suffering. Make them your own and find the Friend who makes you his own.

*7. How can you now live?* What does it mean for you to forgive? What would it mean for you to find a new and constructive purpose for your life? What small things count, no matter how insoluble the large evil? How will you actually help some other person who is going through similar things? "God comforts us in all our afflictions so that we will be able to comfort those who are in any affliction with the comfort with which we ourselves are comforted by God" (2 Corinthians 1:4). You get on with your life by going through what has happened—finding and giving comfort—not by somehow getting over it so you can forget about it and move on. What does this look like now?

*8. What are the consequences of such changes?* Can you imagine gracious circles that might happen? What have you already seen happen?

You have sufferings that you may never get over. But there is a road map for getting to a better place—a place where bitterness is transformed into the constructive displeasure of mercy. May the Lord who hears our cries for mercy continue to rewrite the story of your life.

» » »

## Making It Your Own

1. Which of the books mentioned in this chapter would you like to read next? *Cry, the Beloved Country,* or *When God Weeps,* or *Shame Interrupted*? Each of these tells part of the story of how an

"I'll never get over it" experience is gradually transformed. Take the time to read and think through these stories.

    2. Work through the eight questions. If you are not ready to do all eight, work through the ones you can. Share your answers with the wisest person you know, someone with a deep faith and a sympathetic heart.

CHAPTER 15

# The Everyday Angers

Something frustrating will happen to you sometime today. The world won't go your way. Those "little" things—irritation, frustration, complaining—are hard cases too. Not because they are so hard to get over, but because they are so commonplace. They happen so often that we have trouble seeing them as a problem at all.

Perhaps you make a phone call to solve a simple billing question. You patiently work your way through the menus, finally arriving at the right extension. You're put on hold by the recording, left to hear music and canned announcements you don't want to listen to. Finally, you get through to a real person. You and the customer service representative can barely understand each other's accents. The rep puts you on hold in order to look something up or check with a supervisor. You wait some more. Then the phone goes dead and you hear, "If you want to make a call, please hang up and try again." You feel intense irritation. You complain—in your head and out loud. The urge to commit mayhem beckons. Maybe when you finally get through later, the next service rep gets an edgy customer or an earful. Maybe you grouse throughout the day to everyone you meet. I know this about you because I know this about me!

## The Everyday Problem of Complaining

It's likely that another human being will mistreat you today. You might be lied to, ignored, criticized unfairly, or argued with for reasons that seem willful and pointless. Perhaps that service rep is pigheaded, and won't do a simple reasonable thing to solve the problem. Perhaps a coworker or family member will cross you. A car mechanic will overcharge you. You feel offended and frustrated.

It's likely that you will do or say something wrong today. You will misunderstand what someone else said or meant and react according to your misunderstanding. You will be edgy, or aggressive, or brush someone off. You criticize someone, either mentally or out loud. You will speak with an edge in your voice, an attitude, and a poor choice of words. Perhaps you express frustration on the spot, or later you vent to someone unconnected to the problem. If you aren't wholly self-righteous, you'll feel some wince of regret. You might feel disgusted—at yourself as much as at this unruly world filled with unruly people, unruly technology, unruly weather, and the unruly unfolding of everyday events.

This all comes so easily. From an early age we are talented complainers. We skillfully nurture our talent—and every day presents new opportunities for practice! Yet these small complaints and irritations are a good place to start becoming decisively different.

We often think that an "anger problem" must mean some major personal or interpersonal trouble. We think that the main sins to be solved are the violence, the tantrums, the arguing, the rancor, the deep-seated bitterness, the sour attitude. It's true, these are serious business. If they remain unsolved, human life becomes a living hell. But in my experience, I've found that it's often best to start with little problems. Disentangle your complaining. Come out to the clear, firm alternative. How on earth does a sour, negative attitude become a sweet, constructive spirit? Learn that and you've learned how to live well. You learn the secret of contentment (Philippians 4:11–12). As you learn, ripple effects spread throughout your entire life. You cut the heart out of the deep problems as you learn to address the little problems.

The Bible makes this point: There is no struggle you face that is not common to all people (1 Corinthians 10:13). That levels the playing field. We each face the same temptations—everyday life brings frustration and disappointment, and we react with irritation and complaining. We are more alike than different. Whether my problems appear large or small, I have the same *kind* of struggle as everyone else. Our differences are matters of degree. Obviously, not all of us are consumed by explosive or implosive hostility. But all of us are tempted to grumble. That is the tiny cone and seedling from which giant redwoods grow. Major sins are only minor sins grown up. Complaining has the same DNA as violent rage.

So it makes sense that the life-altering solution to minor complaining has the same DNA as the solution to major bitterness or explosive temper. The discussion in 1 Corinthians 10 helps us see how we are all in the same boat. But the apostle Paul, speaking for Jesus ("apostle" simply means someone's messenger), doesn't leave us there. He leads us by the hand onto solid ground. He goes on to say, "God is faithful and he will not let you to be tempted beyond your ability, but with the temptation he will also provide the way of escape, that you may be able to endure it" (1 Corinthians 10:13). When you and I encounter frustrating circumstances, we are tempted to spiral into a negative attitude. But here is a way out and a way forward.

### Realize that God Is Involved

#### He is faithful.

He will stick with you through the process. He who began a good work in you will follow through until he has finished remaking you into Jesus's image. This is a great comfort when you feel discouraged by low-grade irritability, complaining, or resentment. Everyday angers are *very* difficult to overcome. They become habits we're not even aware of. But habits that have become second nature can change—rarely in an instant, usually in a slow growth process in the right direction. The Lord who creates a new nature in you will stick by you. Our Father loves his children. *Father, you do not give up. Do not give up on me.*

**He will not allow you to be tempted beyond what you are able to bear.**

The harder the struggle, the heavier the temptation to grumpy or bitter words, the more you need help—and the closer he will draw near to you in your need. *Lord, help me.*

**He will provide a way of escape.**

This isn't magic. Affliction and temptation rarely go *POOF!* and vanish. *Holy Spirit, talk with me. Keep your hand on me when I am walking through a dark valley where many things can set me off.*

> *Imagine*—a way of escape from getting all hot and bothered by the daily upsets.
> *Imagine*—a way of peace, not constant turmoil.
> *Imagine*—a way to become a peacemaker in a world at war.
> *Imagine*—a way to step out of the rut of being one more complainer in a world of complainers.

When the everyday angers are your struggle, remember the road map we set forth in chapter 10. Put those eight questions to work. We walked through the irritation and upset of being stuck in a very inconvenient and frustrating traffic jam. The everyday angers make life dark and tangled. That road map orients you to the light and leads you forward.

That way is not a technique, a medication, or an incantation. It is not an insight into yourself or the influences upon you. It is not some form of self-management that enables you to get a grip in the midst of unruly reality. The way for you to go forward is discover a Person who cares for you even in the midst of your everyday struggles.

## Why Is Everyday Anger So Serious?

Everyday anger means we've copped an attitude. If I view and treat other people as subhuman, by that very attitude I'm acting as if I'm some superhuman. God calls that pride. Our pride means that we adopt an attitude that views and treats others as less than human. (The service rep and the phone company may have the same problem toward me, but that's not my biggest problem right now.)

We don't want to be bothered—but this is a bother. We want to be treated with respect—but this is disrespect. We want life to go smoothly—but this is a bumpy road that dead ends into a cul-de-sac. These motives obsess me: *I must have this.* They blind me to the truth that God is faithful. Then I live sleepwalking in unbelief. So I turn my tiff with the phone company into a war. But the real God helps me to awaken and remember. This is not my universe, after all. It is not the customer service rep's universe. Jesus tells it to us straight: grumbling is a most serious sin, a capital crime, a primal offense against the God whose universe this is.

From Jesus's point of view, all everyday disgust and negativity shares DNA with murder, after all. Calling someone an "idiot" is the attitudinal kin to killing that person.

> "But I say to you that everyone who is angry with his brother shall be guilty before the court; and whoever says to his brother, 'You good-for-nothing,' shall be guilty before the supreme court; and whoever says, 'You fool,' shall be guilty enough to *go* into the fiery hell." (Matthew 5:22 NASB)

## Mercy Meets Anger

The God who is faithful promises to be merciful. So we own up. The attitude is wrong, but he is more than generous. Complaining is inexcusable—but forgivable. He who loves us will help us solve that phone bill problem in a way that is patient and kind, even when it must be firm, persistent, or fierce. Kindness can be fiercely executed without getting hostile. You can patiently and energetically express constructive displeasure without ever complaining, whining, and venting. And then you can let it go when the time is right to move on.

Only one antidote to a sour attitude heals as deep as the problem. As we've said before, we must cut to our motives and find specific mercy in Christ. So we own up to the grandiose self-absorption that motors inside the everyday complaining. We take to heart that this universe is home to the living God who is faithful to his merciful purposes in your life. Everything that happens to me—this frustrating phone call, for starters—takes place within God's larger, stated purposes for my good. His love for us will free us from self-obsession, whether or not the service reps help us. What would it mean if we really grasped, right here and now in the hot seat, the truth that he will not allow you to be tempted beyond what you are able to bear?

You can bear this customer service rep, this endless automated maze that routes phone calls. You can learn the constructive displeasure of mercy. You can learn the peace that passes understanding. At all times it is possible to become patient, forgiving, generous. And at the right time, in the right place, in the right way, it is possible to engage a problem candidly and persistently with some constructive and appropriate anger.

## Jesus Changes a Complainer for Good

What will make the decisive difference that calms and transforms your everyday angers into fruitful wisdom? Two things change a complainer for good. One, you are given the supreme Gift: Jesus, God's own Son, comes in person to forgive you and to free you from the blind willfulness that drives your complaining. Two, he gives you the supreme purpose: to love in the same way he loves you.

You and I have been given a gift with a purpose. The gift is life in Christ. That purpose is that we become Exhibit A in demonstrating real love at work in the real world: the constructive displeasure of mercy. It means nothing less than treating people the way Jesus treats you. When we do wrong, *he* demonstrates his constructive displeasure and mercy to us. He is patient with us, not quick on the draw. He forgives us and doesn't turn against us. He is generous to us, giving us grace upon grace. He talks straight to us, bringing what's wrong to light in order to set us free of what blinds and perverts us.

You and I learn to do the same as is being done to us. You may well have gotten a taste of this dynamic from a good parent, a wise boss, an excellent coach, a thoughtful teacher, a mature friend, a genuine pastor. Have you noticed that when you are treated in this fine way, it tends to bring out the same in you? You get a glimpse from someone else of a higher purpose for your life. You get a bigger perspective on troubles and troublesome people.

Everyday complaining is so often about convenience and ease—but you can learn that other things are much more important. You want something better out of life than simply becoming one more complainer and cynic. That human kindness gives a sip of the fresh water of wisdom. God is the spring itself, the mighty river of living water. Jesus said that he went about the work of "making disciples." That's just a fancy way to say making us over so that we become like him in the way we treat people.

Or perhaps you've never had a taste of this from other people. Family, coworkers, friends, or religious folks were manipulative, aggressive, and hypocritical. They either pretended everything was okay or they let you have it with both barrels. God has been either a nonentity, a bigger version of the bogeyman, or an impersonal force supposedly shining in all that's good. But your bad experience can bring an even brighter shine to what ought to be. You've choked down a lot of dirty water and false promises. God is the fresh water and the true promiser. He intends to make you a fresh spring too, to remake your life purpose so that you increasingly treat others the way you've been treated by him—the merciful way he continues to treat you.

Whether you've had good role models or bad, you can know a larger life purpose that is the way it's meant to be. Notice the inner logic of this larger life purpose. Notice what defeats our complaining and bickering:

> Do all things without grumbling or disputing; so that you will prove yourself to be blameless and innocent, children of God above reproach in the midst of a crooked and perverse generation, among whom you appear as lights in the world. (Philippians 2:14–15 NASB)

The gift: God has made you his child. The purpose: to live a shining life, different from what you are by nature and nurture. When we hear a phrase such as "crooked and perverse generation," we might think of some cranky moralist bewailing what's on TV these days. But Paul is not talking here about sexual sleaze or graphic violence. He's talking about everyday angers. Complaining, which rarely makes even a blip on the radar screen, is a perversity. It distorts your humanity.

Complaining characterizes our whole generation (and every generation!). Everybody has bad role models on this issue because we live in the midst of cultures of dissatisfaction. You are called to become so different that you shine. Imagine a non-complainer in an all-complainers world. Imagine a patient, large-hearted person in a hothouse of petty disagreements and dissatisfactions. Imagine a constructive problem-solver in the midst of all the grabbing for goodies. Imagine someone with good reasons for basic gratitude, whose shining purpose comes from drinking of the Gift of gifts.

If you are no longer disagreeable, does this mean you'll suddenly agree to anything? Of course not. The question is *how you will disagree*—with the phone company, your spouse, your parents, your kids, your coworkers. If you are no longer argumentative, *how do you argue well* with what's wrong? If you're no longer a complainer, *how do you complain well* in order to make this world a better and happier place? Growing in these things will open a door to making a difference in this world. Do you want to impact the world around you? Would you like to leave a lasting legacy? Then become someone who does "all things without grumbling or arguing."

We've taken a good look at the everyday angers. I trust that every reader (like this author) has found that his or her name and story fit comfortably in these pages! I hope that each of us also sees a way forward into light. From our limited point of view, complaining doesn't seem like a marquee, red-letter sin. But from God's point of view, it is a death penalty crime—and it is entirely forgivable and entirely changeable. This chapter has a larger personal application section because this is very personal! It's all about how we live in the details and how God might transform you into a large-hearted person who knows the love of God and shares his love through the ups and downs of your daily life.

» » »

## Making It Your Own

1. What was your yellow-highlighter sentence in this chapter? Why did you choose that? Where did you put a question mark, a BWA, something that puzzled you, or say, "I disagree with that"?

2. Choose one of your everyday angers, and work it through our eight questions in detail. Start by personalizing complaining and irritation. The eight questions will be your framework, and you get to fill in the details from your life.

   (1) *Your situation.* What do you complain about? What situations trigger your irritability?

   (2) *Your reaction.* How do you complain? What do you say? How do you say it? What are you thinking? What gestures, body language, or actions show you are one unhappy camper, sulking on the stage of God's universe?

   (3) *Your motives.* What do you want that becomes your claim against the universe? Every complaining word registers the

overflow of "But I want _____ . I insist on _____ ."
What expectations hijack you, own you, master you when
you grouse? How does this exalt you to a god ("pride"), erase
the real God ("unbelief"), and substitute what you want for
what God wills ("lusts of the flesh")?

(4) *Consequences.* How does your complaining affect others?
What vicious circles get created? Do they get testy back at
you, escalating tensions? Do they join you and reinforce
you, making it a pity party and a coven of complaining? Do
they avoid you because a sour person brings no pleasure to
others?

(5) *The God who is there, who is not silent, who acts.* Do you
see your need for his mercy (not in theory, but right now,
caught in the act)? How does mercy come to a grumbler?
What about God's gift is incompatible with any complaining
and bickering? What one truth mentioned in this chapter
will change you as you take it to heart?

(6) *How do you respond?* God is a person to know and talk
with, not a theory to contemplate or discuss. Ask for the help
that you need. Talk out loud. (Jesus himself came with "loud
crying and tears" to his Father.) Confess your sins of grumbling. Express your remorse. Voice genuine gratitude. Turn
over in your mind God's promises of mercy in Jesus Christ.
Ask God to make you wise and to make this situation work
for good.

(7) *How do you act?* Complaining and arguing express destructive actions, words, feelings, and thoughts. What constructive actions, words, feelings, and thoughts are appropriate in
this particular situation? Who do you need to go to? How do
you need to go? What should you say? Jesus never grumbled,
but he faced one hardship after another. He will personally
help you handle this hardship.

(8) *Consequences.* What positive outcome do you hope to see?
If you did change, from grumbling to constructive, what

difference did it make? What gracious circles might replace
the vicious circles?

3. Then you may want to go on and work through one of the
following:

   a. Do you and another person have the same argument over
and over? Arguments where you could mail in the tape ahead
of time are very discouraging when you're stuck in the rut.
But they can be extremely revealing and fruitful for change.
Bickering is more complicated than complaining, only because it takes two to tango. But the causes are often quite
straightforward. Two persons can each walk through our
eight questions. The other person's stuff is always Question
1 for you. The really interesting part comes when you try to
sort out why it sets you off in such a negative direction. That
tells you about you. The typical ruling motives of both parties get expressed. Things that "push your buttons" reveal
your buttons, not just what the button pusher did. If both
parties are willing to face up, then the heart motives of both
can be rewired by God's kindness. Even if only one party is
willing to deal, you can be the one who changes. And when
one person stops dancing, no more tango. The argument
changes when one party starts to become constructive, not
a coconspirator committing arson to the relationship. For
further input, you might want to look back at James 3—4 in
chapter 9, which had repetitive arguments in view.

   b. Is your everyday anger the accumulated product of the grind
and disappointment of life? This form of anger is everyday, but calls for slower analysis. It's not usually tit-for-tat,
trigger-and-response. Older people often get testy or cynical: "grumpy old men" (and women too). This is usually a
dreary, low-grade bitterness and hollowness, not explosive.
Crumbled dreams, disappointed expectations, and disillusionment with other people (and oneself) create that "waste
of our wraths and sorrows" mentioned back in chapter 1.

Work it through our eight questions. The cumulative everyday "vanity of vanities, all is vanity" (Ecclesiastes) is as worthy of careful thought as a flare-up of complaining or bickering. It will reveal motives around which you have built your core life—motives that can't bear the weight of life and death. How can hope shine more brightly than loss? Psalm 73 is a particularly relevant touchstone for this.

c.  Are there ways you underreact? This also is an everyday problem. It can be quite tricky to identify. By definition, if I'm underreacting I'm not seeing what's going on or acknowledging how I'm feeling. Let me give two different everyday examples.

- First, are there things going on around you that should bother you, but you ignore them, or even join in? For example, racist attitudes at work, demeaning to ethnic groups? Lewdness on TV, demeaning to both men and women? Dissing of parents (or teens), of men (or women), of bosses (or workers), of pastors (or parishioners), of Christians (or Muslims), of Americans (or French), of Democrats (or Republicans)? When our conscience is miswired, we go numb and indifferent to attitudes that should bother us. God's passion for justice gives us every reason to take a good hard look around and to join in the pursuit of a more evenhanded and merciful treatment of other people. You might need to get more bothered about what you or others are doing—and thus able to become more constructive in the midst of a world that does such things routinely. The letter of 1 Peter is rich in this regard.

- Second, are there things inside you that bother you, but you tend to deny? Are you angry at some level, but don't quite know how to face it? Does some injustice or betrayal eat at you, but you're trying to pretend everything's OK? Are you angry, but stifling it? There's no magic in our eight questions, but they are a reliable road map that can help keep you oriented as you seek to walk in the right direction. They can help you identify what's what. Non-reaction, confusion, and denial are reactions (Question 2) that arise for motivated reasons (Question 3). So adapt our questions to your struggle. God's kindness gives every reason to face yourself honestly and without fear. There are numerous psalms in the 30s and 50s that give voice to honest distress. You might find that one of them helps you voice the problem and find honest refuge in the love of the God worth loving.

CHAPTER 16

# Do You Ever Get Angry
# at Yourself?

People get mad at just about anything. Of course, *other* people's failings ignite the most passionate and long-lasting hatreds. Meanwhile, day-by-day those staples of news radio—weather and traffic—can bring on hot flashes and muttered curses whenever they mess with your plans. Your dog or cat, your oven or computer . . . you name it, anything can arouse wrath when it crosses your will.

Including yourself.

How do you react to your own failings? Do you ever get down on yourself because you feel inferior or defective? Are you displeased with the person who looks back at you from the mirror? Guilt, shame, and self-reproach are ways anger at self feels and thinks.

I suspect you get mad at yourself sometimes. And anger at oneself can be more than a passing thought. It can become a life-long state of affairs. What is "low self-esteem" but a judgment of self-condemnation that has morphed into a life of chronic self-reproach? *I am such an idiot. I did it again, I can't believe it. I hate myself. Why do I always fail? I am such a loser. Why bother to even try? If people knew who I really am and how I really feel, they'd despise me.*

Of course, the "moral emotion" can get aroused about yourself. We evaluate ourselves continually, just as we evaluate other people, the weather outside, and the song we're listening to. Evaluation is what "conscience" does, and everyone has one, even when it gets distorted. And conscience does get distorted. Sometimes we judge others accurately; other times we misjudge them. In the same way, sometimes we judge ourselves accurately; other times we misjudge ourselves. And whether the judgments we make are true, partly true, or completely false, we always then face the question of mercy. When does my judgment of myself become merciless? How does a conscience become both accurate and full of mercy? That is the question this chapter will explore.

Anger at self broadcasts on a broad bandwidth. The most obvious form is overt self-accusation, but it has many aliases. Relentless guilty feelings? An inferiority complex? Continual self-deprecation? Negative comparisons with others? Self-punishing or self-shaming thoughts? Self-defeating or self-mutilating behaviors? Sometimes anger at self is dramatic and talks out loud. Often it's subtle and owns the thought waves.

Conscience is a gift. But it can become a merciless slavemaster. There is no doubt that anger at self usually runs far, far off the rails. It can become a fruitless, self-destructive routine, in the same way that anger at others can become a fruitless other-destructive obsession. It is a gift of God to be able to evaluate yourself accurately. But conscience can also be a good gift gone bad, a gift that needs redeeming—part of "the renewal of your mind" that the Holy Spirit mercifully undertakes.

This chapter is based on two premises. First, it is possible to clear up the confusion and better understand why you condemn yourself. Second, a clear understanding opens a straight path to the mercies of God. Anger at self can be completely rewired. Fruitless self-reproach can be transformed into healthy fear of God. And true fear of God is inseparable from trust in his compassion, lovingkindness, and forgiveness. Healthy guilt is one component in a life of deeper sanity, truer faith, and growing joy. That's where we are going. Let's take the first step by getting a bead on the problem of anger at yourself.

## Making Sense of Anger at Yourself

For starters, notice that all the themes we've seen operating in other forms of anger also play out in anger at yourself. We react to a perceived wrong in something that matters to us. Anger motivates us to think, talk, and act to punish the wrongdoer—only this time the guilty party is yourself.

You act out the role of an implacable god. *I* set up the standards against which I've failed, so *I* am angry at me. I must bear the punishment to atone for my wrongs against *myself*. And *I* will dish out punishment to the evildoer, who is me.

You also play the role of aggrieved victim. I've failed *myself* by my failure, bringing shame on *myself*. I've offended *me*. The person I think *I ought to be*, the person *I present myself as being*, the person *I like to think I am*, that *good person* has been wounded and dishonored by this bad person. The person who is ruining my life is me.

It's quite a tangle we get ourselves into!

Full disclosure as we unpack this problem: I'm not going to say, "You should never judge yourself. Just accept yourself. You're OK and fine just the way you are. You have intrinsic worth just because you're a person, so you can feel good about yourself." It's part of being human to judge ourselves. The day you stop evaluating yourself is the day you stop breathing. We want to educate the conscience, not neutralize it or pander to it. One part of sanity is to know that you are not OK. So we face a dilemma. I don't want to become blind to my real failings, but I don't want to send myself on a guilt-trip and become obsessed with my failings. How can I know myself as I am before God, and at the same time find my way into true peace, joy, and gratefulness?

We all find ourselves on home ground here. Let's explore the territory together.

## Failings That Bring on Anger with Yourself

As we've seen, anger reacts to something that matters and seems wrong. Let's look at four different reasons that people feel angry at themselves. First, a *specific personal failure* is the most obvious key that turns on the engines of self-condemnation. Consider some examples.

- You blew up at the kids for the umpteenth time. You've sworn many times that you'll never do that again, so your anger does a U-turn and smashes into you. You are angry at yourself because you get angry at others.
- You consumed cookies and ice cream when you were supposed to be on a diet. Now guilt consumes you. You hate yourself for feeling so stuffed, for having so little self-control.
- You used drugs or got drunk—again. Now you feel self-disgust. You call in sick to work because you can't face people. You get surly with your friends, spouse, or kids, though on the inside you're big-time upset with yourself.

Those are a few instances of the simple kind of anger at self where you did something wrong and your conscience takes vengeance.

Is this you? Do you condemn yourself for a specific personal failure?

But it's not always so straightforward. Other factors can complicate the problem of being angry at yourself. These other reasons are more tangled.

Second, you might be angry at yourself over a *failure that feels like something you did, but it was actually a product of circumstances.* For example, you became ill your sophomore year in college and had to leave school. For a variety of reasons, the money and time were never there to complete your education. Though *you* didn't fail, you *perceive* yourself to have failed. You feel ashamed, and get down on yourself. Or, when you were in your fifties, the economy took a downturn. When your company laid off 4,500 workers, you got a pink slip. Some people in that situation might get angry at the boss, the company, or the economy. But you take it personally. You've let down your family and tarnished the family name. The suicides that follow an economic disaster—e.g., Wall Street in 1929, Seoul in 1995—were not always because the person did anything particularly wrong. But self-condemnation, shame, despair, and violence against oneself unite to punish a self-perceived wrongdoer and failure.

Is this you? Do you condemn yourself for something where you were a victim of circumstances?

Third, you might be angry at yourself because of *what someone else did to you.* Your birth mother gave you up for adoption. You think that there must be something wrong with you. An older cousin sexually molested you when you were a preteen. You feel that you must have done something to deserve it, and God was punishing you. Your father always called you "Stupid." It must be true. After twenty years of marriage, your spouse ran off with someone younger and better looking. You feel like a defective person because you were rejected and now you're a divorced single parent. The black mark against you can never be erased. In each of these cases, though the failure was someone else's, you *perceive* yourself to have failed, and you bear the stigma.

Is this you? Do you condemn yourself because of something another person did to you?

Fourth, being down on and angry at yourself might not be tied to any particular wrong you did or any blows that landed on you. Anger at self can be *a global statement of a worthless existence:* "I'm a nobody. My life means nothing." You hate yourself simply for being yourself. Your crime is that you exist. You'll never matter. Your life is pointless. You *are* failure—a hopeless nobody. Though you can't put your finger on any one thing, you live under a pervasive sense of condemnation. Through every waking hour, your conscience broadcasts in the language of reproach and self-negation.

Is this you? Do you condemn yourself because you are you?

So the simple case—I did wrong and I hate myself for it—is not the only case. And simple anger is not the only emotion in play. You may have noticed in my descriptions how closely anger at self intertwines with its kinfolk emotions of despair, disgust, guilt, shame, and fear.

## Three Questions to Help You Understand Anger at Yourself

Let's unpack the deeper reasons for anger at yourself. To start, you have to consider what *standard* you measure your failure against. (By the way, it's the same standard by which you'd measure success.) Think of your standards as ladders you are trying to climb. Answering three questions about your ladders will help you get to the real cause of anger at yourself and sort out where it is appropriate, where it is confused, and what to do about it in any case.

1. What ladder are you climbing?
2. Whose ladder are you climbing?
3. Who can pick you up when you fall?

Let's unpack each of these three questions.

## What Ladder Are You Climbing?

The standard you serve defines the goals you pursue. The ladders you climb give your life meaning. You are climbing toward what you admire, treasure, and live for. Anger at yourself is always in reference to something you think you are supposed to be and do. You climb—you try to reach whatever standard you are pursuing. When you fail, you feel condemned. Consider the following examples.

*1. I hate myself because I'm ugly, weak, and clumsy.*
What is the standard by which I reproach myself? I am climbing a ladder based on physical endowment. Beauty, strength, and agility

define success or failure. If I am not physically perfect and strong, then I feel like I'm a defective person

*2. I condemn myself because I'm not as extroverted as other people, so I feel very self-conscious in social situations.*

What is the standard against which I fail? I'm climbing a ladder of approval from other people, and being at ease in a group is my definition of value.

*3. I feel like a failure because I didn't get straight As, or get married, or rise to the top in my career, and I haven't made the money my parents and siblings make.*

What ladder am I climbing? I must reach a certain level of achievement in school, marriage, status, and money. The definition of what counts stigmatizes me as a loser.

*4. I feel like my life is a mistake because my birth mother gave me up for adoption.*

The standard? To be a valid person, your birth parents must love you. If they rejected you, then you are a reject.

*5. There's something very wrong with me because I was sexually molested.*

The standard? If I am to ever be a valid person, I must not have experienced violation at the hands of an evildoer.

*6. I feel like a second-class person because of my ethnic or cultural background or because I have a disability.*

The ladder I climb says that I am not worthy if my skin is the wrong color, if I come from a certain cultural background, if I have a disability.

7. *I loathe myself because I slept with my girlfriends or boyfriends or both, and use pornography. I feel soiled and humiliated.*

What is the ladder that defines my failure? Love protects the purity of another, so sexual immorality is wrong.

8. *I hate myself because I stole money from my workplace and cheated on my taxes. I'm wracked by guilt, and feel like the word thief is branded on my forehead.*

The standard? Love is honest and trustworthy in financial dealings, so stealing is wrong.

9. *I continually hear a voice of self-condemnation because I had an abortion. All the reasons people give about why it's OK just sound like self-justifying excuses.*

The standard? Love protects and nurtures the life of an innocent and helpless person. But I terminated a boy or girl who was depending on me for life.

Let's do two things with this list. First, it is always helpful to keep things personal. Do any of these nine ladders identify ways you feel displeased with yourself? Or can you identify with other similar ladders? There are commonalities among us, but we each put our own personal touch on the ladders we climb. What standards define whether your conscience commends you or condemns you?

Second, notice something about this list of nine typical ways we evaluate ourselves. It mixes together three very different *kinds* of ladders. It makes a big difference what kind of ladder you are climbing. The reason it makes a difference is that some of these standards are true and others are false. Some standards enable us to evaluate ourselves accurately. Other standards cause us to misjudge ourselves.

The first three express typical social values. We rate ourselves (and others rate us) by physical attributes, social skills, and achievements. Is it true that your looks, social skills, and accomplishments

define you as either a worthy or worthless person? No. These are
false standards. They evaluate you according to what goodies you
get (or don't get) out of life. These are non-moral issues. When such
standards become your criteria, then self-condemnation (or self-
affirmation) is based on a bogus value. It is no sin not to be pretty
or witty. One aspect of sin's deep distorting effect is we think it is
a sin.

The second three describe life-shaping events that some people
experience. We might negatively evaluate ourselves (and so might
others) because we were put up for adoption, were betrayed sexually, or were made routinely uncomfortable because of bigotry. Is it
true that your life is valid only if you did not experience adoption,
rape, or prejudice? Are you somehow invalidated if you did experience such things? No. Such assessments are false. They evaluate you
by the hard things you experienced in life. These are moral issues
(and in the case of adoption, a mix of rights and wrongs). But in no
case was the wrong yours. The standard is false. If such experiences
condemn you, you are being condemned by a lie. One aspect of sin's
enslaving and blinding power is that we believe falsehoods.

The final three items describe sins that people commit. We might
judge ourselves (and so might others) for immorality, theft, or killing. Is it true that you justly condemn yourself if you are lewd, thiev-
ing, or deadly? Yes. These standards evaluate the kind of person you
are. They describe true moral failures. You show good judgment to
see yourself through these eyes. Your conscience is wired to what
is true. If such actions condemn you, you are evaluating yourself
rightly. One aspect of God's liberating mercy and grace is that we see
good and evil for what they are.

It makes a big difference what kind of ladder you are climbing.
Imagine it this way: You are standing in the parking lot beside a big
box store—a Home Depot or Walmart. The building has thirty-foot
high cinder-block walls. You have two ladders, one fifteen feet long
and the other thirty-five feet long. You want to climb up on the roof.
(Warning: Don't try this in real life!) While you are blindfolded, a

friend props both ladders up against the wall. Without looking, you choose a ladder and start to climb.

Now what happens if you start to climb the fifteen-foot ladder? You've got a built-in problem—an insurmountable problem. It reaches less than halfway up the wall! It's a ladder to nowhere. Even if you get to the top rung you haven't actually gotten anywhere. You're just stuck halfway up a thirty-foot precipice. No matter how hard you try, you'll never get to the roof. Each of the first six items on our list is a fifteen-foot ladder. They can never deliver. Hating yourself for failing is a waste of anger and guilt. The actual failure is that we can spend our lives scrambling up ladders to nowhere rather than a ladder to somewhere.

When you're committed to climbing a fifteen-foot ladder, life never really works. You can't undo these "failures" or have the hard things that happen to you go away. You'll feel temporary happiness when you get up a few rungs, only to feel disappointment that success wasn't what you'd hoped it would be. If someone else is higher up the ladder than you, you feel jealous and inferior. You're a relative failure. If there's someone else lower down the ladder, you feel superior. You look down on such people. What if someone tries to pass you? You fight them off and compete like a madman to scramble up—to nowhere. You can never get to the roof. And in the end you wind up in a heap.

The thirty-five-foot ladders reach all the way to the roof. Those items reveal the kind of person you are. Some readers probably noticed that they stated three of the Ten Commandments in street talk: theft and other financial duplicities (the eighth commandment), adultery and other immoralities (the seventh commandment), murder and other aggressions (the sixth commandment). All God's commandments teach us what faith and love look like. Open your heart to him. Open your hands and ask for help. Love your God with all that you are. Trust him. Listen to him, take refuge in him, cling to him, obey him, fear him, rejoice in him. Those ladders reach all the way to the rooftop. And love other people with the same concern you have for yourself. Give to them. Forgive them. Care for them. Help them. Those, too, are thirty-five-footers.

The big ladders do humble us by our failures. And we all fall short in faith and love. It is a great grace when you come to realize that these are your true failures. When what most dismays you about yourself are failures to trust and love, you become aware of the self-absorption that is the deepest plague of your heart. And in the divine paradox of the grace of God, recognizing failure on the big ladders opens your eyes to something unimaginably wonderful. You come to understand the love of Jesus, because you have come to know that you need his mercy, protection, and strength more than anything else in the world.

Our experiment in the Home Depot parking lot teaches something profound about anger at self. Sorting out the standard is the first step to straightening out a distorted conscience and making sense of anger at yourself. *Is your self-evaluation against an accurate or inaccurate standard?* Are you stuck on a ladder to nowhere? Do you hate yourself for falling down a ladder that doesn't get anywhere even if you reach the top? Or are you seeking to climb a ladder that really does go somewhere? Even when you fall short, are you opening your heart to the love of God rather than gnashing your teeth? This is the first question that helps to make us deeply sane.

But there is a second miswiring of the conscience that is equally profound.

## Whose Ladder Are You Climbing?

*Who* created the standard you are serving? Who made the ladder? Before whose *eyes* are you held accountable? Whose opinion matters most? Who is the person you must please? Who is the judge whose opinion most matters? There are only three options. You assess yourself either in your own eyes, in the eyes of other people, or in God's eyes.

Option 1: Are *you* the judge whose opinion matters in your universe? Did you concoct the value system by which you evaluate yourself? Do you fail (or succeed) in your own eyes? Is the meaning of your life defined by your *self*-esteem, by whether or not you accept yourself as good enough?

Option 2: Do *other people* serve as judges in your universe? Did they manufacture the rating system that matters? Do you fail (or succeed) in the eyes of other people? Is the meaning of your life defined by your reputation with *others*, and by whether or not they accept you as good enough?

Option 3: Is *God* the judge whose opinion matters in his universe? Did he design the standard that defines true and flourishing humanness? Do you fail (or succeed) in his eyes? Is the meaning of your life defined by your fidelity when you stand before the judgment seat of *Christ*, and by whether or not God accepts you because he has made you his beloved child?

There are only three options. In the first two the conscience is distorted by living before the wrong eyes. So self-reproach is distorted because it is all about what *I* think about me, or what *you* think about me. The third option is clear-minded. Both my self-reproach and my freedom from reproach flow from God's good judgment and deep mercy. My self-evaluation mirrors what my *Father* thinks about me. This is one implication of the proverb, "The fear of the LORD is the beginning of wisdom" (9:10 NASB). The fear of the Lord means that his eyes matter to you. You stand or fall before him—and knowing that is the first act of standing up. His opinion of you matters. His evaluation makes the life-or-death difference.

Getting the right standard and the right eyes clarifies your self-reproach. But what next? Where do you turn when you are down on yourself? I was recently watching a public television special about elementary education. And a school psychologist said four things to a group of fourth graders:

- Tell yourself you aren't defined by what you look like, by what other people say, or even by what you achieve.
- If you feel down on yourself, learn to give yourself a pep talk every day.
- Tell yourself that you're OK.
- You can accomplish your dreams if you believe in yourself.

She wants to free her students from self-reproaches. So far so good. And I entirely agree with her first point. She is unmasking those first three fifteen-foot ladders from our list earlier in the chapter. She sees that your looks, the opinions of others, and your achievements don't work. But consider her solution. Her last three points assume that you live in your own eyes. In order to save yourself from yourself, she asserts that you are to proclaim that you are your own savior: "You can do it. You're OK. Believe in yourself." She has perceived a few of the wrong standards. But she encourages her students to live before the wrong set of eyes—their own. So her gospel simply asserts a different fifteen-foot ladder as the solution to the fifteen-foot ladders that don't work. She proclaims empty platitudes.

We've got to dig deeper, and think harder, and look more closely at where we turn when condemning voices beset us.

## Where Do You Go When You Are Angry at Yourself?

This is the most important matter of all.

Is it finally on our shoulders to make it all better? Once you get the standard right, once you get the eyes right, then it becomes much easier to see who must save us from our self-condemnation. We are saved outside of ourselves. The supreme joy of being human is knowing your Father, knowing your good Shepherd, knowing your life-giving Spirit. The living, personal God loves you and will right all wrongs, including your own. Our Lord's anger at us is always fair, but his mercies run deeper still.

Who can pick you up when you fall? Who can set you free from your sense of personal failure? Who can rewire your conscience so you evaluate yourself truthfully? Who can rewire your conscience so you think of yourself before the right set of eyes? Who will love you and help you?

His mercies run deeper than whatever dark, accusing voices talk in your head.

Whenever angry voices berate you, the love of Jesus is reaching out to you. The Father of all mercies has mercy on people who need mercy. When your own heart is merciless, and you spiral into yourself, he invites you to reach out and ask for help. He leans in, and listens. He knows your sins and your sorrows. He knows how you think and feel. He cares. He will take you by the hand and lead you back into the light. He warmly welcomes you: "Come to me when you are struggling and weighed down." He gives you a new identity: "You are my own beloved child." He gives you a new purpose: "You are my servant." He gives you grace: "You are truly forgiven." He reassures you: "You are not responsible for what happened to you. It was hard, or even evil. But I will walk beside you through this dark valley."

How can you know these things? Take God's words to you in Romans 8 to heart.

*There is no condemnation for those who are in Christ Jesus (v. 1).* Left to myself, I stand justly condemned by God. The devil, other people, and my conscience all condemn me, too. But standing in the love of Christ, I am free. The devil and other people may still condemn me. But my conscience can freely say, "I am truly forgiven and welcomed home. Thank you, my Savior and my God!"

*If God is for you, who can be against you (v. 31)?* As we have said, the Accuser is always against me, and other people can be against me, and my conscience can be against me. But if God is truly for me, then I need no longer condemn myself.

*Who is to condemn you? Christ Jesus is the one who died—
more than that, who was raised—who is at the right hand of God,
who is in fact interceding on your behalf (v. 34).* Who is to condemn
me? If the one who died in my place is now alive and interceding for
me in love, why should I continue to condemn myself?

The darkest thing you ever did, the most horrifying thing that
ever happened to you—*nothing* can separate you from the love of
Christ (v. 35). Into the nightmare of self-laceration come shining reasons for gratitude, joy, and purpose. A voice of mercy takes the microphone and silences the cruel voices of condemnation. You don't
need to deny anything. You can look it all in the face. Yet you do not
need to despair. Let me say it again: even when self-condemnation
is merciless, the Father of all mercies has mercy for people who need
mercy. He is mercy. And he comes in person looking for you.

» » »

## Making It Your Own

1. Revisit the questions I asked you earlier in the chapter. What
kind of failings start you down the whirlpool of self-condemnation?

    Is it a true moral failing?

    Is it a non-moral issue, a typical social value that doesn't re-
ally matter in the end?

    Is it something that happened to you?

    Is it something someone else did to you?

2. Read and ponder 1 Corinthians 4:1–5. How does Paul describe his freedom from living before the wrong eyes?

3. Take time to ponder Psalm 25. Notice three things in
particular.

- How do these words pull you out of the spiral of self-condemnation for moral failures?

- How does this teach you to talk about the hard things that happen to you?
- What does God show and tell you about himself that makes such a conversation possible?

4. Anger at oneself is a black hole. Self-reproach curves inward and spirals downward. But notice how this honest hymn reverses the flow. How does Christ's grace deliver you from condemnation to joy? Let this song lead you out of yourself to the one whose mercies are new every morning.

## From the Depths of Woe

From depths of woe I raise to thee the voice of lamentation;
Lord, turn a gracious ear to me and hear my supplication;
If thou iniquities dost mark, our secret sins and misdeeds dark,
O who shall stand before thee?

To wash away the crimson stain, grace, grace alone availeth;
Our works, alas are all in vain; in much the best life faileth;
No man can glory in thy sight, all must alike confess thy might,
And live alone by mercy.

Therefore my trust is in the Lord, and not in mine own merit;
On him my soul shall rest, his Word upholds my fainting spirit;
His promised mercy is my fort, my comfort, and my sweet
    support;
I wait for him with patience.

And though my sorrows dark may be, Christ is my consolation.
He is my refuge day by day, high fortress of salvation.
He'll take away my tears of pain, wash dust of death away with
    rain.
And now I sing before thee.

And though I wait the live-long night, until the dawn appeareth,
My heart still trusteth in his might; it doubteth not nor feareth;
Do thus, O you of Israel's seed, you of the Spirit born indeed;
And wait til God appeareth.


Though great our sins and sore our woes, his grace much more
aboundeth;
His helping love no limit knows, our upmost need it soundeth.
Our Shepherd good and true is he, who will at last set Israel
    free
From all their sin and sorrow.


On heights of joy I'll raise to thee a voice of exultation.
Lord, turn thy glorious face to me; receive my adoration.
Thy mercies triumph full and free through Jesus Christ who
        rescued me.
I gladly stand before thee.

Lyrics: Stanzas 1–3, 5–6, Martin Luther; Stanzas 4 and 7,
        anon.
Music: Christopher Miner

# CHAPTER 17

# Anger at God

Most discussions of anger don't mention anger at God. They are right to discuss such things as interpersonal conflict, road rage, vengeance, or bitterness. But anger is explored only as an inward experience and interpersonal event. Usually the profoundly significant stance of anger against God simply doesn't register on the radar screen.

It's a significant blind spot. In reality, enmity toward God is an underlying and defining characteristic of humans. It's the active dynamic at work when we say, Mankind is fallen. But this abiding enmity usually operates quietly in the background. It's like gravity. You rarely notice it, but it's always there. When provoked, it shows its teeth with a surprising degree of hostility. The Bible often flags this anger. For example,

- People will often blame God when what they have lived for comes up empty. "When a man's folly brings his way to ruin, his heart rages against the LORD" (Proverbs 19:3).
- When God's children wandered about in the wilderness, he summed up their attitude as, "They grumble against me" (Numbers 14:27). Quarreling with God is a baseline human characteristic.
- When hardships seem overwhelming, God is often a scapegoat. Job was in unrelenting pain, but his wife's reaction

was, "Do you still hold fast your integrity? Curse God and die" (Job 2:9).

- When God blesses someone we wish he would curse, anger can erupt. God showed mercy to Nineveh, and "it displeased Jonah exceedingly, and he was angry" (Jonah 4:1).
- When men and women reap what they sow, they often harshly judge the One who rightly judges them. People "cursed the God of heaven for their pain and sores. They did not repent of their deeds" (Revelation 16:11).
- Hostility directed toward God often lands on his servants. For example, David and Jesus owned the words, "The reproaches of those who reproach you have fallen on me" (Psalm 69:9; Romans 15:3).

God came on scene in person when the Son of God was conceived in the womb of Mary. The Gospels go on to bear witness to the continual animosity that Jesus faced—at his birth, throughout his ministry, and in his betrayal and death. "The world . . . hates me because I testify about it that its works are evil" (John 7:7).

Human nature has not changed. There is something instinctive, irrational, compulsive, and virulent about anger at God. It makes no sense to bite the hand that feeds you, to hate the Father who gives and sustains life. He is good, and he does good. He is compassionate, gracious, patient, full of loving-kindness and faithfulness. He freely forgives. His mercies are new every morning. But we instinctively hate him anyway because he insists on one thing:

"Listen to me."

His insistence insults our pride and self-will. We are like teenagers with an authority allergy. As we saw when we probed James 3–4, self-exalting desire is the engine of sinful anger. By loving ourselves and loving the world, we don't listen. We operate at enmity to the Lord we were created to love.

Understood this way, we realize that anger at God is not first an emotion. It is the stance a person takes, a core commitment of the heart. Remember what we said many chapters ago about how god-playing motives underlie the judgmental mind, military actions, hot emotions, and agitated body that come together in an "anger outburst"? Sometimes anger at God does erupt into hostile words, angry feelings, and violent actions. That's why many psalms pray for God's protection from those firestorms of open aggression that Jesus continually faced.

But most often people who are deep-down angry at God simply go their own way, building a kingdom with themselves at the center. They go about the business of inventing a virtual reality. They act as if merely human creatures have the power and right to define our identity, purpose in life, worldview, meaning, sexuality, sense of right and wrong, and so forth. Normal life silently and steadily suppresses the fact that we will each give account to the one who actually defines reality. The virtual realities are sand castles, washed away in the next tide. Anger's fight will give way to fear's flight: "Hide us from the presence of Him who sits on the throne, and from the wrath of the Lamb" (Revelation 6:16 NASB).

And yet this Father, and Lamb, and life-giving Spirit alone can save us . . . from ourselves. Our steady, persistent resistance to God is usually an unspectacular madness. But it is the essence of sin, the inner heartbeat of evil. If I might borrow a pungent phrase from Sigmund Freud and turn its meaning upside-down, *pride* is the "universal obsessional neurosis" of humankind. And Jesus Christ performs the one psychotherapy that cures our souls.

I suspect that few readers who have gotten this far are angry at God as a core commitment! We are brothers and sisters whom redeeming love has claimed. But we still struggle, don't we? What about our double-mindedness, the instinct to pride that still works in us who have been humbled by Christ's mercies? Our true self longs to yield wholly to the Lord's will, but what hope is there for us when we find the seeds of resistance to God still very alive in us? When we feel disappointed or disillusioned because life in Christ is harder than we imagined? When we feel indifferent and

dull—"Whatever . . ."—to the things of God? When someone
promises us that this one truth, or this one spiritual discipline, or
this one accountability relationship, or this one great local church
offers the secret that will make everything different, but it doesn't
work? When God's people let us down, or do outright wrong to us,
and we are rightly angry at what they do, and our anger spills over
toward the God and Father of us all? What do we do?

Think with me about two things: a one-liner from the Bible, and
then the life story of one of the greatest pagan kings who ever lived.
Later in the personal application section of this chapter we'll also
listen to an unwed teenage mother who got it right.

First, consider the one-liner. "He gives more grace. Therefore
it says, 'God opposes the proud, but gives grace to the humble'"
(James 4:6). We looked at this when we considered how James 3—4
speaks to our conflicts with other people. It speaks the same message
of hope when we find ourselves fighting on the wrong side against
our God. He does give more grace. He does call us out when we get
proud and angry. And as we listen to him, as we seek him, we find
that he does, indeed, give mercy and grace to help us in our time of
need.

Second, consider the life story of Nebuchadnezzar, a very great
king with a long history of proud hostility against the Most High.
God repeatedly brought him down to earth. At one point the king
forbade his subjects from worshiping anyone or anything except the
golden image he had made. Three men disobeyed, worshiping the
LORD and refusing to bow down to the golden image. In rage, the
king ordered them burned alive. But a fourth man, the LORD, ap-
peared in the fire, walking with his loyal friends through their trial
by fire. Nebuchadnezzar was awestruck.

But he subsequently forgot what he had learned. His insane
pride soared to the heavens. He attacked the God of glory by proclaiming his own glory, majesty, and greatness. Heaven struck him
down with madness. But after seven years, something remarkable
took place, and the king bore witness.

> I, Nebuchadnezzar, lifted my eyes to heaven, and my reason
> returned to me, and I blessed the Most High, and praised and
> honored him who lives forever. (Daniel 4:34)

His sanity and his kingdom were restored in his humility.

> Now I, Nebuchadnezzar, praise and extol and honor the King
> of heaven, for all his works are right and his ways are just; and
> those who walk in pride he is able to humble. (Daniel 4:37)

The King of kings is able to humble those who walk in pride. In
the end, Nebuchadnezzar actually became a role model of desirable
humility to his proud son, Belshazzar (Daniel 5:18–22). The Most
High delivers us from the madness of our enmity, anger, and aggression. He is able to make us sane. We become our proper size, earth-
bound creatures and dependents, who recognize the glory of God.

## When Advice Misses the Core Issue of Anger with God

We've looked at how our Lord discusses anger at him, whether in its
"pure" form among those who live in enmity against him, or in the
mixed form that we his children can and do experience. How does
what we've considered from Scripture compare to the Christian self-
help books that discuss anger at God? They tend to miss the heart of
what's going on in anger so the advice is less than helpful. The standard advice for those who are angry at God runs something like this:

1. Remember anger just is—it's neither good nor bad. It's OK
   to feel angry at God. He made us with angry emotions.
2. God often lets us down and disappoints us. How else can we
   explain the heartaches of life, when hard things happen? If
   he's supposed to be in control, then he could have stopped it,
   and he didn't.
3. You can vent your anger at God. He's a mature lover and
   mature love can absorb the anger of the beloved. Don't be
   afraid to tell him exactly what you feel and think. God wants

an honest relationship. Many of the Psalms portray anger at God, so if other godly people have let out their rage at him, you can too. Don't censor your feelings and language; say it like you feel it so you won't be a hypocrite.

4. You need to forgive God. Forgiveness is the opposite of anger, and you need to let go of the hostility in order to be at peace in yourself and start building a trusting relationship with God. Forgive him for the ways he let you down.

Plausible? Many people find it so. Coherent? It does hang together. True? No, these four doctrines are not true. They confuse the issue, rather than clarifying.

As we have intimated above, anger at God is profitably engaged by treating it like any other anger event. Ask what you want that you aren't getting. Which of your firm beliefs is God contradicting? Which of your expectations have met with disappointment? What demands are you making of life—of God—that are not being answered? Normalize anger at God. You will invariably find particular, life-dominating demands that have been asserted against God and substituted for God himself. To use Bob Dylan's penetrating words, God becomes "an errand boy to satisfy your wandering desires," but he refuses to run our errands.[1]

Sometimes our unmet desires are simply wrong. An atheist is angry because God's claims fundamentally threaten the ground on which he bases his life. He insists on personal autonomy and the supreme authority of his own opinions and willfulness. Wanting to control the world, wanting independence from the one on whom we are made to depend, wanting to make up our own meaning of life, we are fools. In these cases, the anger at God is wrong because the desires are intrinsically and entirely wrong.

Other times our unmet desires are for good things. For example, a child prays for her father, who is dying of cancer. She gets angry at God when her father dies. She wanted him to live, and God did not give her what she asked. A single woman longs to be married. She gets angry at the true God because he has not given her a husband. A homeschooling parent with a rebellious teen gets angry at God because he is supposed to make our kids turn out the way we want. A man rages against God because a church leader sexually molested him when he was a youth. In these cases, anger at God is a more subtle wrong. The object of desire is good: life, marriage, thriving children, trustworthy pastors. But this desire for something good has gone bad by becoming all-important. Some desirable good gift has replaced God, the truly good Giver. He has been reduced to the means to an end.

The Lord wants us to rewind both the bad desires and the good desires gone bad. The Giver of good gifts gives mercy and wisdom as his finest treasures. In giving us mercy and wisdom, in giving us Jesus Christ, he is giving us himself. "Thanks be to God for his inexpressible gift" (2 Corinthians 9:15).

Anger at God can be compelling. In 1979 I met a seventy-year-old man named Armen. Intense anger at God had haunted him since childhood. His wild hatred was driving him into madness and raving. He was from Armenia and had immigrated to the United States as a young man. When he was a child he had witnessed the genocide of his people. He remembered his mother and other women praying fervently in their church for God to spare their lives. Ottoman soldiers came into the sanctuary and butchered the praying women. God had failed to protect people at the very moment they were calling out for his protection.

Is Armen's blind, consuming anger an understandable human reaction? Yes. Is it wrong nevertheless? This is a hard truth, but yes. It was surely not wrong to plead for safety. It is surely not wrong to be shattered, unglued, distraught in the face of atrocities. It would surely be right to rejoice in those times when we find safety. (Armen himself was spared when an uncle scooped him up and bolted for the hills.)

God never promises to protect us from all violence. Jesus himself pleaded, "Let this cup pass from me" in the face of imminent torture, violence, and wrath. But he embedded his plea of faith within deeper faith: "Nevertheless, not my will, but yours be done." Then Jesus was cruelly butchered. God's other children have often experienced what Paul described so vividly: "For your sake we are being killed all the day long; we are regarded as sheep to be slaughtered" (Romans 8:36).

God does promise in that situation that even in the sacrifice of their lives, death is unable to separate us from the love of God, which is in Christ Jesus our Lord. A bigger purpose is being worked out by God. We will not find heaven on earth until heaven comes down.

Countless people have faced brutal death while loving the God whose actual love is bigger than death. Armen's lifelong grievance against God was based on insisting on something God had never promised. Normal, shattering grief (in which hope remains) had degraded into abnormal, maddening grievance (in which all hope was lost). God has promised better than what Armen demanded— not less, but more: the resurrection of the dead and life everlasting. Armen never embraced the reality that we have an inheritance that is imperishable, undefiled, and unfading.

Anger at God is wrong. (We'll discuss those "anger psalms" in a moment.) It overflows with mistrust toward God. It firmly embraces and stubbornly proclaims lies about what God is like. It rationalizes any number of self-destructive and sinful behaviors. However, anger at God also presents a wonderful opportunity for profound personal growth through counseling. Handled rightly, it is the royal road into the dark disorder of the human heart. Like any other commonplace wrong, it must be faced and acknowledged. There is no temptation that overtakes us that is not common to all, but God is merciful. He is faithful to help us come clean. He is faithful to help us when we do come clean. By the grace of God, those who are angry at him discover (often for the first time) who he actually is and who they are.

The Bible's God is a grown-up God. Faith is childlike in its directness of dependency. It is not childish either in superstitious fears or in comforting magic charms. Grown-up, yet childlike faith is bluntly realistic. Job looked his sufferings in the eye and said, "Shall we accept good from God and not accept adversity?" After losing her husband and sons, Naomi said, "The Almighty has dealt very bitterly with me." After the desolation of all earthly good, Ethan the psalmist said, "How long, O LORD? Will you hide yourself forever? How long will your wrath burn like fire? Remember how short my time is! For what vanity you have created all the children of man!"[2]

Unbelief blames God for the bad things, curses him, walks angrily away, and sets about manufacturing other gods who might give us what we want. Faith is unafraid to credit God with controlling both the delightful and the bitter things that happen to us—and faith continues to seek the help of the One who alone can help us. In the first twenty verses of Lamentations 3, Jeremiah agonizes under sufferings that he identifies as coming from God's hand.

> He has driven and brought me into darkness without any light. . . . He has besieged and enveloped me with bitterness and tribulation. . . . He shuts out my prayer. . . . He turned aside my steps and tore me to pieces. . . . He has made my teeth grind on gravel . . . I have forgotten what happiness is. (vv. 2, 5, 8, 11, 16–17)

This is a painful passage, the prophet experiencing a taste of Christ's subsequent suffering. But Jeremiah then finds profound comfort:

> But this I call to mind, and therefore I have hope: The steadfast love of the LORD never ceases; his mercies never come to an end; they are new every morning; great is your faithfulness. (Lamentations 3:21–23)

That's grown-up medicine. It makes your soul healthy.

## What Is the Alternative?

The self-help alternative is not good for you. Let's look briefly at the four doctrines we mentioned: anger "just is"; God lets us down and betrays our trust; you need to vent your anger at God; you need to forgive God.

First, earlier we dealt at length with the fact that anger is never neutral. It never "just is." It's not a neutral capacity that is neither good nor bad. Instead, every anger event comes loaded either right or wrong (or mixed and mixed up!). The first piece of advice ducks the moral dilemma of anger at God.

Second, does God let us down when we suffer? We certainly experience disappointments in life. But one would be hard-pressed to find any evidence that God somehow betrays us. He says what he does and does what he says. Until heaven comes down, this world is a hard place to live. The Christian faith is explicit that believing does not grant immunity from suffering.

When the Bible portrays and discusses suffering, God always embeds the hardships we experience as a subset of his larger purposes. These may not be at all obvious in the moment. But in the long run, all tears will be wiped away and we will live in a world with only love, joy, and peace. Meanwhile, people may seriously let us down. Abusers heinously betray trust, and if hell has gradations, the atrocities they commit merit the deepest pit. That's to cite the worst-case scenarios. Many people who are angry at God have suffered more routine hardships: disappointment in love, financial disaster, a life-threatening illness, death of a loved one.

Afflictions are hard. Sufferings hurt. People who are angry at God typically suffer the exact same kinds of pain (and enjoy many of the same blessings) as people who love God! Groaning about our sufferings (to God, in faith and hope) is heartily warranted. But God has never promised freedom from tears, mourning, crying, and pain—or from the evils that cause them—until the great day when life and joy triumph forever over death and misery.

It is curious how people who don't believe that God sovereignly rules all things become embittered hyper-Calvinists when they face sufferings and say, "God could have changed things for me and he didn't. He had the power, and he didn't use it. It's his fault." To actually believe that God rules for his glory and our welfare is to gain an unshakable foundation for trust and hope, in the midst of hellish torments, as well as amid the milder pains and disappointments.

The doctrine that God lets us down reinforces our self-righteousness and validates our schemes for earthly joy. This congruence with our fallenness makes the teaching plausible and attractive. But it also means that because self-help does not identify the sinfulness within anger at God, no true hope can be offered to the disappointed, disillusioned, and angry. The gospel of a sin-bearing Savior who will deliver his beloved children from the condemnation of their sins, from the corruption of their sins, and from the pain of other people's sins finds no logical landing place in a person whose bad feelings are simply OK.

Third, you do not need to vent your hostility at God in order to deal with it. Instead, name your sin and your need for what it is. Turn away from it. Turn toward God for mercy. It helps a great deal when we come to understand the demands, false beliefs, and self-righteousness that produce and drive our anger. No psalm encourages the venting of hostile anger like the self-help books encourage.

In the supposed "vent your anger" psalms—for example, Psalm 44—what comes through is how faith in who God is and what he promises cries out when it is justly agitated. It's not hostility; it's a passionate cry for help. The writers essentially say, "Things are not going well. In fact, what's happening is terrible. Where are your promises? Why are you so far away from our need? Your enemies— our enemies too!—are walking all over us. We are crying out to you in our dismay, hurt, complaint, upset, grief, grievance. Help us!" In Psalm 44 the sons of Korah are really upset at how bad circumstances are. They really want God to intervene. Their displeasure is the constructive displeasure of faith, however, not destructive raging. It's needy, not dismissive. It's hopeful, not hostile. It's faith speaking out, not pride and self-will passing judgment. They yearn for the well-being of people whom God has promised to love, people who have entrusted themselves to his care.

The psalms where faith is upset yearn for God's name, good-ness, and power to be publicly displayed. They yearn for wrongs to be made right. They yearn for him to be merciful to us. Such loving unhappiness and believing complaint yearns for the Lord, our only hope, to eliminate the sufferings we currently experience. The inten-sity of the complaint arises from the intensity of faith. It contains no cursing, no malevolence, no lies, no hostile belittling. It is an appeal for help, not a damning judgment. Psalmists become dismayed be-cause they know and trust that God is good, because they love God, and because they struggle to reconcile God's promises with current affliction.[3]

Psalmists move toward God in honest faith because they need him and they are anguished about their circumstances. But people who are angry at God shove him away. They don't believe in him or believe in his help. Psalmists want God's glory, want evil to go away, groan and complain in their faith. And typically a psalmist's words also show that he is aware of his own guilt and sin—something ig-nored by the self-help teaching. A complex awareness of our respon-sibility coexists with loathing the evil intentions of those who afflict us. When the Bible teaches how to voice distress to God, it teaches a cry of faith, not a roar of rage. The self-help teaching fails to help troubled people complain to a God they love.

Finally, the notion that we need to "forgive God" heads entirely in the wrong direction. Granted, the person who really deals with anger at God by repentance and faith will no longer feel angry at God. He feels overwhelming gratitude because he has *found* forgive-ness, not because he has *granted* forgiveness. God is good. He never stands in the dock as the accused—even when sinful rage seeks to put him in that place. Who does the forgiving so that a trusting rela-tionship between a human and God can be rebuilt? Does the initiat-ing mercy arise from the man or woman who feels disappointed and angry? Or does it arise with the Lord whose mercies are generous and well-adapted to our complicated need?

The Psalms and Job give no warrant for teachings that we ever need to forgive God. The redemption of "anger at God" comes as we learn how much we need him, not because we give him something we need to get off our chest. Job, a godly man of honest faith, repented for his own particular strand of self-righteousness. To the degree that he had blamed God and sought to justify himself, he admitted that he was wrong.

The person who is honest about his or her anger at God—and gets to the truth about it—will walk a different route from the one prescribed by the popular formula. The repentant and believing heart will not settle for some uneasy truce between past sufferings and current willingness to tolerate some sort of relationship with the God who let me down. The believing heart will find truth, joy, hope, and love unspeakable. The believing heart will find God.

» » »

## Making It Your Own

1. I expect that this chapter has aroused some "But what about _____?" questions for you. And I also imagine that some of the sentences that you note, highlight, and ponder will change you as you take them to heart.

What is grabbing your attention?

2. Shortly after Jesus was conceived, his mother Mary gave voice to one of the most remarkable prayers of joy ever spoken. Luke 1:46–55 captures her song:

> My soul magnifies the Lord,
>     and my spirit rejoices in God my Savior,
>     for he has looked on the humble estate of his servant.
> For behold, from now on all generations will call me blessed
>     because he who is mighty has done great things for me,
>     and holy is his name.

And his mercy is for those who fear him
    from generation to generation.
He has shown strength with his arm;
He has scattered the proud in the thoughts of their hearts;
He has brought down the mighty from their thrones
    and exalted those of humble estate;
He has filled the hungry with good things,
    and the rich he has sent away empty.
He has helped his servant Israel,
    in remembrance of his mercy,
as he spoke to our fathers,
    to Abraham and to his offspring forever.
    (author translation)

There are two things that thread through these living words. Take the time to really look at this prayer and notice them.

First:

- Underline all the words and phrases in Mary's prayer that express the humility, need, weakness, and lowliness that is a fountain of joy and gratitude. She embodies everything that is the opposite of anger.
- How does she expose the pride that is the beating heart of anger at God?
- How does she express humility?
- How does her attitude of humility bring her joy?

Second:
- Underline all the words and phrases that express Mary's understanding of who God is and what he does.
- How does the Lord connect with the lowly? How does he break connection with the arrogant?

# A Final Word

We have come a long way. In these pages we've come at the experience of anger from many different angles. We've looked together at the good and the bad, at the good that goes bad, at the bad that's remade good.

Perhaps you were surprised at different points along the way. You might have expected me to say that anger is bad, and give methods to get rid of it. Instead I said anger can be good, and gave you methods to transform it. You might have expected me to say that anger is neither good nor bad; it just is. Instead I said that anger is always either good or bad (or a mix of both), and here's how to sort it out. You might have expected me to say that anger is good and here's how to let it empower you, but I said anger usually goes bad, and here's how to do the moral calculus more honestly. Through it all, I hope that you have found a coherent vision—faithful to your life, faithful to how human nature works, and worth living out.

You might have been surprised that we talked so much about good and evil, and the image of God, and sin against God, and God's wrath, and God's mercies in Christ. You might not have expected that something so everyday as anger and anger management is so tied in with matters that get shuffled off into theology— as if such matters never touch the ground where you live. But they do touch the ground. These realities *are* the ground on which you live. You can never reckon with anger unless you reckon with the living God.

Perhaps you were surprised at what you found out about yourself. I hope so. If you worked through the application questions, used your yellow highlighter, and thought about your BWAs, then you most likely see the world in a somewhat different light than you did at the beginning of this book. I know that I see the world in a different light than when I began writing.

So what remains to be said?

There is a "final word" on anger. It's well worth saying, but it's hard to put into words. I hope I can do it justice. You won't find this in a self-help book or a psychology class. But except for the graphic immediacies of human experience and the good intentions of trying to make life go a bit better, not much that you've read here is in those places. This final word lives out in plain sight in the Good Book, difficult as it can be to wrap our minds around it. This chapter is important. It rounds out your *understanding* of anger. In fact, it rounds out your *experience* of anger.

The final word is that anger is going somewhere. It will someday be perfected. Then it will be swallowed up in joy.

Through these chapters, we've lived most often in the angry moment. We've looked at the many things that provoke our displeasure. We've looked at varieties of ways that people express anger. We've explored causes, those good or bad motives of the human heart. We've looked at what makes a decisive difference in the storm of the moment. We've repeatedly plunged into the immediacy of human experience. But the ultimate significance of anger is not found in the heat of each present moment. Anger is going somewhere. There will be a climax. Then it will be over.

Why is this? The presence of anger depends on the presence of evil. Wherever there is evil, you find anger. You find both the angers that are evil and angers that oppose evil. Where there is no evil, you find no anger. No possibility of anger. Let me say it again: *Where there is no evil, you will find no anger.* In any time and place of love, of joy, of peace, there are no reasons for anger. Perhaps you've had a small taste of what this is like. The best moments in your best relationship. The best day on your best vacation. It whets your appetite for the day when anger is over and done. The angers that are themselves wrong are no more. The necessity of just anger at wrong is no more.

This is a chapter about the future of anger, when it will first come into its own, and will then be swallowed up. We will look at these two parts of the finale.

## You Will Participate in the Wrath of God

When anger comes clean, it is determined to deal with evil. What is this like? Don't start by trying to imagine some particular *emotion* that might or might not be felt. Don't start by imagining some *individual's* attitude. It is almost impossible to strain out the negative associations we all have to individual expressions of animosity. Instead, start by conceiving of the *task* that needs to be accomplished by a great team of people acting in concert to eliminate a grave wrong. What is this great task that needs to be accomplished?

God is committed to destroying evil and he is committed to remaking his people into the image of Jesus.

Consider how this works. It is the theme of Romans, the most comprehensive apostolic letter. Chapter 12 marks a turning point. Having grasped God's mercies in Christ, we now turn to the transformative implications of those freely given mercies. God is committed to destroying the evil in us. You and I have entered into a lifelong process of learning "the will of God," of actually becoming good (vv. 1–2). Each of us will express this transformation by having a specific part to play within the living body of Jesus Christ on earth (vv. 3–8). After locating us in this big picture, the next three chapters zoom in on details of how goodness comes to life (12:9—15:13). The first line sounds the keynote: Let love be genuine. Hate what is evil. Cling to what is good. You are to love. You are to hate. You are to become good. We are aiming high with Jesus as our model, the very character of God himself. Jesus's love is without flaw. He utterly abhors what is wrong. He is glued to what is good.

Paul comes back to this central point toward the end of his letter: "Be wise as to what is good and innocent as to what is evil" (16:19). We know all too well the taint and folly. Haltingly, we are learning the purity and wisdom. We know that when Jesus died for you and for me, he willingly died for an enemy (5:6–10). Now you and I are learning to hate evil—over a lifetime, with many missteps along the way. But we will be complete when we see his face. The displeasure, anger, and hate that are our worst characteristics are being purified and made wise. And in the end, we will be good with the good- ness of God. Imagine that. Psalm 126:1–2 captures something of the experience:

> When the LORD restored the fortunes of Zion,
>     we were like those who dream.
> Then our mouth was filled with laughter,
>     and our tongue with shouts of joy

Imagine that.

Here is what it means for the task that defines us. The trans- formation process doesn't end with making us fit to live with God and with each other. This is not some glorified moral self-improve- ment project. God is committed to destroying all evil everywhere. He hates evil. Changing those whom he has chosen to love is one aspect. But ultimately he is out to destroy evil down to its roots. "The God of peace will soon crush Satan under your feet" (Romans 16:20). You are being made fit to participate in the good wrath of the only-good God.

We have almost no words to describe something this good. We need a careful definition, as with all words used for important, life- and-death matters. Defining how you are to "hate what is evil" is as tricky as defining how you are to "love what is good." For example, what is the love that is genuine? Is it a passion for cheesecake? Is it

the head-over-heels infatuation of "being in love"? Is it erotic attraction, however immoral? Is it self-sacrificing generosity that considers
and seeks the true welfare of another? Those are four very different
loves. The same word does duty for the finest goodness, for a typical
evil, and for many things in between!

So it is with words describing anger, displeasure, and hate. Most
of the anger words come bristling with negative connotations. When
I say you will participate in the wrath of God, it's hard to think
straight. But imagine something high and noble. Imagine the day of
liberation after a long slavery. Imagine a supreme honor and joyous
triumph. Imagine something utterly good and long-awaited. That's
what the wrath of God brings to pass. Evil is erased forever. Every
cause of pain is no more. There are no more lies. All tears are wiped
away. One of the great lines in *The Lord of the Rings* is Sam's question, "Is everything sad going to come untrue?" The answer is yes.

The most accurate word for untainted anger is *indignation*.
Indignation means strong, unselfish displeasure at wrong. Add to
that the good meanings of *wrath*—the bringing of justice, truth,
and liberty to people oppressed by injustice, falsehood, and slavery.
Imagine then *displeasure at evil that is deep, determined, lasting,
strong, and unselfish*. Imagine a displeasure that accomplishes what
most needs doing on behalf of the oppressed. Imagine the wrath of
God. As you are remade into the image of God, then one day you
also will both feel and act on a displeasure at evil that is deep, determined, lasting, strong, and unselfish.

Exactly what the "great Day of the wrath of God"—*dies irae*—
will look like is beyond our imagination. It is also the great Day of
salvation.

> What no eye has seen, nor ear heard, nor the heart of man
> imagined, what God has prepared for those who love him.
> (1 Corinthians 2:9)

It is good. All good. But what exactly it means that we will participate in that day of deliverance I cannot say. Meanwhile, we are to

hate evil, but love our enemies. We never know which enemies might become our dearest friends. After all, Christ loved us when we were his enemies. Until the Day comes, the door of life is open. Enter all who will.

## The Wrath of God Will Be Swallowed Up

And the Day will come. The Bible treats us to vivid images and metaphors, evoking the sense of significance and drama. We're given no video trailer. We aren't meant to know the details. But it is unmistakable that God does act within history to destroy evil. The plagues on Egypt—reptiles, epidemics, insects, violent weather, the angel of death—expressed God's real-time indignation against tyrants because of their policy of genocide and enslavement. He heard his afflicted people crying out for mercy. He acted to set them free: the wrath of God.

The armies of Israel were agents of God's indignation against degraded, child-sacrificing Canaanite idolatry. (But there were Canaanites who came through the door of salvation—including Rahab who is in the line of Jesus.) The Babylonian military was an agent of God's indignation against Israel for their insolence, drift, and injustice. (But God never gave up on his promises to the line of Abraham, Isaac, and Jacob.) Sometimes the Bible doesn't even cite secondary causes who were agents of the Lord's indignation. It simply reads, "Er, Judah's firstborn, was wicked in the sight of the LORD, and the LORD put him to death. . . . What Onan did was wicked in the sight of the LORD and he put him to death also" (Genesis 38:7, 10).

In many people's minds, "God" has no capacity for just anger. God is a three-letter word for a vague, bodiless, all-accepting energy without an angry bone. But don't these same people loathe predatory pedophilia? Don't they hate terrorists who slaughter innocent people? Aren't they angry that a drunk driver with twenty previous arrests drives head-on into another car, killing the parents and leaving two children as orphans? Don't they get upset when their spouse and their best friend betray them by committing adultery? Doesn't their higher power care about evil as much as they do?

The real God made us for himself. He sustains our every breath. He loathes careful predators and careless killers. He hates the gods people make up according to their own fancy. He made us for himself, to love him utterly. So he is "jealous"—love and anger perfectly united—at our immoralities and betrayals. He is indignant at evil. He came as flesh and bone, loving good, hating evil, dying for evildoers, calling all to repentance and life. Behold the Lamb of God, who takes away the sins of the world. He freely forgives all who seek mercy. He will act decisively against evil. If you love him, join in a cause that is deep, determined, lasting, strong, and unselfish.

Often in good literature or film, and occasionally on the stage of history, we get a taste for the conflict between good and evil. These stories resonate deeply with us (even though everyday human relations and most of human history give us good reasons for cynicism). People love *Les Misérables* and *Star Wars* and *The Lord of the Rings*. We love any great adventure where good overcomes evil at great odds, where evil that looked triumphant is destroyed in the end.

Our experience of real life is more complicated, of course. Still, history can give us a taste for what it looks like. Most conflicts are morally ambiguous mixed cases. But some situations are less mixed up than others. World War II comes the closest to a clear-cut case study. It is good that people rallied to the task of destroying Hitler and Nazism. Nations allied because they hated the evil that threatened them. After great hardship and death, VE Day in England and America was one of the most joyous days the world has ever known.

To understand anger that has come clean, start by conceiving the *task* that needed to be accomplished. Every human being is embroiled in The Great War between good and evil. The outcome means life or death. The defeat of darkness is sheer joy. Imagine that spirit, the high cause that brings freedom for the oppressed and destruction of the oppressor. The task of indignation is not an emotion first and foremost. In World War II, Nazi evil needed to be destroyed. We might say that the 101$^{st}$ Airborne, the Royal Navy, the 4$^{th}$ Army, and the RAF participated in "the wrath of Churchill and Roosevelt." That's not defined by feelings of personal animosity. It is defined by the fierceness of their commitment to root out real evil.

In daily life, we continually deal with the reality that all human actors are morally ambiguous. Those who generally do right are compromised by imperfections and moral contradictions. We have clay feet. And those who generally do wrong come with redeeming qualities, good intentions, and extenuating circumstances. We aren't as bad as we could be. Naturally, this is congruent with Scripture. Every lead actor in the Bible disappoints us—Abraham, Moses, David, Peter, and so forth. And those outside the covenant often surprise us—Ruth, Naaman, the Ninevites, the Samaritan woman at the well, and so on. There are only two pure cases in Scripture: Jesus and Satan.

But along the way, the actors do finally tilt either toward good or toward evil. And from God's viewpoint, and in the end, that tilt will prove defining and decisive. C. S. Lewis's famous essay *The Weight of Glory* captures what it is like when all the mixed-up-ness finally gets sorted out. All the good in essentially bad people is no more when God's common grace is removed. And all the bad in essentially good people is no more when indwelling sin is purified away.

> It is a serious thing to live in a society of possible gods and goddesses, to remember that the dullest and most uninteresting person you talk to may one day be a creature which if you saw it now, you would be strongly tempted to worship, or else a horror and a corruption such as you now meet, if at all, only in a nightmare. All day long we are, in some degree, helping each other to one or other of these destinations. . . . There are no *ordinary* people. You have never talked to a mere mortal. . . . It is immortals whom we joke with, work with, marry, snub, and exploit—immortal horrors or everlasting splendours.[1]

In other words, some people are being purified. The clinging darkness contradictory to their essential faith will finally be swept away. And other people are being *im*purified. The gift of light contradictory to their essential selfishness will finally be withdrawn.

Are you being remade into the image of God? Is your anger something that you grieve, because you see how your irritations and resentments are so often reckless and self-serving? With good reason, anger is one of Seven Deadly Sins and is one of the sins chosen to list in the Ten Commandments. Does this matter to you? If you are fighting your unruly angers and finding mercy from God, then someday your anger will be clean and bright.

God's anger against evil must be openly expressed because it is integral to the task of making right all that is wrong. This theme is everywhere in Psalms. The most tender psalms of refuge and safety also contain promises of God's wrath against his enemies. Why is this? Because you are only safe when evil is destroyed. If you are being remade into his image, then you will join his battle to rid the world of wrong. You will participate in the wrath of God. If you are not being remade into his image, then you are his enemy. You will experience the wrath of God against you.

If at your core you say, "Not my will, but yours be done," then, to your everlasting joy, contradictory self-will shall finally be destroyed. Humility will win, and your anger will be purified of all its spite, pettiness, and bitterness. But if at your core you say, "My will be done," then, grievously, to your everlasting woe, self-will is finally unchecked. You will become your pride, hatreds, and malice.

Again, listen to how C. S. Lewis captures the decisive factor.

> In the end, that Face which is the delight or the terror of the universe must be turned upon each of us either with one expression or with the other, either conferring glory inexpressible or inflicting shame that can never be cured or disguised. I read in a periodical the other day that the fundamental thing is how we think of God. By God Himself, it is not! How God thinks of us is not only more important, but infinitely more important.

Indeed, how we think of him is of no importance except in so far as it is related to how he thinks of us.[2]

The stakes are high. Life or death, freedom or slavery, good or evil, God's glory or our vanity and vainglory. In that light, if God wills to include us in his cause, then our participation in his wrath makes complete sense.

Yet we still find anger confusing, don't we? Our experience is so mixed, so colored by pettiness and self-serving bias. But here's one more principle that I find helpful in sorting it out. The pettier the battle, the more bizarre it sounds to participate in the wrath of God. To whatever degree it's me against my competition, me against the people that I don't like, the notion of God's wrath seems offensive. But the bigger the battle, the more that's at stake, then the more it makes sense that we participate in the active indignation of God. We are either on his side or not. By nature we are not. It is mercy that causes us to switch sides. We are talking about how God includes us on *his* side, not about us welcoming him to whatever cause or loyalty claims our affections and ignites our passions. The complications of our mixed motives are finally washed away. We can join him as he finishes what he began.

Psalm 149 is second to last for a reason. For five verses we sing in simple joy, gladness, and hallelujahs: "The LORD takes pleasure in his people. He adorns the humble with salvation" (v. 4). But there is one scene more. The last four verses enlist us as participants in the judgment of the world, describing this as an honor: "Let the high praises of God be in their mouth and a two-edged sword in their hand, to execute vengeance on the nations and punishment on the peoples" (vv. 6–7, author translation). We will actually be good and angry.

It is significant that the Psalms wait until just before the end to reveal, briefly, this most peculiar honor. We can't handle it any earlier. We need those other 148 psalms to disciple our hearts into the realities of the Word of God: the character of the Lord God, the place of Scripture, godlessness versus godliness, mercy and justice, neediness and joy, sin and suffering, life and death, redemption and struggle, the path and the destination, the Messiah. And then Psalm 149 makes sense.

## Swallowed by Joy

And then there is one more psalm:

> Praise the LORD!
>
> Praise God in his sanctuary;
>     praise him in his mighty heavens!
> Praise him for his mighty deeds;
>     praise him according to his excellent greatness!
> Praise him with trumpet sound;
>     praise him with lute and harp!
> Praise him with tambourine and dance;
>     praise him with strings and pipe!
> Praise him with sounding cymbals;
>     praise him with loud clashing cymbals!
> Let everything that has breath praise the LORD!
>
> Praise the LORD!

Here in Psalm 150 there are no more conflicts. "The wrath of God is finished" (Revelation 15:1). So Psalm 150 is pure joy.

And pure joy continues forever.

# Endnotes

## Chapter 1

1. Jean-Paul Sartre, *No Exit*, in *No Exit and Three Other Plays* (USA: Vintage, 1989), 45.

## Chapter 6

1. I've selected items particularly relevant to anger from the list in Mark 7:21–22.

## Chapter 7

1. Samuel Crossman, "My Song Is Love Unknown," *Trinity Hymnal, Revised Edition* (Suwanee, GA: Great Commission, 1990), Hymn 182.

## Chapter 8

1. Doris Kearns Goodwin, *Team of Rivals: The Political Genius of Abraham Lincoln* (New York: Simon & Schuster, 2005), 679–80.
2. Story and citations from Winston Churchill, *The Grand Alliance* (Boston: Houghton-Mifflin, 1950), 457f.
3. Ibid.
4. For the incident with Stalin himself, see Churchill's *The Hinge of Fate* (Boston: Houghton-Mifflin, 1950), 486–87.

## Chapter 10

1. B. B. Warfield, "The Emotional Life of Our Lord," *The Person and Work of Christ* (Philadelphia: Presbyterian & Reformed, 1950, pp. 93–145), 107.

2. Removal of indwelling sin is a work that will be completed when we see Jesus return on the day of joy and the day of life, death, and wrath. See, for example, Philippians 1:6; 1 Thessalonians 5:23; 1 John 3:2.

3. Consider Psalms 3, 5, 7, 9, and 10.

## Chapter 11

1. Martin Luther, "Defense and Explanation of All the Articles," Second Article, Lazareth transl., as found in Grace Brame, *Receptive Prayer* (Chalice Press, 1985), 119.

## Chapter 12

1. Augustus Toplady, "Rock of Ages, Cleft for Me," *Trinity Hymnal, Revised Edition* (Suwanee, GA: Great Commission, 1990), Hymn 499, 500.

2. George MacDonald, *The Marquis' Secret* (Minneapolis, MN: Bethany House, 1982), 58.

3. I am indebted to Andrée Seu for this phrase.

4. I am indebted to Bob DeMoss for this phrase and for the metaphor in the preceding paragraph.

## Chapter 13

1. This basic framework of eight questions applies to other problems besides anger. These questions summarize the basic pattern for truly understanding yourself and how change works. They can be adapted, for example, to incidents of anxiety, or to escapes into drinking or TV watching, and so forth.

2. If you want to study further, there are many examples of this in the Bible. Consider Psalm 73:3–12; Jeremiah 50:11; Habakkuk 1:15; Luke 6:24–26; 16:19, 25; Revelation 11:10.

3. A line from Samuel Crossman's hymn, "My Song Is Love Unknown" (1664).

## Chapter 14

1. For a fuller discussion, see my minibook *Recovering from Child Abuse* (Greensboro, NC: New Growth Press, 2008).

2. Ibid.

## Chapter 17

1. Bob Dylan, "When You Gonna Wake Up" on *Slow Train Coming* (New York: Special Rider Music, 1979).

2. Job 2:10; Ruth 1:20; Psalm 89:46–47

3. Outside the Psalms, Habakkuk most intensely does the same.

## A Final Word

1. C. S. Lewis, *The Weight of Glory and Other Addresses* (Grand Rapids: William B. Eerdmans, 1949), 14f.

2. Ibid., 10.